International Safety Guide for Oil Tankers & Terminals

(ISGOTT)

FOURTH EDITION

INTERNATIONAL CHAMBER OF SHIPPING

OIL COMPANIES INTERNATIONAL MARINE FORUM

INTERNATIONAL ASSOCIATION OF PORTS AND HARBORS

The International Chamber of Shipping (ICS) is a voluntary organisation of national shipowners' associations. It was established as long ago as 1921 and represents more than half of the world's merchant tonnage. The interests of ICS cover all aspects of maritime affairs, but it is particularly active in the fields of marine safety, ship design and construction, pollution prevention and maritime law. ICS has consultative status with several inter-governmental organisations, notably IMO.

The Oil Companies International Marine Forum (OCIMF) is a voluntary association of oil companies having an interest in the shipment and terminalling of crude oil and oil products. OCIMF is organised to represent its membership before, and consult with, the International Maritime Organisation (IMO) and other government bodies on matters relating to the shipment and terminalling of crude oil and oil products, including marine pollution and safety.

The International Association of Ports and Harbors (IAPH) is a voluntary world-wide association of port authorities, founded in 1955. Current membership includes 230 regular and 154 associate members encompassing 77 countries. IAPH is committed to the exchange and promotion of ideas and technical knowledge on issues of concern to those who work in ports and related industries. Its consultative status with UN and other organisations, including IMO, is a positive benefit in this regard.

First Published in 1978 by
Witherby & Co. Ltd., 32/36 Aylesbury Street,
London, EC1R 0ET, England
Tel no: +44 171 251 5341
Fax no: +44 171 251 1296

Reprinted April 1979

Second Edition 1984

Reprinted April 1986

Third Edition 1988

Reprinted March 1990

Third Edition Revised 1991

Fourth Edition 1996

© *International Chamber of Shipping, London*
and
Oil Companies International Marine Forum, Bermuda
1978, 1979, 1984, 1986, 1988, 1990, 1991, 1996

ISBN 1 85609 081 7

British Library Cataloguing in Publication Data
International Chamber of Shipping, Oil Companies International Marine Forum,
International Association of Ports and Harbors,
International Safety Guide for Oil Tankers and Terminals

Fourth Edition – I Title
ISBN 1 85609 081 7

D
623.8245
INT

Printed in England by
Witherby & Co. Ltd.,
32/36 Aylesbury Street, London, EC1R 0ET

Foreword to Fourth Edition

Safety is critical to the well-being and reputation of the tanker industry. The International Safety Guide for Oil Tankers and Terminals, or ISGOTT as it is now widely known, is the standard reference work on the safe operation of oil tankers and the terminals they serve. To remain current, the Guide must keep abreast of changes in vessel design and operating practice and reflect the latest technology.

This fourth edition includes much new guidance on recent developments within the industry. Principal among them is the advent of the double hull tanker as the standard ship. Double hull tankers are not new, but hitherto they have been specialised vessels, generally smaller ships and confined to certain trades.

As time passes a growing number of tanker operators will need to familiarise themselves with the special characteristics of double hull vessels. Therefore this new edition addresses such questions as the possibility of hydrocarbon gas leakage into double hull spaces and the stability of some double hull designs during simultaneous ballast and cargo handling.

Account has been taken in this revision of the growing awareness of air pollution and the use of vapour return lines to avoid venting all hydrocarbon vapours to the atmosphere. The potential problems created by over-pressurisation or under-pressurisation of cargo tanks have also been addressed.

The opportunity has been taken to improve and update the text in a number of other respects to ensure that ISGOTT continues to provide the best technical guidance on tanker and terminal operations. All operators are urged to ensure that the recommendations in this guide are not only read and fully understood, but also followed.

Contents

PART II: TECHNICAL INFORMATION

APPENDICES

Purpose and Scope

This guide makes recommendations for tanker and terminal personnel on the safe carriage and handling of crude oil and petroleum products on tankers and at terminals. It was prepared originally by combining the contents of the 'Tanker Safety Guide (Petroleum)' published by the International Chamber of Shipping (ICS) and the 'International Oil Tanker and Terminal Safety Guide' published on behalf of the Oil Companies International Marine Forum (OCIMF). In producing this fourth edition the content has been reviewed by these organisations, together with the International Association of Ports and Harbors (IAPH), to ensure that it reflects current practices and legislation. This latest edition takes account of certain changes in recommended operating procedures. Comments made by the International Maritime Organization (IMO) on the terminology used in the guide have also been noted and changes made in order to avoid possible misinterpretation.

The purpose of the guide is to provide operational advice to assist personnel directly involved in tanker and terminal operations. It is emphasised that the ship's operator should always be in a position to provide positive support, information and guidance to the master who is in charge of the day-to-day running of the ship, and that the terminal management should ensure that its concern for safe operating practices is known to the terminal personnel. It should be borne in mind that in all cases the advice in the guide is subject to any local or national terminal regulations that may be applicable, and those concerned should ensure that they are aware of any such requirements.

It is recommended that a copy of the guide be kept — and used — on board every tanker and in every terminal to provide advice on operational procedures and the shared responsibility for port operations.

The contents of the guide are arranged in two parts. Part I covers operational procedures and is designed to provide guidance on safe operating practices. The approach adopted has been to arrange the material so that each chapter is concerned with a particular type of operation. However, some chapters deal with the general precautions to be observed in conjunction with the specific guidance for the particular operation concerned. Each chapter has a small introductory paragraph describing its scope and drawing attention to related advice contained in other chapters. Part II contains more detailed technical information and provides the reasons for many of the precautions described in Part I.

Certain subjects are dealt with in greater detail in other publications issued by ICS and OCIMF or by IMO. Where this is the case an appropriate reference is made, and a list of these and other related publications is given in the bibliography.

It is not the purpose of the guide to make recommendations on design or construction. Information on these matters may be obtained from national authorities and from authorised bodies such as classification societies. Similarly, the guide does not attempt to deal with certain other safety related matters — e.g. navigation, helicopter operations, and shipyard safety — although some aspects are inevitably touched upon. It should also be noted that the guide does not relate to cargoes other than crude oil and petroleum products which may be carried in tankers and combination carriers. It therefore does not cover the carriage of chemicals or liquefied gases, which are the subject of other industry guides.

Comments and suggestions for improvement are always welcome for possible inclusion in future editions. They may be addressed to any of the three sponsoring organisations, as follows:

International Chamber of Shipping,
12 Carthusian Street,
London EC1M 6EB
United Kingdom

Oil Companies International Marine Forum,
15th Floor,
96, Victoria Street,
London SW1E 5JW
United Kingdom

International Association of Ports & Harbors,
Kotohira-Kaikan Bldg.,
2-8, Toranomon 1-chome, Minato-ku,
Tokyo 105,
Japan

Bibliography

The following publications of the International Chamber of Shipping (ICS), the Oil Companies International Marine Forum (OCIMF), the Society of International Gas Tanker and Terminal Operators (SIGTTO), the Tanker Structure Co-operative Forum (TSCF) and the International Maritime Organization (IMO), most of which are mentioned in the guide, should be referred to as appropriate for additional information and guidance:

OCIMF	Anchoring Systems and Procedures for Large Tankers (1st Edition 1982)
ICS	Bridge Procedures Guide (3rd Edition)
ICS/OCIMF	Clean Seas Guide for Oil Tankers (4th Edition 1994)
TSCF	Condition Evaluation and Maintenance of Tanker Structures (1st Edition 1992)
ICS/OCIMF/ SIGTTO	Contingency Planning and Crew Response Guide for Gas Carrier Damage at Sea and in Port Approaches (2nd Edition 1989)
ICS	Correct Use of VHF Channels (Revised Edition in preparation 1996)
IMO	Crude Oil Washing Systems
OCIMF	Design and Construction Specification for Marine Loading Arms (3rd Edition in preparation 1996)
OCIMF	Disabled Tankers – Report of Studies on Ship Drift and Towage (1st Edition 1981)
OCIMF	Drift Characteristics of 50,000 to 70,000 DWT Tankers (1st Edition 1982)
ICS	Drug Trafficking and Drug Abuse: Guidelines for Owners and Masters on Recognition and Detection (2nd Edition 1994)
OCIMF	Effective Mooring (1st Edition 1989)
IMO	Emergency Procedures for Ships Carrying Dangerous Goods — Group Emergency Schedules
ICS/OCIMF	Guidance Manual for the Inspection and Condition Assessment of Tanker Structures (1st Edition 1986)
OCIMF	Guidelines for the Handling, Storage, Inspection and Testing of Hoses in the Field (formerly Buoy Mooring Forum Hose Guide) (2nd Edition 1995)
OCIMF	Guide on Marine Terminal Fire Protection and Emergency Evacuation (1st Edition 1987)
ICS/OCIMF/ SIGTTO	Guide to Contingency Planning for the Gas Carrier Alongside and Within Port Limits (1st Edition 1987)
ICS/OCIMF/ SIGTTO	Guide to Contingency Planning for Marine Terminals Handling Liquefied Gases in Bulk (1st Edition 1989)
ICS	Guide to Helicopter/Ship Operations (3rd Edition 1989)
OCIMF	Guide to Purchasing, Manufacturing and Testing of Loading and Discharge Hoses for Offshore Moorings (4th Edition 1991)
TSCF	Guidelines for the Inspection and Maintenance of Double Hull Tanker Structures (1st Edition 1995)
OCIMF	Hawser Guidelines (1st Edition 1987)
OCIMF	Hawser Test Report (1st Edition 1982)
IMO	Inert Gas Systems
OCIMF	Inspection Guidelines for Bulk Oil Carriers (2nd Edition 1994)

OCIMF/ SIGTTO	Inspection Guidelines for Ships Carrying Liquefied Gases in Bulk (1st Edition 1990)
IMO	International Maritime Dangerous Goods (IMDG) Code
OCIMF	Marine Terminal Survey Guidelines (2nd Edition 1995)
OCIMF	Mooring Equipment Guidelines (1st Edition 1992)
ICS/OCIMF	Peril at Sea and Salvage – A Guide for Masters (4th Edition 1992)
OCIMF	Prediction of Wind and Current Loads on VLCCs (2nd Edition 1994)
OCIMF/ SIGTTO	Prediction of Wind Loads of Large Liquefied Gas Carriers (1st Edition 1985)
ICS/OCIMF	Prevention of Oil Spillages through Cargo Pumproom Sea Valves (Second Edition 1991)
OCIMF	Recommendations for Equipment Employed in the Mooring of Ships at Single Point Moorings (3rd Edition 1993)
OCIMF	Recommendations for Oil Tanker Manifolds and Associated Equipment (4th Edition 1991)
OCIMF	Recommendations for Manifolds for Refrigerated Liquefied Gas Carriers for Cargoes from 0°C to minus 104°C (2nd Edition 1987)
OCIMF	Recommendations for Manifolds for Refrigerated Liquefied Natural Gas Carriers (LNG) (2nd Edition 1994)
OCIMF	Recommendations on Equipment for the Towing of Disabled Tankers (1st Edition 1981)
IMO	Recommendations on the Safe Transport, Handling and Storage of Dangerous Substances in Port Areas
OCIMF	Safety Guide for Terminals Handling Ships Carrying Liquefied Gases in Bulk (2nd Edition 1993)
ICS	Safety in Chemical Tankers (1st Edition 1977)
ICS	Safety in Liquefied Gas Tankers (1st Edition 1980)
ICS	Safety in Oil Tankers (2nd Edition 1978)
OCIMF	Ship Information Questionnaire for Bulk Oil Carriers (1st Edition 1989)
OCIMF/ SIGTTO	Ship Information Questionnaire for Gas Carriers (1st Edition 1990)
ICS/OCIMF/ SIGTTO	Ship to Ship Transfer Guide (Liquefied Gases) (2nd Edition 1995)
ICS/OCIMF	Ship to Ship Transfer Guide (Petroleum) (2nd Edition 1988)
OCIMF	Single Point Mooring Maintenance and Operations Guide (2nd Edition 1995)
OCIMF	SPM Hose Ancillary Equipment Guide (3rd Edition 1987)
OCIMF	SPM Hose System Design Commentary (2nd Edition 1993)
ICS	Steering Gear: Test Routines and Check Lists (Revised 1987)
ICS/OCIMF	Straits of Malacca & Singapore – Guide to Planned Transits by Deep Draught Vessels (3rd Edition 1990)
ICS	Tanker Safety Guide (Chemicals) (2nd Edition in preparation)
ICS	Tanker Safety Guide (Liquefied Gas) (2nd Edition 1995)

Definitions

For the purpose of this safety guide the following definitions apply:

Administration

Means the Government of the State whose flag the ship is entitled to fly.

Anti-static additive

A substance added to a petroleum product to raise its electrical conductivity above 100 pico Siemens/metre (pS/m) to prevent accumulation of static electricity.

Approved equipment

Equipment of a design that has been tested and approved by an appropriate authority such as a government department or classification society. The authority should have certified the equipment as safe for use in a specified hazardous atmosphere.

Auto-ignition

The ignition of a combustible material without initiation by a spark or flame, when the material has been raised to a temperature at which self-sustaining combustion occurs.

Bonding

The connecting together of metal parts to ensure electrical continuity.

Cathodic protection

The prevention of corrosion by electrochemical techniques. On tankers it may be applied either externally to the hull or internally to the surfaces of tanks. At terminals, it is frequently applied to steel piles and fender panels.

Clingage

Oil remaining on the walls of a pipe or on the internal surfaces of tanks after the bulk of the oil has been removed.

Cold work

Work which cannot create a source of ignition.

Combination carrier

A ship which is designed to carry either petroleum cargoes or dry bulk cargoes.

Combustible (also referred to as 'Flammable')

Capable of being ignited and of burning. For the purposes of this guide the terms 'combustible' and 'flammable' are synonymous.

Combustible gas indicator

An instrument for measuring the composition of hydrocarbon gas/air mixtures, usually giving the result as a percentage of the lower flammable limit (LFL).

Dangerous area

An area on a tanker which for the purposes of the installation and use of electrical equipment is regarded as dangerous.

Dry chemical powder

A flame inhibiting powder used in fire fighting.

Earthing (also referred to as 'Grounding')

The electrical connection of equipment to the main body of the earth to ensure that it is at earth potential. On board ship, the connection is made to the main metallic structure of the ship which is at earth potential because of the conductivity of the sea.

Entry permit

A document issued by a responsible person permitting entry to a space or compartment during a specific time interval.

Explosimeter

See 'Combustible gas indicator'.

Explosion-proof ('Flame-proof')

Electrical equipment is defined and certified as explosion- (flame-) proof when it is enclosed in a case which is capable of withstanding the explosion within it of a hydrocarbon gas/air mixture or other specified flammable gas mixture. It must also prevent the ignition of such a mixture outside the case either by spark or flame from the internal explosion or as a result of the temperature rise of the case following the internal explosion. The equipment must operate at such an external temperature that a surrounding flammable atmosphere will not be ignited.

Explosive range

See 'Flammable range'.

Flame arrester

A permeable matrix of metal, ceramic or other heat resisting materials which can cool a deflagration flame, and any following combustion products, below the temperature required for the ignition of the flammable gas on the other side of the arrester.

Flame screen

A portable or fitted device incorporating one or more corrosion resistant wire woven fabrics of very small mesh which is used for preventing sparks from entering a tank or vent opening or, for a short time, preventing the passage of flame. (Not to be confused with flame arrester.)

Flammable (also referred to as 'Combustible')

Capable of being ignited and of burning. For the purposes of this guide the terms 'flammable' and 'combustible' are synonymous.

Flammable range (also referred to as 'Explosive range')

The range of hydrocarbon gas concentrations in air between the lower and upper flammable (explosive) limits. Mixtures within this range are capable of being ignited and of burning.

Flashlight (also referred to as 'Torch')

A battery operated hand lamp. An approved flashlight is one which is approved by a competent authority for use in a flammable atmosphere.

Flashpoint

The lowest temperature at which a liquid gives off sufficient gas to form a flammable gas mixture near the surface of the liquid. It is measured in a laboratory in standard apparatus using a prescribed procedure.

Foam (also referred to as 'Froth')

An aerated solution which is used for fire prevention and fire fighting.

Foam concentrate (also referred to as 'Foam compound')

The full strength liquid received from the supplier which is diluted and processed to produce foam.

Foam solution

The mixture produced by diluting foam concentrate with water before processing to make foam.

Free fall

The unrestricted fall of liquid into a tank.

Froth

See 'Foam'.

Gas free

A tank, compartment or container is gas free when sufficient fresh air has been introduced into it to lower the level of any flammable, toxic, or inert gas to that required for a specific purpose, e.g. hot work, entry, etc.

Gas free certificate

A certificate issued by an authorised responsible person confirming that, at the time of testing, a tank, compartment or container was gas free for a specific purpose.

Grounding

See 'Earthing'.

Halon

A halogenated hydrocarbon used in fire fighting which inhibits flame propagation.

Hazardous area

An area on shore which for the purposes of the installation and use of electrical equipment is regarded as dangerous. Such hazardous areas are graded into hazardous zones depending upon the probability of the presence of a flammable gas mixture.

Hazardous zone

See 'Hazardous area'.

Hot work

Work involving sources of ignition or temperatures sufficiently high to cause the ignition of a flammable gas mixture. This includes any work requiring the use of welding, burning or soldering equipment, blow torches, some power driven tools, portable electrical equipment which is not intrinsically safe or contained within an approved explosion-proof housing, and internal combustion engines.

Hot work permit

A document issued by a responsible person permitting specific hot work to be done during a specific time interval in a defined area.

Hydrocarbon gas

A gas composed entirely of hydrocarbons.

Inert condition

A condition in which the oxygen content throughout the atmosphere of a tank has been reduced to 8 per cent or less by volume by the addition of inert gas.

Inert gas

A gas or a mixture of gases, such as flue gas, containing insufficient oxygen to support the combustion of hydrocarbons.

Inert gas distribution system

All piping, valves, and associated fittings to distribute inert gas from the inert gas plant to the cargo tanks, to vent gases to atmosphere and to protect tanks against excessive pressure or vacuum.

Inert gas plant

All equipment fitted to supply, cool, clean, pressurise, monitor and control the delivery of inert gas to the cargo tank systems.

Inert gas system (IGS)

An inert gas plant and inert gas distribution system together with means for preventing backflow of cargo gases to the machinery spaces, fixed and portable measuring instruments and control devices.

Inerting

The introduction of inert gas into a tank with the object of attaining the inert condition.

Insulating flange

A flanged joint incorporating an insulating gasket, sleeves and washers to prevent electrical continuity between pipelines, hose strings or loading arms.

Interface detector

An electrical instrument for detecting the boundary between oil and water.

Intrinsically safe

An electrical circuit or part of a circuit is intrinsically safe if any spark or thermal effect produced normally (ie, by breaking or closing the circuit) or accidentally (e.g. by short circuit or earth fault) is incapable, under prescribed test conditions, of igniting a prescribed gas mixture.

Loading overall

The loading of cargo or ballast 'over the top' through an open ended pipe or by means of an open ended hose entering a tank through a hatch or other deck opening, resulting in the free fall of liquid.

Lower flammable limit (LFL)

The concentration of a hydrocarbon gas in air below which there is insufficient hydrocarbon to support and propagate combustion. Sometimes referred to as lower explosive limit (LEL).

Mooring winch brake design capacity

The percentage of the minimum breaking load (MBL) of a new mooring rope or wire it carries, at which the winch brake is designed to render. Winch brakes will normally be designed to hold 80% of the line's MBL and will be set in service to hold 60% of the mooring line's MBL. Brake holding capacity may be expressed either in tonnes or as a percentage of a line's MBL.

Mooring winch design heaving capacity

The power of a mooring winch to heave in or put a load on its mooring rope or wire. Usually expressed in tonnes.

Naked lights

Open flames or fires, lighted cigarettes, cigars, pipes or similar smoking materials, any other unconfined sources of ignition, electrical and other equipment liable to cause sparking while in use, and unprotected light bulbs.

Non-volatile petroleum

Petroleum having a flash point of 60°C or above as determined by the closed cup method of test.

OBO, OIL/ORE

See 'Combination Carrier'.

Oxygen analyser/meter

An instrument for determining the percentage of oxygen in a sample of the atmosphere drawn from a tank, pipe or compartment.

Packaged cargo

Petroleum or other cargo in drums, packages or other containers.

Permissible Exposure Limits (PEL)

The maximum exposure to a toxic substance that is allowed by appropriate regulatory standards, including those of flag States. PEL's are usually expressed as:

Time Weighted Average (TWA) – the airborne concentrations of a toxic substance averaged over an 8 hour period, usually expressed in parts per million (ppm).

Short Term Exposure Limit (STEL) – the airborne concentration of a toxic substance averaged over any 15 minute period, usually expressed in parts per million (ppm).

Petroleum

Crude oil and liquid hydrocarbon products derived from it.

Petroleum gas

A gas evolved from petroleum. The main constituents of petroleum gases are hydrocarbons, but they may also contain other substances, such as hydrogen sulphide or lead alkyls, as minor constituents.

Pour point

The lowest temperature at which a petroleum oil will remain fluid.

Pressure surge

A sudden increase in the pressure of the liquid in a pipeline brought about by an abrupt change in flow velocity.

Pressure/vacuum relief valve (P/V valve)

A device which provides for the flow of the small volumes of vapour, air or inert gas mixtures caused by thermal variations in a cargo tank.

Purging

The introduction of inert gas into a tank already in the inert condition with the object of:
(1) further reducing the existing oxygen content; and/or
(2) reducing the existing hydrocarbon gas content to a level below which combustion cannot be supported if air is subsequently introduced into the tank.

Pyrophoric iron sulphide

Iron sulphide capable of a rapid exothermic oxidation causing incandescence when exposed to air and potential ignition of flammable hydrocarbon gas/air mixtures.

Reid vapour pressure (RVP)

The vapour pressure of a liquid determined in a standard manner in the Reid apparatus at a temperature of 37.8°C and with a ratio of gas to liquid volume of 4:1. Used for comparison purposes only. See 'True Vapour Pressure'.

Responsible officer (or person)

A person appointed by the employer or the master of the ship and empowered to take all decisions relating to a specific task, having the necessary knowledge and experience for that purpose.

Resuscitator

Equipment to assist or restore the breathing of personnel overcome by gas or lack of oxygen.

Self stowing mooring winch

A mooring winch fitted with a drum on which a wire or rope is made fast and automatically stowed.

SOLAS

The International Convention for the Safety of Life at Sea.

Sour crude oil

A crude oil containing appreciable amounts of hydrogen sulphide and/or mercaptans.

Spontaneous combustion

The ignition of material brought about by a heat producing (exothermic) chemical reaction within the material itself without exposure to an external source of ignition.

Static accumulator oil

An oil with an electrical conductivity less than 50 picoSiemens/metre (pS/m), so that it is capable of retaining a significant electrostatic charge.

Static electricity

The electricity produced by dissimilar materials through physical contact and separation.

Static non-accumulator oil

An oil with an electrical conductivity greater than 50 picoSiemens/metre (pS/m), which renders it incapable of retaining a significant electrostatic charge.

Stripping

The final operation in pumping bulk liquid from a tank or pipeline.

Tanker

A ship designed to carry liquid petroleum cargo in bulk, including a combination carrier when being used for this purpose.

Tank Cleaning

The process of removing hydrocarbon vapours, liquid or residue. Usually carried out so that tanks can be entered for inspection or hot work.

Tension winch (automated or self tensioning mooring system)

A mooring winch fitted with a device which may be set to automatically maintain the tension on a mooring line.

Terminal

A place where tankers are berthed or moored for the purpose of loading or discharging petroleum cargo.

Terminal representative

A person designated by the terminal to take responsibility for an operation or duty.

Threshold limit value (TLV)

The time-weighted average concentration of a substance to which workers may be repeatedly exposed, for a normal 8-hour workday or 40-hour workweek, day after day, without adverse effect. (See also Permissible Exposure Limits.)

Topping off

The operation of completing the loading of a tank to a required ullage.

Topping up

The introduction of inert gas into a tank which is already in the inert condition with the object of raising the tank pressure to prevent any ingress of air.

Torch

See 'Flashlight'.

Toxic

Poisonous to human life.

True vapour pressure (TVP)

The true vapour pressure of a liquid is the absolute pressure exerted by the gas produced by evaporation from a liquid when gas and liquid are in equilibrium at the prevailing temperature and the gas/liquid ratio is effectively zero.

Ullage

The depth of the space above the liquid in a tank.

Upper flammable limit (UFL)

The concentration of a hydrocarbon gas in air above which there is insufficient oxygen to support and propagate combustion. Sometimes referred to as upper explosive limit (UEL).

Vapour

A gas below its critical temperature.

Vapour emission control system

An arrangement of piping and equipment used to control vapour emissions during tanker operations, including ship and shore vapour collection systems, monitoring and control devices and vapour processing arrangements.

Vapour lock system

Equipment fitted to a tank to enable the measuring and sampling of cargoes without release of vapour/inert gas pressure.

Volatile petroleum

Petroleum, having a flash point below 60°C as determined by the closed cup method of testing.

Water fog

A suspension in the atmosphere of very fine droplets of water usually delivered at a high pressure through a fog nozzle for use in fire fighting.

Water spray

A suspension in the atmosphere of water divided into coarse drops by delivery through a special nozzle for use in fire fighting.

Work permit

A document issued by a responsible person permitting specific work to be done during a specific period in a defined area.

Part I

Operations

Chapter 1

Hazards of Petroleum

In order to appreciate the reasons for the practices adopted to ensure safety in tanker and terminal operations, all personnel should be familiar with the flammable properties of petroleum, the effects of the density of petroleum gases and their toxic properties. This Chapter contains a brief summary, and more detailed information is given in Chapters 15 and 16.

1.1 FLAMMABILITY

When petroleum is ignited, it is the gas progressively given off by the liquid which burns as a visible flame. The quantity of gas available to be given off by a petroleum liquid depends on its volatility which is frequently expressed for purposes of comparison in terms of Reid vapour pressure. A more informative measure of volatility is the true vapour pressure but unfortunately this is not easily measured. It is referred to in this guide only in connection with venting problems associated with very volatile cargoes, such as some crude oils and natural gasolines.

Petroleum gases can be ignited and will burn only when mixed with air in certain proportions. If there is too little or too much petroleum gas the mixture cannot burn. The limiting proportions, expressed as percentage by volume of petroleum gas in air, are known as the lower and upper flammable limits. They vary amongst the different possible components of petroleum gases. For the gas mixtures from the petroleum liquids encountered in normal tanker practice the overall range is from a minimum lower flammable limit of about 1% gas by volume in air to a maximum upper flammable limit of about 10% gas by volume in air.

As a petroleum liquid is heated the concentration of gas in air above it increases. The temperature of the liquid at which this concentration, using a specific measuring technique, reaches the lower flammable limit is known as the flashpoint of the liquid.

1.2 FLAMMABILITY CLASSIFICATION

There are many classification systems for defining the flammability characteristics of petroleum liquids, most of which are based on flashpoint and Reid vapour pressure data. For the purpose of this guide, which deals only with the particular conditions in petroleum tanker cargo handling, the division of such liquids into the two broad categories of non-volatile and volatile, as defined below, is in general sufficient to ensure that proper precautions can be specified.

- **Non-Volatile**

  Flashpoint of 60°C or above as determined by the closed cup method of testing.

- **Volatile**

  Flashpoint below 60°C as determined by the closed cup method of testing.

If there is any doubt as to the characteristics of a cargo, or if a non-volatile cargo is being handled at a temperature above its flashpoint minus 10°C, it should be treated as volatile petroleum. Owing to their particular characteristics, residual fuel oils should always be treated as volatile (see Chapter 24).

1.3   GAS DENSITY

The gases from normal petroleum liquids are heavier than air and inert gas, thus the possibility of layering of gases is very important in cargo handling operations. The density of the undiluted gas from a high vapour pressure distillate, such as motor gasoline, is likely to be about twice that of air and about 1.5 times that from a typical crude oil. These density differences diminish as the gases are diluted with air. Flammable mixtures usually contain at least 90% by volume of air and consequently have densities almost indistinguishable from that of air.

More detailed information on the density of petroleum gases is given in Chapter 15.

1.4   TOXICITY

Comparatively small quantities of petroleum gas when inhaled can cause symptoms of diminished responsibility and dizziness similar to drunkenness, with headache and irritation of the eyes. The inhalation of a sufficient quantity can be fatal.

These symptoms can occur at concentrations well below the lower flammable limit. However, petroleum gases vary in their physiological effects and human tolerance to these effects also varies widely. It should not be assumed that because conditions can be tolerated the gas concentration is within safe limits.

The smell of petroleum gas mixtures is very variable, and in some cases the gases may dull the sense of smell. The impairment of smell is especially likely and particularly serious if the mixture contains hydrogen sulphide.

The absence of smell should never be taken to indicate the absence of gas.

More detailed information on the toxic properties of petroleum, and of substances associated with the carriage of petroleum, is given in Chapter 16.

Chapter 2

General Precautions on Tankers

This Chapter deals primarily with the precautions to be taken on board a tanker whenever operational at sea or in port. Reference should be made to the appropriate Chapters for precautions relating to specific operations such as cargo handling, ballasting, tank cleaning, inerting or entry into enclosed spaces. Chapter 4 should be consulted for additional precautions to be taken while the vessel is in port.

2.1   GENERAL PRINCIPLES

In order to eliminate the risk of fire and explosion on a tanker, it is necessary to avoid a source of ignition and a flammable atmosphere being present in the same place at the same time. It is not always possible to exclude both these factors and precautions are therefore directed towards excluding or controlling one of them.

In the case of cargo compartments, pumprooms, and at times the tank deck, flammable gases are to be expected and the strict elimination of all possible sources of ignition in these locations is essential.

Cabins, galleys and other areas within the accommodation block inevitably contain ignition sources such as electrical equipment, matches and cigarette lighters. While it is sound practice to minimise and control such sources of ignition, it is essential to avoid the entry of flammable gas.

In engine and boiler rooms, ignition sources such as those arising from boiler operations and electrical equipment cannot be avoided. It is therefore essential to prevent the entry of flammable gases into such compartments. The contamination of bunker fuel by volatile cargo through bulkhead leaks, pipeline mixture or any other cause will introduce an additional danger. The routine checking of bunker spaces for flammability by tanker and terminal personnel is therefore to be encouraged.

It is possible, by good design and operational practice, for both flammable gases and ignition sources to be safely controlled in deck workshops, store rooms, forecastle, centre castle, dry cargo holds etc. The means for such control must, however, be rigorously maintained. In this connection it should be realized that an additional danger would be introduced into such areas by the contamination of bunker tanks with volatile cargo.

Although the installation and the correct operation of an inert gas system provides an added measure of safety, it does not preclude the need for close attention to the precautions set out in this chapter.

2.2 SMOKING AND NAKED LIGHTS

2.2.1 Smoking at Sea

While a tanker is at sea, smoking should be permitted only at times and in places specified by the master. Section 4.8.2 lists criteria which should be taken into account in determining the location of smoking places. Smoking must be prohibited on the tank deck or any other place where petroleum gas may be encountered. Additional restrictions on smoking in port are contained in Section 4.8.

2.2.2 Matches and Cigarette Lighters

The use of matches and cigarette lighters outside accommodation spaces should be prohibited, except in places where smoking is permitted. Matches and cigarette lighters should not be taken outside these places by personnel, nor should they be carried on the tank deck or in any other place where petroleum gas may be encountered.

The risk involved in carrying matches, and more particularly cigarette lighters, should be impressed on all personnel. Matches used on board should only be of the 'safety' type.

2.2.3 Naked Lights (Open Flame)

Naked lights must be prohibited on the tank deck and in any other place where there is a risk that petroleum gas may be present.

2.2.4 Notices

Portable and permanent notices prohibiting smoking and the use of naked lights should be conspicuously displayed at the point of access to the vessel and at the exits from the accommodation area. Within the accommodation area, instructions concerning smoking should be conspicuously displayed.

2.3 GALLEY

It is essential that galley personnel be instructed in the safe operation of galley equipment. Unauthorised and inexperienced persons should not be allowed to use such facilities.

A frequent cause of fires is the accumulation of unburnt fuel or fatty deposits in galley ranges, within flue pipes and filter cowls of galley vents. Such areas require frequent inspection to ensure that they are maintained in a clean condition. Oil and deep fat friers should be fitted with thermostats to cut off the electrical power and so prevent accidental fires.

Galley staff should be trained in handling fire emergencies. The appropriate fire extinguishers and fire blankets should be provided.

Additional restrictions on the use of galleys while in port are contained in Section 4.9.

2.4 PORTABLE LAMPS AND ELECTRICAL EQUIPMENT

2.4.1 General

All portable electrical equipment including lamps should be approved by a competent authority and must be carefully examined for possible defects before being used. Special care should be taken to ensure that the insulation is undamaged and that cables are securely attached and will remain so while the equipment is in use. Special care should also be taken to prevent mechanical damage to flexible cables (wandering leads).

2.4.2 Lamps and Other Electrical Equipment on Flexible Cables (Wandering Leads)

The use of portable electrical equipment on wandering leads should be prohibited within cargo tanks and adjacent spaces, or over the tank deck, unless throughout the period the equipment is in use:

- The compartment within which or over which the equipment and the lead are to be used is safe for hot work (see Section 2.8), and

- The adjacent compartments are also safe for hot work, or have been purged of hydrocarbon to less than 2% by volume and inerted, or are completely filled with ballast water, or any combination of these, (see Section 2.8) and

- All tank openings to other compartments not safe for hot work or purged as previous point are closed and remain so; or

- The equipment, including all wandering leads, is intrinsically safe; or

- The equipment, is contained within an approved explosion-proof housing. Any flexible cables should be of a type approved for extra hard usage, have an earth conductor, and be permanently attached to the explosion-proof housing in an approved manner.

In addition there are certain types of equipment which are approved for use over the tank deck only.

The foregoing does not apply to the proper use of flexible cables used with signal or navigation lights or with approved types of telephones.

2.4.3 Air Driven Lamps

Air driven lamps of an approved type may be used in non-gas free atmospheres although, to avoid the accumulation of static electricity at the appliance, the following precautions should be observed:

- The air supply should be fitted with a water trap; and

- The supply hose should be of a low electrical resistance.

Permanently installed units should be earthed.

2.4.4 Flashlights (Torches), Lamps and Portable Battery Powered Equipment

Only flashlights that have been approved by a competent authority for use in flammable atmospheres must be used on board tankers.

UHF/VHF portable transceivers must be of an intrinsically safe type.

Small battery powered personal items such as watches, miniature hearing aids and heart pacemakers are not significant ignition sources.

Unless approved for use in a flammable atmosphere, portable radios, tape recorders, electronic calculators, cameras containing batteries, photographic flash units, portable telephones and radio pagers must not be used on the tank deck or in areas where flammable gas may be present (see Section 4.10.2).

2.5 FIXED ELECTRICAL EQUIPMENT

Fixed electrical equipment in dangerous areas, and even in locations where a flammable atmosphere is to be expected infrequently, must be of an approved type and be properly maintained so as to ensure that neither the equipment nor the wiring becomes a source of ignition.

2.6 SYNTHETIC CLOTHING

Experience has shown that clothing made from synthetic material does not give rise to any significant electrostatic hazard under conditions normally encountered on tankers.

However, the tendency for synthetic material to melt and fuse together when exposed to high temperatures leads to a concentrated heat source which causes severe damage to body tissue. Clothing made of such material is therefore not considered suitable for persons who may in the course of their duties be exposed to flame or hot surfaces.

2.7 RADIO TRANSMITTING ANTENNAE

During medium and high frequency radio transmission (300 kHz – 30 MHz), significant energy is radiated which can, at distances extending to 500 metres from the transmitting antennae, induce an electrical potential in unearthed 'receivers' (derricks, rigging, mast stays etc.) capable of producing an incendive discharge. Transmissions can also cause arcing over the surface of antenna insulators when they have a surface coating of salt, dirt or water. It is therefore recommended that:

• All stays, derricks, and fittings should be earthed. Bearings of booms should be treated with a graphite grease to maintain electrical continuity.

• Transmissions should not be permitted during periods when there is likely to be a flammable gas in the region of the transmitting antennae.

Low energy transmissions, such as are used for satellite and VHF communications, do not produce the same sources of ignition. Further restrictions on the use of radio communications when at a petroleum berth are given in Section 4.11.

2.8 HOT WORK

2.8.1 General

Hot work is any work involving welding or burning, and other work including certain drilling and grinding operations, electrical work and the use of non-intrinsically safe electrical equipment, which might produce an incendive spark.

Hot work outside the main machinery spaces (and in the main machinery spaces when associated with fuel tanks and fuel pipelines) must take into account the possible presence of hydrocarbon vapours in the atmosphere, and the existence of potential ignition sources. Hot work should only be carried out outside the main machinery spaces if no other viable means of repair exists. Alternatives to be considered include cold work, or removal of the work piece to the main machinery spaces.

Hot work outside the main machinery spaces should only be permitted in accordance with prevailing national or international regulations and/or port/terminal requirements and should be subject to the restrictions of a shipboard hot work permit procedure.

Hot work for which a hot work permit is required should be prohibited during cargo, ballast, tank cleaning, gas freeing, purging or inerting operations.

2.8.2 Assessment of Hot Work

The master should decide whether the hot work is justifiable, and safe, and on the extent of the precautions necessary. Hot work in areas outside the main machinery spaces and other areas designated by the operator should not be proceeded with until the master has informed the operator's shore office of details of the work proposed, and a procedure has been discussed and agreed.

Before hot work is started a safety meeting under the chairmanship of the master should be held, at which the planned work and the safety precautions should be carefully reviewed. The meeting should be attended at least by all those who will have responsibilities in connection with the work. An agreed plan for the work and the related safety precautions should be made. The plan must clearly and unambiguously designate one officer who is responsible for the supervision of the work, and another officer who is responsible for safety precautions including means of communication between all parties involved.

All personnel involved in the preparations and in the hot work operation, must be briefed and instructed in their own role. They must clearly understand which officer is responsible for work supervision and which for safety precautions. A written hot work permit (see Appendix F) should be issued for each intended task. The permit should specify the duration of validity, which should not exceed a working day.

A flow-chart for guidance is shown in Figure 2-1.

2.8.3. Preparations for Hot Work

All operations utilizing the cargo or ballast system, including tank cleaning, gas freeing, purging or inerting should be stopped before hot work is undertaken, and throughout the duration of the hot work. If hot work is interrupted to permit pumping of ballast or other operations using the cargo, venting or inerting system, hot work should not be re-started until all precautions have been re-checked, and a new hot work permit has been issued.

No hot work should be carried out on bulkheads of bunker tanks containing bunkers, or within 0.5 metres from such bulkheads.

2.8.4. Hot Work in Enclosed Spaces

A compartment in which hot work is to be undertaken should be cleaned and ventilated until tests of the atmosphere indicate 21% oxygen content by volume and not more than 1% LFL. It is important to continue ventilation during hot work.

Adjacent cargo tanks, including diagonally positioned cargo tanks, should either have been cleaned and gas freed to hot work standard, or cleaned and hydrocarbon vapour content reduced to not more than 1% by volume and kept inerted, or completely filled with water. Other cargo tanks which are not gas free should be purged of hydrocarbon vapour to less than 2% by volume and kept inerted and secured.

On a vessel without an inert gas system, all cargo tanks except tanks containing slops should be cleaned and gas freed. Slops should be placed in a tank as far as possible from the hot work area, and the tank kept closed.

Adjacent ballast tanks, and compartments other than cargo tanks, should be checked to ensure they are gas free and safe for hot work. If found to be contaminated by hydrocarbon liquid or vapours, the cause of the contamination should be determined and the tank(s) cleaned and gas freed.

All interconnecting pipelines to other compartments should be flushed through with water, drained, vented and isolated from the compartment where hot work will take place. Cargo lines may be subsequently inerted or completely filled with water if considered necessary. Vapour lines and inert gas lines to the compartment should also be ventilated and isolated. Heating coils should be flushed.

All sludge, cargo-impregnated scale, sediment or other material likely to give off vapour which is flammable, should be removed from an area of at least 10 metres around the area of hot work. Special attention must be given to the reverse sides of frames and bulkheads. Other areas that may be affected by the hot work, such as the area immediately below, should also be cleaned.

This flowchart assumes the work is considered essential for safety or the immediate operational capability of the ship, and that it cannot be deferred until the next planned visit to a repair yard

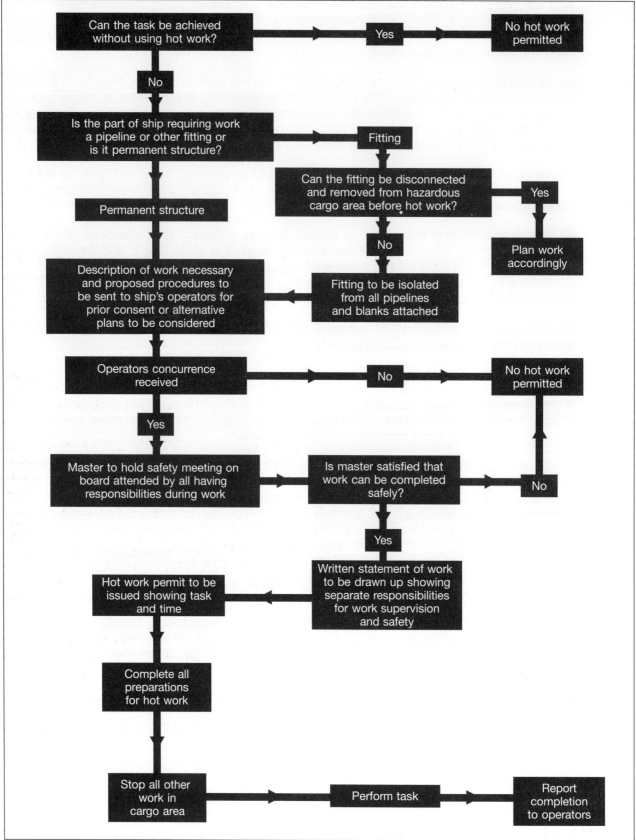

Figure 2-1. *Hot Work Flowchart*

An adjacent fuel oil bunker tank may be considered safe if tests using a combustible gas indicator give a reading of not more than 1% LFL in the ullage space of the bunker tank, and no heat transfer through the bulkhead of the bunker tank will be caused by the hot work.

2.8.5. Hot Work on the Open Deck

If hot work is to be undertaken on the open deck, cargo and slop tanks within a radius of at least 30 metres around the working area must be cleaned and hydrocarbon vapour content reduced to less than 1% by volume and inerted. All other cargo tanks in the cargo area must be inerted with openings closed.

Adjacent ballast tanks, and compartments other than cargo tanks, should be checked to ensure they are gas-free and safe for hot work. If found to be contaminated by hydrocarbon liquid or vapours they should be cleaned and gas freed.

On a vessel without an inert gas system all cargo tanks except those containing slops, must be cleaned and freed of hydrocarbon vapour to less than 1% LFL. Tanks containing slops should be kept closed and be beyond 30 metres from the work area.

2.8.6 Hot Work on Pipelines

Hot work on pipelines and valves should only be permitted when the appropriate item has been detached from the system by cold work, and the remaining system blanked off. The item to be worked on should be cleaned and gas freed to a "safe for hot work" standard, regardless of whether or not it is removed from the hazardous cargo area. Heating coils should be flushed and opened to ensure that they are clean and free of hydrocarbons.

2.8.7 Checks by Officer Responsible for Safety

Immediately before hot work is started the officer responsible for safety precautions should examine the area where hot work is to be undertaken, and ensure that the oxygen content is 21% by volume and that tests with a combustible gas indicator show not more than 1% LFL.

Adequate fire-fighting equipment must be laid out and be ready for immediate use. Fire watch procedures must be established for the area of hot work, and in adjacent, non-inerted spaces where the transfer of heat, or accidental damage, may create a hazard eg damage to hydraulic lines, electrical cables, thermal oil lines etc. Monitoring should be continued for sufficient time after completion of hot work. Effective means of containing and extinguishing welding sparks and molten slag must be established.

The work area must be adequately and continuously ventilated. The frequency of atmosphere monitoring must be established. Atmospheres should be re-tested after each break in work periods, and at regular intervals. Checks should be made to ensure there is no ingress of flammable vapours or liquids, toxic gases or inert gas from adjacent or connected spaces.

Welding and other equipment employed should be carefully inspected before each occasion of use to ensure it is in good condition. Where required it must be correctly earthed. Special attention must be paid when using electric-arc equipment ensuring:

- That electrical supply connections are made in a gas free space;

- That existing supply wiring is adequate to carry the electrical current demanded without overloading, causing heating;

- The insulation of flexible electric cables laid across the deck is in good condition;

- The cable route to the worksite is the safest possible, only passing over gas free or inerted spaces; and

- The earthing connection is adjacent to the work site with the earth return cable led directly back to the welding machine.

> Any changes in the conditions which formed the basis for issuing the original hotwork permit should invalidate it. Hot work should cease, and not be restarted until all safety precautions have been re-checked and a new hot work permit has been issued.

2.9 USE OF TOOLS

2.9.1 Grit Blasting and Mechanically Powered Tools

It should be noted that grit blasting and use of mechanically powered tools are not normally considered as coming within the definition of hot work. However, both these operations should only be permitted under the following conditions:

- The work area should not be subject to vapour release, or a concentration of combustible vapours, and should be free of combustible material.

- The area should be gas-free, and tests with a combustible gas indicator should give a reading of not more than 1% LFL.

- The ship must not be alongside at a terminal.

- There must be no cargo, bunkering, ballasting, tank cleaning, gas-freeing, purging or inerting operations in progress.

Adequate fire-fighting equipment must be laid out, and ready for immediate use.

The hopper and hose nozzle of a grit blasting machine should be electrically bonded and earthed to the deck or fitting being worked on.

There is a risk of perforation of pipelines when gritblasting or chipping, and great care must be taken when planning such work. Before work on cargo lines on deck commences they should be flushed, drop line valves closed, bottom lines filled with water, and the atmosphere inside the part to be worked on confirmed as either inerted to less than 8% oxygen by volume or gas-free to not more than 1% LFL. Similar precautions should be adopted as appropriate for inert gas and crude oil washing lines.

2.9.2 Hand Tools

The use of hand tools such as chipping hammers and scrapers for steel preparation and maintenance may be permitted without a hot work permit. Their use must be restricted to the actual deck areas and fittings not connected to the cargo system.

The work area should be gas-free and clear of combustible materials. The ship must not be engaged in any cargo, bunker, ballasting, tank cleaning, gas-freeing, purging or inerting operations.

Non-ferrous, so called non-sparking, tools are only marginally less likely to give rise to an incendive spark, and, because of their comparative softness, are not as efficient as their ferrous equivalents. Particles of concrete, sand or other rock-like substances are likely to become embedded in the working face or edge of such tools, and can then cause incendive sparks on impact with ferrous or other hard metals. The use of non-ferrous tools is therefore not recommended.

2.10 ALUMINIUM

Aluminium equipment should not be dragged or rubbed across steel since it may leave a smear which, if it is on rusty steel and is subsequently struck, can cause an incendive spark.

It is therefore recommended that the undersides of aluminium gangways and other heavy portable aluminium structures be protected with a hard plastic or wooden strip.

2.11 CATHODIC PROTECTION ANODES IN CARGO TANKS

Magnesium anodes are very likely to produce incendive sparks on impact with rusty steel. Such anodes must not be fitted in tanks where flammable gases can be present.

Aluminium anodes give rise to incendive sparking on violent impact and should therefore be installed only at approved locations within cargo tanks, and should never be moved to another location without proper supervision. Moreover, as aluminium anodes could easily be mistaken for zinc anodes and installed in potentially dangerous locations, it is advisable to restrict their use to permanent ballast tanks.

Zinc anodes do not generate an incendive spark on impact with rusty steel and therefore are not subject to the above restrictions.

The location, securing and type of anode are subject to approval by the appropriate authorities. Their recommendations should be observed and inspections made as frequently as possible to check the security of the anodes and mountings. With the advent of high capacity tank washing machines, anodes are more liable to physical damage.

2.12 SPONTANEOUS COMBUSTION

Some materials when damp or soaked with oil, especially oil of vegetable origin, are liable to ignite without the external application of heat as the result of gradual heating within the material produced by oxidation. The risk of spontaneous combustion is smaller with petroleum oils than with vegetable oils, but it can still occur, particularly if the material is kept warm, for example by proximity to a hot pipe.

Cotton waste, rags, canvas, bedding, jute sacking or any similar absorbent material should therefore not be stowed near oil, paint, etc. and should not be left lying on the jetty, on decks, on equipment, on or around pipelines etc. If such materials become damp, they should be dried before being stowed away. If soaked with oil they should be cleaned or destroyed.

Certain chemicals used for boiler treatment are also oxidising agents and although carried in diluted form, are capable of spontaneous combustion if permitted to evaporate.

2.13 AUTO-IGNITION

Petroleum liquids when heated sufficiently will ignite without the application of a naked flame. This process of auto-ignition is most common where fuel or lubricating oil under pressure sprays onto a hot surface. It also occurs when oil spills onto lagging, vaporises and bursts into flame. Both instances have been responsible for serious engine room fires. Oil feeder lines require particular attention to avoid oil being sprayed from leaks. Oil saturated lagging should be removed and personnel protected from any re-ignition of vapours during the process.

2.14 ENGINE AND BOILER ROOMS

2.14.1 Combustion Equipment

As a precaution against funnel fires and sparks, burners, tubes, uptakes, exhaust manifolds and spark arresters should be maintained in good working condition. If there is a funnel fire or sparks are emitted from the funnel, the tanker should, if necessary, alter course as soon as possible to avoid sparks falling on the tank deck. Any cargo, ballasting or tank cleaning operations that are taking place must be stopped and all tank openings closed.

2.14.2 Blowing Boiler Tubes

Boiler tubes should be soot blown prior to arrival and after departure from a port. The officer on bridge watch should be consulted prior to the operation commencing and the vessel's course altered if necessary. Boiler tubes should not be soot blown when the vessel is in port.

2.14.3 Cleaning Liquids

It is preferable that cleaning liquids be non-toxic and non-flammable. If flammable liquids are used, they should have a high flashpoint. Highly volatile liquids such as gasoline or naphtha should never be used.

Cleaning liquids which are flammable should be kept in closed, unbreakable, correctly labelled containers and stored in a suitable compartment when not in use.

Cleaning liquids should only be used in places where ventilation is adequate taking into consideration the volatility of the liquids being used. All such liquids should be stowed and used in compliance with the manufacturer's instructions.

Direct skin contact with, or the contamination of clothing by, cleaning liquids should be avoided.

2.14.4 Oil Spillage and Leakage

Oil spillage and leakage in the engine and boiler rooms is not only a fire hazard, but can also cause slips and falls. Spills and leaks should therefore be avoided. Floor plates should be kept clean and bilges should be kept free of oil and waste.

2.14.5 Personal Hygiene

In view of the danger to health which may arise from prolonged contact with oil, personal hygiene is most important. Direct skin contact with oil or with oily clothing should be avoided.

2.14.6 Bunker Safety

Although residual fuel oil normally has a flashpoint above 60°C, it should be remembered that it is often stored and managed at temperatures close to, or even above, its flashpoint. High flashpoint fuels sometimes contain residual quantities of light components which slowly migrate into vapour spaces after loading, so raising the flammability. It must therefore never be assumed that the vapour spaces in, and emissions from, bunker tanks will always be safe simply on account of a high specified flashpoint. For this reason, ullaging, dipping and sampling procedures must follow the recommendations given in Chapter 7, Table 7-1.

2.15 COLD WEATHER PRECAUTIONS

During cold weather the functioning of pressure/vacuum relief valves and high velocity vents should be checked. It is also possible that humid air vented from a cargo tank may condense and freeze on gauze screens thus inhibiting ventilation.

On vessels fitted with inert gas systems, care must be taken to maintain the water supply to the deck water seal, to prevent freezing of static water and to control the heating of such water to prevent boiling. In addition the pressure/vacuum breaker, if filled with water, must be protected from freezing by adding glycol.

Precautions should be taken to ensure that the fire main system is kept operational. Steam operated winches and windlasses should be rotated slowly to avoid damage.

2.16   ENTRY INTO ENCLOSED SPACES

Because of the possibility of oxygen deficiency, as well as the presence of hydrocarbon or toxic gas in a cargo tank, cofferdam, double bottom tank or any enclosed space, it is the master's responsibility to identify such spaces and to establish procedures for safe entry. Guidance is to be found in Chapter 11.

Personnel should consult the responsible officer to determine whether entry into such enclosed spaces is permitted. It is the duty of the responsible officer to check the atmosphere in the compartment, ventilate the space, ensure the appropriate procedures are followed, ensure the safety of the personnel concerned, and issue an entry permit.

2.17   PUMPROOMS

2.17.1   General Precautions

Cargo pumprooms, by virtue of their location, design and operation which require the space to be routinely entered by personnel, constitute a particular hazard and therefore necessitate special precautions. A pumproom contains the largest concentration of cargo pipelines of any space within the ship and leakage of a volatile product from any part of this system could lead to the rapid generation of a flammable or toxic atmosphere. The pumproom may also contain a number of potential ignition sources unless formal, structured maintenance, inspection and monitoring procedures are strictly adhered to.

2.17.2   Routine Maintenance and Housekeeping Issues

Pumproom bilges should be kept clean and dry. Particular care should be taken to prevent the escape of hydrocarbon liquids or vapour into the pumproom.

It is important that the integrity of pipelines and pumps is maintained and any leaks are detected and rectified in a timely fashion. Pipelines should be visually examined and subjected to routine pressure tests to verify their condition. Other means of non-destructive testing or examination, such as ultra-sonic wall thickness measurement, may be considered appropriate, but should always be supplemented by visual examination.

Procedures should be established to verify that mud boxes and filters are properly sealed after they have been opened up for routine cleaning or examination.

Valve glands and drain cocks should be regularly inspected to ensure that they do not leak.

Bulkhead penetrations should be routinely checked to ensure their effectiveness.

The security of critical bolts on the cargo pumps and associated fittings, such as pedestal fixing bolts, pump casing bolts and bolts securing shaft guards, should be ensured. In addition, requirements for their examination should be included in routine maintenance procedures.

2.17.3   Ventilation

Because of the potential for the presence of hydrocarbon gas in the pumproom, SOLAS (Chapter II-2, Regulation 59.3) requires the use of mechanical ventilation to maintain the atmosphere in a safe condition.

The pumproom should be continuously ventilated during all cargo operations.

Before anyone enters a pumproom it should be thoroughly ventilated, the oxygen content of the atmosphere should be verified and the atmosphere checked for the presence of hydrocabon and toxic gases.

Ventilation should be continuous until access is no longer required or cargo operations have been completed.

2.17.4 Pumproom Entry

It is strongly recommended that operators develop procedures to control pumproom entry, regardless of whether or not a fixed gas detection system is in use. Clear procedures should be established with regard to undertaking pre-entry checks, gas testing, and subsequent regular atmosphere monitoring.

In addition to detailing pre-entry checks, procedures should include the use of personal gas monitors for those entering the space.

A communications system should provide links between the pumproom, navigation bridge, engine room and cargo control room. In addition, audible and visual repeaters for essential alarm systems, such as the general alarm, should be provided within the pumproom.

Arrangements should be established to enable effective communication to be maintained at all times between personnel within the pumproom and those outside. Regular communication checks should be made at pre-agreed intervals and failure to respond should be cause to raise the alarm.

The frequency of pumproom entry for routine inspection purposes during cargo operations should be reviewed with a view to minimising personnel exposure.

Notices should be displayed at the pumproom entrance prohibiting entry without permission.

2.17.5 Maintenance of Electrical Equipment

The integrity of the protection afforded by the design of explosion proof or intrinsically safe electrical equipment may be compromised by incorrect maintenance procedures. Even the simplest of repair and maintenance operations must be carried out in strict compliance with the manufacturers instructions in order to ensure that such equipment remains in a safe condition. This is particularly relevant in the case of explosion proof lights where incorrect closing after simply changing a light bulb could compromise the integrity of the light.

In order to assist with routine servicing and repair, ships should be provided with detailed maintenance manuals for the specific systems and arrangements as fitted on board.

2.17.6 Inspection and Maintenance of Ventilation Fans

Pumproom ventilation fans are required to operate by drawing air out of the space. As a consequence, should gas be present in the pumproom the vapours will be drawn through the blades of the fan impeller and could be ignited if the blades contacted the casing or if the fan's bearings or seals over-heated.

Pumproom extractor fans, including impellers, shafts and gas seals, should be inspected on a regular basis. At the same time, the condition of the fan trunking should be inspected and the proper operation of change-over flaps and fire dampers confirmed. Routine vibration monitoring and analysis should be considered as a means for providing early detection of component wear.

2.17.7 Cargo Draining Procedures

On some existing tankers, no provision is made for effective line draining and, in order to meet the demands of certain product trades, final line contents are drained to the pumproom bilge. This is an unsafe practice and it is recommended that cargo procedures are reviewed with the aim of preventing a volatile product being drained to the bilge.

It is recommended that consideration be given to the provision of a comprehensive stripping arrangement to enable all lines and pumps to be effectively drained to a cargo tank, slop tank or dedicated reception tank for subsequent discharge ashore.

2.17.8 Miscellaneous

There are a number of ways to enhance the safety of pumprooms which operators may wish to consider, including:

- A fixed gas detection system capable of continuously monitoring for the presence of hydrocarbon gas. Where such equipment is fitted, procedures should be developed in respect of its regular testing and calibration and with regard to the action to be taken in the event of an alarm occurring, especially relating to vacating the space and stopping cargo pumps.

- A fixed sampling arrangement to enable the oxygen content within the pumproom to be monitored from the deck by portable meter prior to pumproom entry. Any such arrangement utilised should ensure the effective monitoring of the remoter parts of the pumproom.

- Temperature monitoring devices fitted to main cargo pumps in order to provide remote indication of the temperature of pump casings, bearings and bulkhead seals. Where such equipment is fitted, procedures should be developed with regard to the action to be taken in the event of an alarm occurring.

- A high level alarm in pumproom bilges which activates audible and visual alarms in the cargo control room, engine room and the navigating bridge.

- Manually activated trips for the main cargo pumps provided at the lower pumproom level.

- Spray arrestors around the glands of all rotary cargo pumps in order to reduce the formation of mists in the event of minor leakage from the gland.

- Examining the feasibility of retro-fitting a double seal arrangement to contain any leakage from the primary seal and to activate a remote alarm to indicate that leakage has occurred. However, the impact of any proposed retro-fit on the integrity of the pump will need to be clearly assessed in conjunction with the pump manufacturers.

- Particular attention to be given to the adequacy of fire protection in the immediate vicinity of the cargo pumps.

- Because of the problems associated with flashback re-ignition after the use of the primary fire fighting medium, consideration to be given to the need to provide a back-up system, such as high expansion foam or water drenching, to supplement the existing system. On ships fitted with an inert gas system, the provision of an emergency facility for inerting the pumproom could be an option, although careful attention must be paid to the safety and integrity of the arrangement.

- The provision of an escape breathing apparatus set located within the pumproom and readily accessible.

Chapter 3

Arrival in Port

This Chapter deals with the preparations and procedures for the arrival of a tanker in port, with particular reference to mooring and unmooring arrangements. Precautions to be taken when entering or leaving port are also given.

3.1 EXCHANGE OF INFORMATION

3.1.1 General

Before the tanker arrives at the terminal there should be an exchange of information as necessary on the following matters.

3.1.2 Tanker to the Appropriate Competent Authority

Information as required by international, regional, and national regulations and recommendations.

The information, some of which may be required in the form of a check list, should include at least the following:

- Name and call sign of vessel.

- Country of registration.

- Overall length, draught and beam of vessel.

- Name of harbour and estimated time of arrival.

- Nature of cargo, correct technical name, name in common usage, UN number (if applicable), flashpoint (as appropriate) and quantity.

- Distribution of cargo on board, indicating that to be unloaded and that to be left on board.

- Whether vessel is fitted with an inert gas system and, if fitted, whether fully operational.

- Whether vessel has any requirements for tank cleaning or slops disposal.

- Any defect of hull, machinery or equipment which may:

  - Affect the safe manoeuvrability of the tanker.

  - Affect the safety of other vessels.

- Constitute a hazard to the marine environment.

- Constitute a hazard to persons or property on land or in the vicinity of the harbour.

- Details of statutory certificates and their period of validity.

3.1.3 Tanker to Terminal

- Ship's draught and trim on arrival.

- Maximum draught and trim expected during and upon completion of cargo handling.

- Advice from master on tug assistance required.

- If fitted with an inert gas system, confirmation that the ship's tanks are in an inert condition and that the system is fully operational.

- Oxygen content of cargo tanks.

- Whether the ship has any requirement for tank cleaning.

- Any hull, bulkhead, valve or pipeline leaks which could affect cargo handling or cause pollution.

- Any repairs which could delay commencement of cargo handling.

- Whether crude oil washing is to be employed.

- Ship's manifold details, including type, number, size, and material of connections to be presented.

- Whether the ship has external impressed cathodic protection.

- Advance information on proposed cargo handling operations or advance information on changes in existing plans for cargo handling operations and distribution of cargo.

- Information as required on quantity and nature of slops and dirty ballast, and of any contamination by chemical additives.

3.1.4 Terminal to Tanker

- Depth of water at the berth at low water and range of salinity that can be expected at the berth.

- Availability of tugs and mooring craft, when they are required to assist in manoeuvring and mooring.

- Whether the ship's or the tugs' lines are to be used.

- Mooring lines and accessories which the ship is required to have available for all mooring operations.

- Details of any shore moorings which will be provided.

- Which side to be moored alongside.

- Number and size of hose connections/manifolds.

- Inert gas requirements for cargo measurement.

- Any particular feature of a jetty berth or buoy mooring which it is considered essential to bring to the prior notice of the master.

- Maximum allowable speed and angle of approach to the jetty.

- Any code of visual or audible signals for use during mooring, including availability of berthing approach velocity indicators.

- For jetty berths, arrangement of gangway landing space or availability of terminal access equipment.

- Advance information on proposed cargo handling operations or changes in existing plans for cargo handling operations.

- Requirements for crude oil washing procedures and tank cleaning, if applicable.

- Whether tanks are to be gas free of hydrocarbon vapours for loading non-volatile static accumulator products.

- Advice on environmental and load restrictions applicable to the berth.

- Arrangements for the reception of slops and/or oily ballast residues.

3.2 PREPARATION FOR ARRIVAL

3.2.1 Port Information

The terminal should ensure that the tanker is provided with general port information as soon as practicable.

3.2.2 Berthing Information

Before berthing, the terminal should provide the master, through the pilot or berthing master, with details of the mooring plan. The procedure for mooring the vessel should be specified and this should be reviewed by the master and pilot or berthing master and agreed between them. Any deviation from the agreed mooring plan made necessary by changing weather conditions should be given to the master as soon as possible.

Additional information should include:

- For jetty berths: the minimum number of tanker's moorings and a diagram showing the relative positions of bollards or quick release hooks and the cargo handling manifold.

- For conventional, multi-buoy moorings, the minimum number of shackles of cable that may be required on each anchor that may be used during the course of mooring and the number and position of mooring lines, shackles and other mooring equipment likely to be needed.

- For Single Point Moorings (SPMs): the diameter of the chafe chain links used in the mooring, the weight of each of the moorings which has to be lifted on board, the length and size of any messenger lines which have to be used to pick up the moorings, the minimum requisite dimension of bow chock or lead required, the method used to make the SPM fast to the tanker and details of any equipment which must be provided by the tanker.

- For all offshore berths: the required Safe Working Load (SWL) of the ship's hose handling derrick, the number and flange size of the hoses to be connected and details of any equipment which the ship must provide to assist in hose handling.

3.2.3 Tanker's Mooring Equipment

Before arrival at a port or a berth, all necessary mooring equipment should be ready for use. The terminal and the port authority should be informed of any deficiencies or incompatibilities in the equipment which might affect the safety of the mooring. Anchors should be ready for use if required, unless anchoring is prohibited. There should always be an adequate number of personnel available to handle the moorings.

3.3 ENTERING OR LEAVING PORT

3.3.1 Security of Buoyancy

When entering or leaving port in a loaded condition it is important that the tanker's buoyancy remains secure against ingress of water resulting from damage. Ullage ports, forepeak, afterpeak, foredeep covers and ventilators should be securely closed, and cargo, bunker, cofferdam and pumproom openings also secured.

3.3.2 Tugs Alongside

Before tugs come alongside to assist a tanker, all cargo and ballast tank lids and ullage ports should be closed, no matter what grade of oil is being or has been carried, unless all the cargo tanks are gas free of hydrocarbon vapour. Tugs and other craft must not be permitted to come alongside before the master has satisfied himself that it is safe for them to do so.

Tugs should have adequate fendering to avoid causing damage and should push the tanker at appropriate positions which should be indicated by markings.

3.4 CAPACITY OF JETTY FENDERING

The capacity of the fendering system to absorb energy is limited. Masters, berthing masters and pilots should be advised by the terminal of the limitations of the fendering system and of the maximum displacement, approach velocity and angle of approach for which the berth and the fendering system have been designed.

3.5 MOORING AT JETTY BERTHS

3.5.1 Personnel Safety

Mooring and unmooring operations including tug line handling are dangerous operations. It is important that everybody concerned realises this and takes appropriate precautions to prevent accidents.

3.5.2 Security of Moorings

Any excessive movement, or the breaking adrift from the berth, of a tanker owing to inadequate moorings could cause severe damage to the jetty installations and the vessel. For all tankers above 16,000 tonnes deadweight intended for general worldwide trading, the mooring restraint available on board the ship as permanent equipment should satisfy the following conditions:

60 knots wind from any direction simultaneously with either:
- 3 knots current from directly ahead or astern (0 deg or 180 deg), or
- 2 knots current at 10 deg or 170 deg. or
- 0.75 knots current from the direction of maximum beam current loading.

The above criteria are intended to cover conditions that could readily be encountered on worldwide trade, but they cannot possibly cater for the most extreme combination of environmental conditions at every terminal. At exposed terminals, or those where for some reason the criteria are likely to be exceeded, the ship's mooring restraint should be supplemented with appropriate shore-based equipment.

Although responsibility for the adequate mooring of a tanker rests with the master, the terminal has an interest in ensuring that vessels are securely and safely moored. Cargo hoses or arms should not be connected until both the terminal representative and the master are satisfied that the ship is safely moored.

For further information on ship and terminal mooring arrangements and procedures, reference should be made to the OCIMF publication "Mooring Equipment Guidelines".

3.5.3   Type and Quality of Mooring Lines

The mooring lines used to secure the tanker should preferably all be of the same materials and construction. Wire ropes are recommended for larger tankers as they limit the tanker's movement at the berth. Moorings composed entirely of high elasticity ropes are not recommended as they can allow excessive movement from strong wind or current forces, or from suction caused by passing ships. Within a given mooring pattern, ropes of different elasticity should never be used together in the same direction.

It should be realised that mooring conditions and regulations may differ from port to port.

Where dynamic (shock) loading on moorings can be caused by swell conditions or the close passing of ships, fibre tails on the ends of mooring wires can provide sufficient elasticity to prevent failure of wires and other components of the mooring system. Such tails, whose length should not exceed one third of the distance between the ship's fairlead and the shore mooring bollard, may be provided by the tanker or the terminal.

Because fibre tails deteriorate more rapidly than wires they should be at least 25% stronger than the wires to which they are attached. They should be inspected frequently, particularly in way of their connection to the wire, and replaced at regular intervals.

3.5.4   Tension Winches

Self tensioning winches fitted with automatic rendering and hauling capability should not be used in the automatic mode while the vessel is moored because they may not always hold it in position at a berth.

3.5.5   Self Stowing Mooring Winches

Because their weight and size make manual handling difficult, mooring wires used by tankers are normally stored on self stowing mooring winches which may be either single drum or split drum.

A number of features of these winches need to be clearly understood by ships' personnel in order to avoid vessels breaking adrift from berths as the result of slipping winch brakes.

The holding power of the brake depends on several factors, the first being its designed holding capacity. This may either have been specified by the shipowner or be the standard design of the winch manufacturer. Some winches have brakes which are designed to slip or render under loads which are less than 60% of the breaking load of the mooring line (MBL) handled. Every ship's officer should be aware of the designed brake holding capacity of the self-stowing mooring winches installed on his vessel.

In addition, deterioration of the brake holding capacity will be caused by wear down of the brake linings or blocks, and it should therefore be tested at regular intervals (not exceeding twelve months). A record, both of regular maintenance and inspections and tests, should be kept on the vessel. If the deterioration is significant, particularly if the initial designed holding capacity was low in relation to the breaking load of the mooring, the linings or blocks must be renewed. Some of the newer self-stowing mooring winches are fitted with disc brakes which are less affected by wear.

Kits are available for testing winch brake holding capacity which can be placed on board for use by the crew.

There are also a number of operational procedures which can seriously reduce the holding capacity of winch brakes if they are not correctly carried out.

- **The number of layers of wire on the drum.**

  The holding capacity of a winch brake is in inverse proportion to the number of layers of the mooring wire or rope on the drum. The designed holding capacity is usually calculated with reference to the first layer and there is a reduction in the holding capacity for each additional layer. This can be substantial – as much as an 11% reduction for the second layer.

  If the rated brake holding capacity of a split drum winch is not to be reduced, only one layer should be permitted on the working drum.

- **The direction of reeling on the winch drum.**

  On both undivided and split drum winches, the holding power of the brake is decreased substantially if the mooring line is reeled on the winch drum in the wrong direction. Before arrival at the berth, it is important that the mooring line is reeled so that its pull will be against the fixed end of the brake strap rather than the pinned end. Reeling in the contrary direction can seriously reduce the brake holding capacity, in some cases by as much as 50%. The correct reeling direction to assist the brake should be permanently marked on the drum to avoid misunderstanding.

  Winches fitted with disc brakes are not subject to this limitation.

- **The condition of brake linings and drum.**

  Oil, moisture or heavy rust on the brake linings or drum can seriously reduce the brake holding capacity. Moisture may be removed by running the winch with the brake applied lightly but care must be taken not to cause excessive wear. Oil impregnation cannot be removed so linings should, in that case, be renewed.

- **The application of the brake.**

  Brakes must be adequately tightened to achieve the designed holding capacity. The use of hydraulic brake applicators or a torque wrench showing the degree of torque applied is desirable. If brakes are applied manually, they should be checked for tightness.

3.5.6 Shore Moorings

At some terminals, shore moorings are used to supplement the tanker's moorings. If the adjustable ends are on board the tanker these moorings should be tended by the tanker's personnel in conjunction with its own moorings. If shore based wires with winches are provided, agreement should be reached over the responsibility for tending. If shore based pulleys are provided, the tanker should tend the mooring since both ends of the line are on board.

3.6 BUOY MOORINGS

3.6.1 General

All the normal precautions taken during berthing alongside a jetty should also be taken when berthing at a buoy mooring.

At terminals with buoy moorings for ocean going tankers it is desirable to have professional advice on those aspects of safety related to the marine operations. This may be by the assignment of a berthing master (mooring master) to the terminal, or by consultation with a port or pilotage authority if available.

3.6.2 Conventional, Multi Buoy Moorings

At conventional buoy moorings, good communication between bridge and poop is essential to avoid moorings or mooring boats being caught up in the ship's propeller.

Severe loads can sometimes develop in certain mooring lines during the mooring operation. It is essential that good quality moorings of adequate length are used and personnel are closely supervised so as to ensure their safety.

At many conventional buoy mooring berths the ship's moorings are supplemented by shore moorings run from the buoys or by ground moorings. The handling of these often heavy wires around the warping drum of a winch should only be undertaken by experienced seamen.

3.6.3 Single Point Moorings (SPM)

Complicated and non-standard mooring arrangements at SPMs frequently lead to dangerous and protracted operations. Therefore the fitting, both on ships and on SPMs, of well designed and, in the case of the ship, accurately positioned, items of standard equipment will considerably reduce the risk of injury to personnel. The proper fitting of such equipment will also provide a more efficient method of securing ships to SPMs at offshore terminals.

OCIMF has produced guidelines for SPM mooring equipment entitled "Recommendations for Equipment Employed in the Mooring of Ships at Single Point Moorings" and it is recommended that these are used by all SPM terminals and the ships using them.

When mooring to an SPM, it is essential that a good communications system between bridge and bow is established and maintained.

The ship should be fully aware of the type of mooring it will be making fast and of the weight to be lifted. The terminal should advise the length and size of the messenger line required.

When the messenger (pick up rope) is being used to heave the mooring on board and, in the case of ships without bow stoppers, during the making fast operation, it is very important that no additional load resulting from the ship falling back or yawing is allowed to develop. Sheaves, pedestal rollers, etc. around which the messenger is led to the warping or storage drum must be free to rotate so as to avoid excessive chafing on the messenger. Care must be taken to ensure that personnel do not stand in positions in which they could be injured by a parting messenger. At some SPMs tankers of over 150,000 dwt are moored by two identical moorings. It is not advisable to pass both moorings through the same bow lead.

3.7 EMERGENCY RELEASE PROCEDURES

3.7.1 General

Means should be provided to permit the quick and safe release of the ship in case of need in an emergency. The method used for the emergency release operation should be discussed and agreed, taking into account the possible risks involved.

3.7.2 Emergency Towing Off Wires (Fire Wires)

Except at terminals where no tugs are available, towing off wires of adequate strength and condition should be made fast to bollards on the tanker, forward and aft, and their eyes run out and maintained at, or about, the waterline.

On tankers alongside a jetty the wires should be hung in positions which tugs can reach without difficulty, usually the offshore side; for tankers at buoy berths, they should be hung on the side opposite to the hose strings.

In order that sufficient wire can pay out to enable the tugs to tow effectively, enough slack should be retained between the bollard and the fairlead and be prevented from running out by a rope yarn or other easily broken means.

There are various methods for rigging emergency towing wires currently in use and the arrangement may vary from port to port. Some terminals may require a particular method to be used and the ship should be advised accordingly.

Chapter 4

General Precautions While a Tanker is at a Petroleum Berth

This Chapter deals with the precautions to be taken both on a tanker and ashore while the tanker is at a petroleum berth. These are additional to the general precautions described in Chapter 2 but do not include precautions that are related to specific operations such as cargo handling, ballasting, bunkering or tank cleaning for which reference to the appropriate Chapter should be made.

4.1 SAFETY PRECAUTIONS AND EMERGENCY PROCEDURES

4.1.1 Compliance with Terminal and Local Regulations

Terminals should have safety and pollution regulations which must be complied with by both tanker and terminal personnel. All tankers at the terminal should be aware of such regulations, together with any other regulations relating to the safety of shipping which may be issued by the appropriate port authority. Regulations regarding work in shore hazardous zones should be carefully noted (see Sections 4.12.4 and 4.12.5).

4.1.2 Manning Requirements

A sufficient number of personnel to deal with an emergency should be present on board the ship and in the shore installation at all times during the ship's stay at a terminal.

Those personnel involved with the operations should be familiar with the risks associated with handling petroleum.

4.1.3 At Buoy Moorings

All the normal precautions taken during cargo handling operations alongside a jetty should be taken when a tanker is at a buoy mooring.

It is essential that good communications between the tanker and the terminal be maintained during the cargo transfer operation. If the buoy mooring is in an exposed location the berthing master should remain on board throughout the operation.

Where mooring loads at an SPM are remotely monitored the terminal should, particularly in deteriorating conditions, keep the vessel regularly advised of the load read-outs being received.

4.1.4 Tanker and Terminal Liaison on Safety Procedures

After the tanker has berthed the terminal representative should contact the responsible officer to:

- Agree designated smoking places.

- Agree galley equipment and cooking appliance limitations.

- Advise on 'Work Permit' and 'Hot Work Permit' procedures.

- Advise on other relevant activities in the vicinity.

- Provide information about other terminal or local safety and pollution regulations.

- Advise means of summoning assistance from terminal, fire, medical, police and other emergency services.

- Exchange information on the availability and use of fire-fighting and emergency equipment on the terminal and the tanker.

- Discuss the action to be taken (both on board and ashore) in case of fire or other emergency (see Section 14.5 and Appendix B).

- Discuss arrangements for the orderly evacuation of the berth in an emergency, e.g. muster points and ship to shore access routes.

The other safety precautions to be observed before cargo handling begins, including implementation of the Ship/Shore Safety Check List, are given in Chapter 5.

4.1.5 Anchors

Anchors not in use should be properly secured but available for immediate use.

4.2 MANAGEMENT OF MOORINGS WHILE ALONGSIDE

Ship personnel are responsible for the frequent monitoring and careful tending of the tanker's moorings, but suitably qualified shore personnel should check the moorings periodically to satisfy themselves that they are being properly tended.

When tending moorings which have become slack or too taut, an overall view of the mooring system should be taken so that the tightening or slackening of individual lines does not allow the tanker to move or place undue loading on other lines. The tanker should maintain contact with the fenders and moorings should not be slackened if the tanker is lying off the fenders.

The possibility of using tugs to maintain position should be considered whenever the following conditions exist or are expected:

- Significant increase in wind speed or change in wind direction, particularly if the tanker has substantial freeboard.

- Swell.

- Periods of maximum tidal flow.

- Limited underkeel clearance.

- The close passing of other ships.

Advice on the responsibility for tending shore moorings is given in Section 3.5.6.

4.3   MANAGEMENT OF MOORINGS AT BUOY BERTHS

While the tanker is at a conventional, multi-buoy mooring, frequent and regular inspection is essential to ensure that mooring lines are kept taut and that movement of the tanker is kept to a minimum. Excessive movement may cause rupture of the cargo connections.

At single point moorings a watchman should be stationed on the forecastle head to report any failure or imminent failure of moorings or leakage of oil. He should also report immediately if the tanker 'rides up' to the buoy. He should be equipped with appropriate means to communicate with the officer of the watch.

4.4   STATE OF READINESS

4.4.1   Fire-Fighting Equipment

Immediately before, or on, arrival at a terminal at which it is intended to load or discharge cargo, fire hoses should be connected to the ship's fire main, one forward and one aft of the ship's manifold. When monitors are provided they should be pointed towards the manifold and be ready for immediate use. Portable fire extinguishers, preferably of the dry chemical type, should be conveniently placed near the ship's manifold. If a stern loading/discharge manifold is used, sufficient fire-fighting equipment must be available in the vicinity to provide an adequate level of protection at that location.

If practicable, a pump should maintain pressure on the ship's fire main while cargo or ballast is being handled. If this is not possible the fire pump should be in a standby condition and ready for immediate operation.

In cold weather, the freezing of fire mains and hydrants should be prevented by continuously bleeding water overboard from hydrants at the extreme end of each fire main. Alternatively, all low points of the fire main may be kept drained.

A check should be made to confirm that both the ship and shore have an international shore fire connection for the transfer of water for fire-fighting (see Appendix E).

The terminal fire-fighting appliances should be operational and ready for immediate use and fire mains should be pressurised or be capable of being pressurised at short notice.

4.4.2   Readiness to Move Under Own Power

While a tanker is berthed at a terminal its boilers, main engines, steering machinery and other equipment essential for manoeuvring should normally be maintained in a condition that will permit the ship to move away from the berth at short notice.

Repairs and other work which may immobilise the tanker should not be undertaken at a berth without prior, written agreement with the terminal. Before carrying out repairs it may also be necessary to obtain permission from the local port authority. Certain conditions may have to be met before permission can be granted.

4.5   COMMUNICATIONS

Telephone, portable VHF/UHF and radio telephone systems should comply with the appropriate safety requirements.

The provision of adequate means of communication, including a back-up system between ship and shore, is the responsibility of the terminal.

Communication between the responsible officer on duty and the responsible person ashore should be maintained in the most efficient way.

When telephones are used, the telephone both on board and ashore should be continuously manned by persons who can immediately contact their superior. Additionally, it should be possible for that superior to override all calls. When VHF/UHF or radiotelephone systems are used, units should preferably be portable and carried by the responsible officer on duty and the responsible person ashore, or by persons who can contact their respective superior immediately. Where fixed systems are used, the above guidance for telephones should be followed.

The selected system of communication together with the necessary information on telephone numbers and/or channels to be used should be recorded on an appropriate form. This form should be signed by both ship and shore representatives.

Where there are difficulties in verbal communication, these can be overcome by appointing a person with adequate technical and operational knowledge and a sufficient command of a language understood by both ship and shore personnel.

4.6 ACCESS BETWEEN SHIP AND SHORE

4.6.1 Means of Access

Personnel should use only the designated means of access between ship and shore.

Gangways or other means of access should be provided with an effective safety net where appropriate. Lifebuoys with lifelines should be available in the vicinity of the gangway or other means of access. In addition, suitable life saving equipment should be available near the access point ashore.

Means of access should be placed as close as possible to crew accommodation and as far away as possible from the manifold.

4.6.2 Gangway Landing

When terminal access facilities are not available and a tanker's gangway is used, the berth must have sufficient landing area to provide the gangway with an adequate clear run in order to maintain safe, convenient access to the tanker at all states of tide and changes in freeboard.

Particular attention to safe access should be given where the difference in level between the decks of the tanker and jetty becomes large. There should be special facilities at berths where the level of a tanker's deck can fall well below that of the jetty. For emergency escape provision see Chapter 14.

4.6.3. Lighting

During darkness, the means of access to the tanker should be well lit.

4.6.4 Unauthorised Persons

Persons who have no legitimate business on board, or who do not have the master's permission, should be refused access to a tanker. The terminal, in agreement with the master, should restrict access to the jetty or berth.

A crew list should be given to the terminal security personnel.

4.6.5 Persons Smoking or Intoxicated

Personnel on duty on a jetty or on watch on a tanker must ensure that no one who is smoking approaches the jetty or boards a tanker. Persons apparently intoxicated should not be allowed to board a tanker unless they can be properly supervised.

4.7 NOTICES

4.7.1 Notices on the Tanker

On arrival at a terminal, a tanker should display notices at the gangway in appropriate languages stating:

> **WARNING**
>
> NO NAKED LIGHTS
>
> NO SMOKING
>
> NO UNAUTHORISED PERSONS

Alternative wording containing the same warnings may also be used.

Photoluminescent notices stating "EMERGENCY ESCAPE ROUTES" (with directional signs) should also be displayed at appropriate locations.

In addition, notices are displayed on board tankers which are primarily for the information of the crew. Shore personnel should also observe these requirements when on board the tanker.

4.7.2 Notices on the Terminal

Permanent notices and signs indicating that smoking and naked lights are prohibited should be conspicuously displayed on a jetty in appropriate languages. Similar permanent notices and signs should be displayed at the entrance to the terminal area or the shore approaches to a jetty.

In buildings and other shore locations where smoking is allowed, appropriate notices should be conspicuously displayed.

Emergency escape routes from the tanker berth to the shore should be clearly indicated.

4.8 SMOKING

4.8.1 Controlled Smoking

Smoking should only be permitted under controlled conditions. A total prohibition on smoking at terminals and on a tanker at a berth is in general unrealistic and unenforceable and may give rise to surreptitious smoking. There may, however, be occasions when, owing to the nature of the cargo being transferred or other factors, a total prohibition on smoking will be necessary. In such cases a regular inspection should be made by a responsible officer to ensure that this prohibition is enforced.

Smoking should be strictly prohibited within the restricted area enclosing all tanker berths and on board any tanker while at a berth, except in designated smoking places.

4.8.2 Location of Designated Smoking Places

The designated smoking places on a tanker or on shore should be agreed in writing between the master and the terminal representative before operations start. The master is responsible for ensuring that all persons on board the tanker are informed of the selected places for smoking and for posting suitable notices in addition to the tanker's permanent notices.

Certain criteria should be followed in the selection of smoking places whenever petroleum cargoes are being handled or when ballasting, purging with inert gas, gas freeing and tank cleaning operations are taking place.

The criteria are:

- The agreed smoking places should be confined to locations abaft the cargo tanks, except when the entry of petroleum gas into amidships accommodation is highly improbable.

- The agreed smoking places should not have doors or ports which open directly on to open decks.

- Account should be taken of conditions that may suggest danger, such as an indication of unusually high petroleum gas concentrations, particularly in the absence of wind, and when there are operations on adjacent tankers or on the jetty berth.

In the designated smoking places all ports should be kept closed and doors into passageways should be kept closed except when in use.

While the tanker is moored at the terminal, even when no operations are in progress, smoking can only be permitted in designated smoking places or, after there has been prior agreement in writing between master and terminal representative, in any other closed accommodation.

When stern loading/discharge connections are being used particular care must be taken to ensure that no smoking is allowed in any accommodation or space the door or ports of which open on to the deck where the stern loading/discharge manifold is located.

4.9 GALLEY STOVES AND COOKING APPLIANCES

4.9.1 Use of Galley Stoves and Cooking Appliances

Before permitting the use of galley stoves and other cooking appliances while a tanker is at a petroleum berth, the ship's master and the terminal representative must, after taking into consideration the location, construction and ventilation of the galley, jointly agree that no danger exists. Particular care must be taken when making this judgment if the stern loading/discharge manifold is to be used to transfer cargo.

If the use of the galley is agreed, the precautions set out in Section 2.3 must be taken.

4.9.2 Steam Cookers and Water Boilers

Cookers and other equipment heated by steam may be used at all times.

4.10 FIXED AND PORTABLE ELECTRICAL EQUIPMENT

4.10.1 Area Classifications

Different criteria are employed for classifying areas on board a tanker and ashore in relation to the use of electrical equipment. Details of the area classifications are given in Chapter 19.

When a tanker is at a berth it is possible that an area on the tanker which is regarded as safe may fall within one of the hazardous zones of the terminal. If such a situation should arise and if the area in question contains unapproved electrical equipment, this equipment may have to be isolated while the tanker is at the berth, or other specific precautions taken.

Where stern loading/discharge connections are fitted the area containing these connections should be designated a hazardous or dangerous area as appropriate. All permanent electrical equipment fitted within the area should be classified for use in a flammable atmosphere. These fittings should be maintained in the same manner as if they were sited on the main cargo deck. Similarly, all portable electrical equipment used in the area must be of an approved type or used under the terms of a hot work permit.

4.10.2 Use of Portable Electrical Equipment in Hazardous Areas

> **Portable electric lamps and portable electric equipment for use in hazardous areas must be of an approved type. Special care should be taken to prevent any mechanical damage to flexible cables or wandering leads.**

Any other electrical or electronic equipment of non-approved type, whether mains or battery powered, must not be active, switched on or used within hazardous areas. This includes radios, mobile telephones, radio pagers, calculators, photographic equipment and any other portable equipment that is electrically powered but not approved for operation in hazardous areas. It should be borne in mind that equipment such as mobile telephones and radio pagers, if switched on, can be activated remotely and a hazard can be generated by the alerting or calling mechanism and, in the case of telephones, by the natural response to answer the call.

In view of the ready availability and widespread use of such equipment, appropriate measures should be taken to prevent its use within hazardous areas. Personnel must be advised of the prohibition of non-approved equipment and terminals should have a policy for informing visitors of the potential dangers associated with the use of electrical equipment. Terminals should also reserve the right to require any non-approved items of equipment to be deposited at the entrance to the port area or other appropriate boundary within the terminal.

> **Items such as mobile telephones and radio pagers should only be re-commissioned once they are in a safe area, such as within the ship's accommodation.**

4.11 COMMUNICATIONS EQUIPMENT

4.11.1 General

Unless certified as intrinsically safe or of other approved design, all communications equipment on board ships such as telephones, talk-back systems, signalling lamps, search lights, loud hailers, and electrical controls for ship's whistles should neither be used nor connected or disconnected when the areas in which they are positioned come within the boundary of a shore hazardous zone.

4.11.2 Radio Equipment

The use of a tanker's radio equipment during cargo or ballast handling operations is potentially dangerous (see Section 2.7). This does not apply to the use of permanently and correctly installed VHF and UHF equipment, provided the power output is reduced to one watt or less.

The use of VHF/UHF radio equipment as a means of communication should be encouraged whenever possible.

When a tanker is at a berth, its main transmitting antennae should be earthed.

If it is necessary to operate the ship's radio in port for servicing purposes, there should be agreement between tanker and terminal on the procedures necessary to ensure safety. These procedures may require the issue of a work permit. Among the precautions that might be agreed are operating at low power, use of a dummy antenna load and confining the transmission to times when the transmitting antennae do not come within the shore hazardous zone.

4.11.3 Ship's Radar Equipment

The radiation of radar waves from a properly sited radar scanner presents no ignition hazard on board a vessel, but the operation of high powered 10cm radar may induce an electrical potential into nearby conductors at the berth. The operation of a tanker's radar will also involve running non-approved electrical equipment. Consultation between the tanker and the terminal is therefore essential before using or repairing this equipment if the area near the scanner mechanism falls within a shore hazardous zone.

4.11.4 Satellite Communications Equipment

This equipment normally operates at 1.6 GHz and the power levels generated are not considered to present an ignition hazard. As the positioning of the antennae may, however, involve the running of non-approved electrical equipment, consultation between the tanker and the terminal is advisable before the satellite terminal is operated.

4.11.5 Closed Circuit Television

If closed circuit television is fitted on a tanker or on a jetty, the cameras and associated equipment must be of an approved design for the areas in which they are located. If of an approved design, there is no restriction upon their use (see Section 4.11.1).

When a tanker is at a berth the servicing of this equipment should be agreed between the ship and the shore.

4.11.6 Telephones

When there is a direct telephone connection from the ship to the shore control room or elsewhere, telephone cables should preferably be routed outside the dangerous zone. Whenever this is not feasible, the cable should be routed and fixed in position by qualified shore personnel and so protected that no danger can arise from its use.

4.12 WORK ON A JETTY OR PETROLEUM BERTH OR ON A TANKER AT A BERTH

4.12.1 Permit to Work Systems – General Considerations

Permit to work systems are widely used throughout the petroleum industry. The permit is essentially a document which describes the work to be done and the precautions to be taken in doing it, and which sets out all the necessary safety procedures and equipment.

Permits should normally be used for hot work, electrical work and cold work undertaken in hazardous and dangerous areas.

The permit should specify clearly the particular item of equipment or area involved, the extent of work permitted, what conditions are to be observed, and the time and duration of validity. This should not normally exceed a working day. At least two copies of the permit should be made; one for the issuer and one for the person at the work site.

The layout of the permit should include a check list giving both the issuer and the user a methodical procedure to ensure that it is safe for work to begin and to stipulate all the necessary conditions. If any of the conditions cannot be met the permit should not be issued until remedial measures have been taken. Specific examples are given in Appendix F and G.

It is advisable to have distinctive 'permits to work' for different hazards. The number of permits will vary with complexity of the operation. Care must be taken not to issue a permit for subsequent work which negates the safety conditions of an earlier permit; for example, a permit should not be issued to break a flange adjacent to an area where a hot work permit is in force. Before issuing a permit the responsible person must be satisfied that the conditions at the site, or of the equipment to be worked on, are safe for the work to be undertaken.

Procedures for hot work are fully described in Section 2.8 but many of the conditions considered are common to all permits.

4.12.2 Hot Work Permits

This form of permit is intended to ensure a high degree of control and supervision when it is required to carry out hot work on board (see Section 2.8 for general precautions and approval for hot work; see Appendix F for hot work permit).

4.12.3 Permit to Work on a Tanker Berth

No construction, repair, maintenance, dismantling or modification of facilities should be carried out on a tanker berth without the permission of the terminal manager. If a tanker is moored at the berth, the agreement of the master should also be obtained by the terminal representative.

In all cases, except for routine work of a non-hazardous nature, this permission must be given in the written form of a permit to work.

4.12.4 Permit to Work on Board a Tanker

When any repair or maintenance is to be done on board a tanker moored at a berth, the responsible officer must inform the terminal representative. Agreement should be reached on the safety precautions to be taken, with due regard to the nature of the work.

4.12.5 Approval for Hot Work on Board Ship

Hot work on board ship must be prohibited until all applicable regulations and safety requirements have been met and a permit to work has been issued (see Section 2.8 for general precautions and approval for hot work). This may involve the master, operator, chemist, shore contractor, terminal representative and port authority as appropriate.

When alongside a terminal, no hot work should be allowed until the terminal representative and, where appropriate, the port authority have been consulted and approval obtained.

A hot work permit should only be issued after obtaining a gas free certificate from an authorised chemist.

4.12.6 Isolation of Electrical Equipment

Whenever work is to be carried out on electrical equipment, or on equipment powered by electricity, a permit to work should be issued indicating that the electrical supply of the equipment has been isolated. An example of an Electrical Isolation Certificate is given in Appendix H.

Isolation can be effected by locking off switchgear or the complete removal of fuses. Consideration should be given to a system of control which prevents the accidental reconnection of supply – for example by installing a locking arrangement, labelling of switches and the display of warning notices.

4.12.7 Use of Tools

No hammering, chipping, or grit blasting should take place, nor should any power tool be used, outside the boiler room, engine room, or accommodation spaces on a tanker, or on a jetty at which a tanker is berthed, without agreement between the terminal representative and the responsible officer, and unless a permit to work has been issued.

In all cases the terminal representative and the responsible officer should satisfy themselves that the area is gas free, and remains so while the tools are in use. The precautions in Section 2.9 should be observed.

4.12.8 Access to Berth

The use of vehicles and equipment should be controlled, particularly in hazardous zones, and the routes to and from work places and parking areas should be clearly indicated. Temporary barriers or movable fencing should be provided, where necessary, to prevent unauthorised access.

Chapter 5

Liaison Between Tanker and Terminal Before Cargo Handling

Emphasis is placed on the fact that the completion of a safe and successful cargo handling operation is dependent upon effective co-operation and co-ordination between all the parties involved. Exchange of information between the tanker and the terminal concerning mooring arrangements is dealt with in Chapter 3. Certain additional information relating to cargo, ballast and bunker handling should be exchanged before these operations begin. This Chapter covers the subjects about which additional information should be available, and the aspects upon which agreement should be reached.

5.1 TERMINAL'S ADVICE TO THE TANKER

The following information should be made available to the responsible officer:

5.1.1 Information in Preparation for Loading and Bunkering:

- Cargo specifications and preferred order of loading.

- Whether or not the cargo includes toxic components, for example H_2S, benzene, lead additives, mercaptans etc.

- Tank venting requirements.

- Any other characteristics of the cargo requiring attention, for example high true vapour pressure.

- Flashpoints (where applicable) of products and their estimated loading temperatures, particularly when the cargo is non-volatile.

- Bunker specifications including H_2S content.

- Nominated quantities of cargo to be loaded.

- Maximum shore loading rates.

- Standby time for normal pump stopping.

- Maximum pressure available at the ship/shore cargo connection.

- Number and sizes of hoses or arms available and manifold connections required for each product cr grade of the cargo.

- Proposed bunker loading rate.

- Communication system for loading control, including the signal for emergency stop.

- Limitations on the movement of hoses or arms.

5.1.2 Information in preparation for discharge:

- Order of discharge of cargo acceptable to terminal.

- Nominated quantities of cargo to be discharged.

- Maximum acceptable discharge rates.

- Maximum pressure acceptable at ship/shore cargo connection.

- Any booster pumps that may be on stream.

- Number and sizes of hoses or arms available and manifold connections required for each product or grade of the cargo and whether or not these arms are common with each other.

- Limitations on the movement of hoses or arms.

- Any other limitations at the terminal.

- Communication system for discharge control including the signal for emergency stop.

5.2 TANKER'S ADVICE TO THE TERMINAL

Before cargo handling commences the responsible officer should inform the terminal of the general arrangement of the cargo, ballast and bunker tanks, and should have available the information listed below:

5.2.1 Information in Preparation for Loading and Bunkering:

- Details of last cargo carried, method of tank cleaning (if any) and state of the cargo tanks and lines.

- Where the vessel has part cargoes on board, grade, volume and tank distribution.

- Maximum acceptable loading rates and topping off rates.

- Maximum acceptable pressure at the ship/shore cargo connection during loading.

- Cargo quantities acceptable from terminal nominations.

- Proposed disposition of nominated cargo and preferred order of loading.

- Maximum acceptable cargo temperature (where applicable).

- Maximum acceptable true vapour pressure (where applicable).

- Proposed method of venting.

- Quantities and specifications of bunkers required.

- Disposition, composition and quantities of ballast together with time required for discharge and maximum light freeboard.

- Quantity, quality and disposition of slops.
- Quality of inert gas (if applicable).

5.2.2   Information in Preparation for Discharge:

- Cargo specifications.
- Whether or not the cargo includes toxic components, for example H_2S, benzene, lead additives, mercaptans etc.
- Any other characteristics of the cargo requiring special attention, for example, high true vapour pressure (TVP).
- Flashpoint (where applicable) of products and their temperatures upon arrival, particularly when the cargo is non-volatile.
- Cargo quantities loaded and disposition in ship's tanks.
- Quantity and disposition of slops.
- Any unaccountable change of ullage in ship's tanks since loading.
- Water dips in cargo tanks (where applicable).
- Preferred order of discharge.
- Maximum attainable discharge rates and pressures.
- Whether tank cleaning, including crude oil washing, is required.
- Approximate time of commencement and duration of ballasting into permanent ballast tanks and cargo tanks.

5.3   AGREED LOADING PLAN

On the basis of the information exchanged, an operational agreement should be made in writing between the responsible officer and the terminal representative covering the following:

- Ship's name, berth, date and time.
- Name and signature of ship and shore representative.
- Cargo distribution on arrival and departure.
- The following information on each product:
  - Quantity.
  - Ship's tank(s) to be loaded.
  - Shore tank(s) to be discharged.
  - Lines to be used ship/shore.
  - Cargo transfer rate.
  - Operating pressure.
  - Maximum allowable pressure.
  - Temperature limits.
  - Venting system.

- Restrictions necessary because of:
  - Electrostatic properties.
  - Use of automatic shut-down valves.

This agreement should include a loading plan indicating the expected timing and covering the following:

- The sequence in which ship's tanks are to be loaded, taking into account:
  - Deballasting operations.
  - Ship and shore tank change over.
  - Avoidance of contamination of cargo.
  - Pipeline clearing for loading.
  - Other movements or operations which may affect flow rates.
  - Trim and draught of the tanker.
  - The need to ensure that permitted stresses will not be exceeded.

- The initial and maximum loading rates, topping off rates and normal stopping times, having regard to:
  - The nature of the cargo to be loaded.
  - The arrangement and capacity of the ship's cargo lines and gas venting system.
  - The maximum allowable pressure and flow rate in the ship/shore hoses or arms.
  - Precautions to avoid accumulation of static electricity.
  - Any other flow control limitations.

- The method of tank venting to avoid or reduce gas emissions at deck level, taking into account:
  - The true vapour pressure of the cargo to be loaded.
  - The loading rates.
  - Atmospheric conditions.

- Any bunkering or storing operations.
- Emergency stop procedure.

A bar diagram is considered to be one of the best means of depicting this plan.

5.4.   INSPECTION OF SHIP'S CARGO TANKS BEFORE LOADING

Where possible, inspection of ship's tanks before loading cargo should be made without entering the tanks.

A tank inspection can be made from the deck using ullage or sighting ports with, where applicable, the inert gas within the tank maintained at its minimum positive pressure. Care must be taken by the person inspecting not to inhale vapours or inert gas when inspecting tanks which have not been gas freed. Frequently tank atmospheres which are, or have been, inerted have a blue haze which, together with the size of the tanks, makes it difficult to see the bottom even with the aid of a powerful torch or strong sunlight reflected by a mirror. Other methods such as dipping and measuring the heel, or having the stripping line or eductors opened in the tank and listening for suction, may have to be used. It may sometimes be necessary to remove tank cleaning opening covers to sight parts of the tank not visible from the ullage ports but this should only be done when the tank is gas free, and the covers must be replaced and secured immediately after the inspection.

If, because the cargo to be loaded has a critical specification, it is necessary for the inspector to enter a tank, all the precautions contained in Section 11.4.2 must be followed.

Before entering a tank which has been inerted, it must be gas freed for entry and, unless all tanks are gas freed and the IGS completely isolated, each individual tank to be entered for inspection must be isolated from the IGS (see Sections 10.6.10 and 10.6.11).

5.5   AGREED DISCHARGE PLAN

On the basis of the information exchanged, an operational agreement should be made in writing between the responsible officer and the terminal representative covering the following:

- Ship's name, berth, date and time.

- Names and signatures of ship and shore representatives.

- Cargo distribution on arrival and departure.

- The following information on each product:
  - Quantity.
  - Shore tank(s) to be filled.
  - Ship's tank(s) to be discharged.
  - Lines to be used ship/shore.
  - Cargo transfer rate.
  - Operating pressure.
  - Maximum allowable pressure.
  - Temperature limits.
  - Venting systems.

- Restrictions necessary because of:
  - Electrostatic properties.
  - Use of automatic shut-down valves.

This agreement should include a discharge plan indicating the expected timing and covering the following:

- The sequence in which the ship's tanks are to be discharged, taking account of:
  - Ship and shore tank change over.
  - Avoidance of contamination of cargo.
  - Pipeline clearing for discharge.
  - Crude oil washing, if employed, or other tank cleaning.
  - Other movements or operations which may affect flow rates.
  - Trim and freeboard of the tanker.

- The need to ensure that permitted stresses will not be exceeded.

- Ballasting operations.

• The initial and maximum discharge rates, having regard to:

- The specification of the cargo to be discharged.

- The arrangements and capacity of the ship's cargo lines, shore pipelines and tanks.

- The maximum allowable pressure and flow rate in the ship/shore hoses or arms.

- Precautions to avoid accumulation of static electricity.

- Any other limitations.

• Bunkering or storing operations.

• Emergency stop procedure.

A bar diagram is considered to be one of the best means of depicting this plan.

5.6 COMMUNICATIONS

To ensure the safe control of operations at all times, it should be the responsibility of both parties to establish, agree in writing and maintain a reliable communications system.

Before loading or discharging commences, the system should be adequately tested. A secondary stand-by system should also be established and agreed. Allowance should be made for the time required for action in response to signals.

These systems should include signals for:

• Identification of vessel, berth and cargo.

• Stand by.

• Start loading or start discharging.

• Slow down.

• Stop loading or stop discharging.

• Emergency stop.

Any other necessary signals should be agreed and understood.

When different products or grades are to be handled their names and descriptions should be clearly understood by the ship and shore personnel on duty during cargo handling operations.

The use of one VHF/UHF channel by more than one ship/shore combination should be avoided.

5.7 SHIP/SHORE SAFETY CHECK LIST

The recommended Ship/Shore Safety Check List should be completed in accordance with Appendix A.

The purpose of the Ship/Shore Safety Check List is to ensure the safety of both ship and terminal and of all personnel and it should be completed jointly by a responsible officer and the terminal representative. Each item should be verified before it is ticked. This will entail a physical check by the two persons concerned and will be conducted jointly where appropriate. It is of no value if it is merely regarded as a paper exercise.

It is emphasised that some of the items on the Ship/Shore Safety Check List will require several physical checks or even continuous supervision during the operation.

The Ship/Shore Safety Check List may be accompanied by an explanatory letter, for which a recommended text is given in Appendix A, inviting the co-operation and understanding of the tanker's personnel. The letter should be given to the master or responsible officer by the terminal representative. The recipient should acknowledge receipt of the letter on a copy which should then be retained by the terminal representative.

Chapter 6

Precautions Before and During Cargo Handling and Other Cargo Tank Operations

This Chapter sets out the precautions to be taken before and during cargo handling, ballasting, bunkering, tank cleaning, gas freeing and purging operations. These precautions are additional to those given in Chapters 2 and 4, but do not include precautions and procedures related to specific operations which are dealt with in Chapters 7, 9, and 10.

6.1. OPENINGS IN SUPERSTRUCTURES

6.1.1. General

A tanker's accommodation normally contains equipment which is not suitable for use in flammable atmospheres. It is therefore imperative that petroleum gas is kept out of the accommodation.

All external openings should be closed when the tanker, or a ship at an adjacent berth, is conducting any of the following operations:

- Handling volatile petroleum or non-volatile petroleum near to or above its flashpoint.

- Loading non-volatile petroleum into tanks containing hydrocarbon vapour.

- Crude oil washing.

- Ballasting, purging, gas freeing or tank washing after discharge of volatile petroleum.

Although discomfort may be caused to personnel in accommodation that is completely closed during conditions of high temperatures and humidity, this discomfort should be accepted in the interests of safety.

6.1.2 Doors, Ports and Windows

In the accommodation, all external doors, ports and similar openings which lead directly from the tank deck to the accommodation or machinery spaces (other than the pumproom), or which overlook the tank deck at any level, or which overlook the poop deck forward of the funnel should be kept closed. A screen door cannot be considered a safe substitute for an external door.

Additional doors and ports may have to be closed in special circumstances, such as during stern loading, or due to structural peculiarities of the tanker.

If doors have to be opened for access they should be closed immediately after use.

Doors that must be kept closed should be clearly marked, but in no case should doors be locked.

6.1.3 Ventilators

Ventilators should be kept trimmed to prevent the entry of petroleum gas, particularly on tankers which depend on natural ventilation. If ventilators are located so that petroleum gas can enter regardless of the direction in which they are trimmed, they should be covered, plugged or closed.

6.1.4 Central Air Conditioning and Mechanical Ventilating Systems

Intakes of central air conditioning or mechanical ventilating systems should be adjusted to prevent the entry of petroleum gas, if possible by recirculation of air within the enclosed spaces.

If at any time it is suspected that gas is being drawn into the accommodation, central air conditioning and mechanical ventilating systems should be stopped and the intakes closed and/or covered.

6.1.5 Window Type Air Conditioning Units

Window type air conditioning units which are not certified as safe for use in the presence of flammable gas or which draw in air from outside the superstructure must be electrically disconnected and any external vents or intakes covered or closed.

6.2 OPENINGS IN CARGO TANKS

6.2.1 Cargo Tank Lids

During the handling of volatile petroleum and loading of non-volatile petroleum into tanks containing hydrocarbon vapour, and while ballasting after the discharge of volatile cargo, all cargo tank lids should be closed and secured.

Cargo tank lids or coamings should be clearly marked with the number and location (port, centre or starboard) of the tank they serve.

Tank openings of cargo tanks which are not gas free should be kept closed unless gas freeing alongside by agreement.

6.2.2 Sighting and Ullage Ports

During any of the cargo and ballast handling operations referred to in Section 6.2.1, sighting and ullage ports should be kept closed unless required to be open for those operational purposes indicated in Section 7.2. If for design reasons they are required to be open for venting purposes, the openings should be protected by a flame screen which may be removed for a short period during ullaging, sighting, sounding and sampling. These screens should be a good fit and be kept clean and in good condition. Closed loading of cargoes having toxic effects should be adopted (see Section 7.2.4). For vessels fitted with an inert gas system see Section 7.2.3.

6.2.3 Cargo Tank Vent Outlets

The cargo tank venting system should be set for the operation concerned and, if required, the outlets should be protected by a device to prevent the passage of flame. High velocity vents should be set in the operational position to ensure the high exit velocity of vented gas.

When volatile cargo is being loaded into tanks connected to a venting system which also serves tanks into which non-volatile cargo is to be loaded, particular attention should be paid to the setting of p/v valves and the associated venting system, including any inert gas system, in order to prevent flammable gas entering the tanks to be loaded with non-volatile cargo.

6.2.4 Tank Washing Openings

During tank cleaning or gas freeing operations tank washing covers should only be removed from the tanks in which these operations are taking place and should be replaced as soon as these operations are completed. Other tank washing covers may be loosened in preparation but they should be left in their fully closed position.

6.2.5 Segregated Ballast Tank Lids

Segregated ballast tank lids should be kept closed when cargo or ballast is being handled as petroleum gas could be drawn into these tanks. Segregated ballast tank lids must be clearly marked as such.

6.3 PUMPROOM PRECAUTIONS

6.3.1 General

The pumproom precautions set out in Section 2.17 should be observed before and during all cargo handling operations.

Tanks or pipelines should not be drained into the pumproom bilges but if, on completion of deballasting this has to be done, care must be taken to ensure that such drainings do not contain petroleum. Tanks or lines containing petroleum must not be drained into the pumproom bilges.

Loading through or pressurisation of pumproom pipelines should be avoided if possible.

No repairs are to be undertaken on cargo pumps, their associated relief valves or control systems, while the pumps are running.

Throughout cargo handling operations, the pumproom ventilation system must be in continuous operation.

6.3.2 Inspection of Glands, Bearings, etc.

Before starting any cargo operation, an inspection should be made to ensure that strainer covers, inspection plates and drain plugs are in position and secure.

Drain valves in the pumproom cargo system, especially those on cargo oil pumps, should be firmly shut.

Any bulkhead glands should be checked and adjusted or lubricated as necessary to ensure an efficient gas tight seal between the pumproom and the machinery space.

During all cargo operations, including loading, the pumproom should be inspected at regular intervals to check for leakages from glands, drain plugs and drain valves, especially those fitted to the cargo oil pumps. If the pumps are in use, pump glands, bearings and the bulkhead glands (if fitted) should be checked for overheating. In the event of leakage or overheating the pump should be stopped. No attempt should be made to adjust the pump glands on rotating shafts while the pump is in service.

6.4   TESTING OF CARGO SYSTEM ALARMS AND TRIPS

Pump alarms and trips, level alarms etc., where fitted, should be tested regularly to ensure that they are functioning correctly, and the results of these tests should be recorded.

6.5   SHIP AND SHORE CARGO CONNECTIONS

6.5.1   Flange Connections

Flanges for ship to shore cargo connections, at the end of the terminal pipelines and on the ship's manifold, should be in accordance with the OCIMF publication 'Recommendations for Oil Tanker Manifolds and Associated Equipment'.

Flange faces, gaskets and seals should be clean and in good condition.

Where bolted connections are made, all bolt holes should be used and care taken in tightening bolts as uneven or over tightening of bolts could result in leakage or fracture. Improvised arrangements using 'G' clamps or similar devices must not be used for flange connections.

6.5.2.   Removal of Blank Flanges

Each tanker and terminal manifold flange should have a removable blank flange, made of steel or other approved material such as phenol resin, and preferably fitted with handles.

Precautions should be taken to ensure that, prior to the removal of blanks from tanker and terminal pipelines, the section between the last valve and blank does not contain oil under pressure. Precautions must also be taken to prevent any spillage.

6.5.3   Reducers and Spools

Reducers and spools should be made of steel and fitted with flanges conforming with BS 1560, ANSI B16.5 or equivalent. Ordinary cast iron should not be used. (See OCIMF 'Recommendations for Oil Tanker Manifolds and Associated Equipment'.)

There should be an exchange of information between the ship and terminal when manifold reducers or spools are made of any material other than steel since particular attention is necessary in their manufacture to achieve the equivalent strength of steel and to avoid the possibility of fracture.

6.5.4   Lighting

During darkness, adequate lighting should be arranged to cover the area of the ship to shore cargo connection and any hose handling equipment so that the need for any adjustment can be seen in good time and any leakage or spillage of oil detected.

6.5.5   Emergency Release

A special release device may be used for the emergency disconnection of cargo hoses or arms.

If possible the hoses or arms should be drained, purged or isolated as appropriate before emergency disconnection, so that spillage is minimised.

Periodic checks should be made to ensure that all safety features are operational.

6.6 CARGO HOSES

6.6.1 Examination Before Use

It is the responsibility of the terminal to provide hoses which are in good condition but the master of a tanker may reject any which appear to be defective.

Before being connected, hose strings should be examined for any possible defect which may be visible in the bore or outer covers such as blistering, abrasion, flattening of the hose or evidence of leaks.

Hoses for which the rated pressure has been exceeded must be removed and re-tested before further use.

Hoses to be used should have been pressure tested to manufacturer's specifications at intervals which are in accordance with the manufacturer's recommendations or as recommended in the OCIMF publication "Guidelines for the Handling, Storage, Inspection and Testing of Hoses in the Field". Intervals between tests should not in any case exceed one year. The date of such pressure testing should be indicated on the hose. (See Appendix C).

6.6.2 Handling, Lifting and Suspending

Hoses should always be handled with care and should not be dragged over a surface or rolled in a manner which twists the body of the hose. Hoses should not be allowed to come into contact with a hot surface such as a steam pipe. Protection should be provided at any point where chafing or rubbing can occur.

Lifting bridles and saddles should be provided. The use of steel wires in direct contact with the hose cover should not be permitted. Hoses should not be lifted at a single point with ends hanging down but should be supported at a number of places so that they are not bent to a radius less than that recommended by the manufacturer.

Excessive weight on the ship's manifold should be avoided. If there is an excessive overhang, or the ship's valve is outside the stool support, additional support should be given to the manifold. A horizontal curved plate or pipe section should be fitted at the ship's side to protect the hose from sharp edges and obstructions. Adequate support for the hose when connected to the manifold should be provided. Where this is a single lifting point, such as a derrick, the hose string should be supported by bridles or saddles.

6.6.3 Adjustment During Cargo Handling Operations

As the tanker rises or falls as a result of tide or cargo operations, the hose strings should be adjusted so as to avoid undue strain on the hoses, connections and ship's manifold and to ensure that the radius of curvature of the hose remains within the limits recommended by the manufacturer.

6.6.4 Submarine and Floating Hose Strings

Hoses in service at offshore mooring installations should be inspected periodically by divers. Particular attention should be paid to kinked or damaged sections, oil seepage from the hose flange areas, heavy marine growth and scuffing on the sea bed. Where hose strings are lowered and raised repeatedly from the sea bed, care should be taken to avoid damage caused by chains and lifting plates.

Particular attention should be paid when lowering hose strings to avoid coiling down. Dragging of hoses over the sea bed should be minimised.

Before attempting to lift a hose string on board the responsible officer should check that the total weight involved does not exceed the safe working load of the ship's derrick or crane which it is proposed to use. The terminal should advise the total weight of the hose string to be lifted in relation to the height of the lift, which could be as much as 8 metres above deck level for a tanker's manifold connection situated 4.6 metres inboard. In wave and/or swell conditions greater than 1 metre significant height, dynamic loads may be imposed by the movement of the hose. In these circumstances the load to be lifted may be as much as 1.5 times the static weight of the hose and its contents.

Appendix C lists representative weights of hose strings when full of oil for submarine pipeline connections at conventional buoy moorings and for floating hose strings at single point moorings. These tables are for general guidance only and a check should be made with the terminal.

During the lifting of hose strings, contact with the ship's side and any sharp edges should be avoided.

When the hose string has been lifted to the required height for connecting to the manifold, and while it remains connected, the vertical section of the hose string should be supported by hang off chains or wires made fast to a strong point on the ship's deck.

In order to prevent spillage, precautions must be taken to ensure that, prior to the removal of blanks from submarine or floating pipelines, the pipeline does not contain petroleum under pressure (see Section 6.5.2).

A visual inspection of each floating hose string should be made before connecting it to the tanker manifold to determine if damage has been caused by contact with other vessels, crossed lines, possible kinking, oil seepage etc.

If any damage to the hose is found which is considered to be critical to the intended operation, the hose should be withdrawn from use to allow further inspection and repair.

6.7 METAL CARGO ARMS

6.7.1 Operating Envelope

Each installation of metal arms has a designed operating envelope which takes into account the elevation changes resulting from the tide, the freeboard of the largest and smallest tankers for which the berth was intended, minimum and maximum manifold setbacks, limited changes in horizontal position due to drift off and ranging, and maximum and minimum spacing when operating with other arms in the bank. The limits of this envelope should be thoroughly understood by operators because operating outside it can cause undue stress. Metal arm installations should have alarms for excessive range and drift.

The person in charge of operations on a berth should ensure that the tanker's manifolds are kept within the operating envelope during all stages of loading and discharging operations.

6.7.2 Forces on Manifolds

Most arms are counterbalanced so that no weight other than that of the liquid content of the arm is placed on the manifold. As the weight of oil in the arms, particularly the larger diameter arms, can be considerable it may be advisable for this weight to be relieved by a support or jack. Some arms have integral jacks which are also used to avoid overstressing of the tanker's manifold by the weight of the arm or other external forces such as the wind.

Some counterbalanced arms are made slightly 'tail heavy' to compensate for clingage of oil and so that arms will normally return to the parked position if released, not under power, from the ship's manifold. Additionally, in some aspects of the operating envelope there can be an uplift on the manifold. For both these reasons manifolds should also be secured against upward forces.

6.7.3 Tanker Manifold Restrictions

The material of manufacture, support and cantilever length of a manifold and the spacing intervals of adjacent outlets must be checked for compatibility with the arms. Manifold flanges should be vertical and parallel to the ship's side. The spacing of the manifold outlets sometimes dictates the number of arms which can be connected if interference between adjacent arms is to be avoided. In most cases cast iron manifolds will be subjected to excessive stress unless jacks are used.

6.7.4 Inadvertent Filling of Arms While Parked

To avoid the possibility of an inadvertently filled loading arm crashing on to the ship's deck, the parking lock should not be removed before checking that the arm is empty.

6.7.5 Ice Formation

As ice formation affects the balance of the arm, any ice should be cleared before removing the parking lock.

6.7.6 Mechanical Couplers

For most mechanical couplers the ship's manifold flange face must be smooth and free of rust for a tight seal to be achieved.

Care should be taken when connecting to ensure that the coupler is centrally placed on the manifold flange and that all claws or wedges are pulling up on the flange.

6.7.7 Wind Forces

Wind loading of metal arms may place an excessive strain on the tanker manifolds as well as on the arms. At those terminals where wind loading is critical a close watch should be kept on wind speed and direction. Operations should be suspended and arms drained and disconnected if wind limits are approached.

6.7.8 Precautions While Arms are Connected

The following precautions should be taken during the period that arms are connected:

- The ship's moorings should be monitored frequently by ship and shore personnel and tended as necessary so that any movement of the ship is restricted to within the limits of the metal arm operating envelope.

- If drift or range alarms are activated all transfer operations should be stopped and remedial measures taken.

- The arms should be free to move with the motion of the ship. Care should be taken to ensure that hydraulic or mechanical locks cannot be inadvertently engaged.

- The arms should not foul each other.

- Excessive vibration should be avoided.

6.8 CLIMATIC CONDITIONS

6.8.1 Terminal Advice of Adverse Weather Conditions

The terminal representative should warn the tanker of any forecast of imminent adverse weather conditions which may require operations to be stopped, or loading or discharge rates to be reduced.

6.8.2 Wind Conditions

If there is little air movement, petroleum gas may persist on deck in heavy concentrations. If there is a wind, eddies can be created on the lee side of a tanker's house or deck structure which can carry vented gas towards the house or structure.

Either of these effects may result in heavy local petroleum gas concentrations and it may then be necessary to extend the precautions set out in Section 6.1, or to stop loading, ballasting of non-gas free tanks, purging, tank cleaning or gas freeing while these conditions persist. These operations should also be stopped if wind conditions cause funnel sparks to fall on deck.

6.8.3 Electrical Storms (Lightning)

When an electrical storm is anticipated in the vicinity of the tanker or terminal the following operations must be stopped, whether or not the ship's cargo tanks are inerted:

- Handling of volatile petroleum;

- Handling of non-volatile petroleum in tanks not free of hydrocarbon vapour;

- Ballasting of tanks not free of hydrocarbon vapour;

- Purging, tank cleaning or gas freeing after the discharge of volatile petroleum.

All tank openings and ventilation valves must be closed, including any bypass valve fitted on the tank venting system.

6.9   ACCIDENTAL OIL SPILLAGE AND LEAKAGE

6.9.1   General

Both ship and shore personnel should maintain a close watch for the escape of oil at the commencement of and during loading or discharging operations. In particular, care should be taken to ensure that pipeline valves, including drop valves, are closed if not in use.

Cargo or bunker tanks which have been topped up should be checked frequently during the remaining loading operations to avoid an overflow.

If leakage occurs from a pipeline, valve, hose or metal arm, operations through that connection should be stopped until the cause has been ascertained and the defect remedied. If a pipeline, hose or arm bursts, or if there is an overflow, all cargo and bunker operations should be stopped immediately and should not be restarted until the fault has been rectified and all hazards from the released oil eliminated. If there is any possibility of the released oil or of petroleum gas entering an engine room or accommodation space intake, appropriate preventive steps must be taken quickly.

Means should be provided for the prompt removal of any spillage on deck. Any oil spill should be reported to the terminal and port authorities and the relevant ship and shore oil pollution emergency plans (SOPEP) should be activated.

Harbour authorities and any adjacent ship or shore installation should be warned of any hazard.

6.9.2   Sea and Overboard Discharge Valves

At the start of and at regular intervals throughout loading, discharging, ballasting and tank washing watch should be kept to ensure that oil is not escaping though sea valves.

When not in use, sea and overboard discharge valves connected to the cargo and ballast systems must be securely closed and lashed and may be sealed. In-line blanks should be inserted where provided. When lashing is not practical, as with hydraulic valves, some suitable means of marking should be used to indicate clearly that the valves are to remain closed.

For further information on this subject reference should be made to the ICS/OCIMF publication "Prevention of Oil Spillages through Cargo Pumproom Sea Valves".

6.9.3   Scupper Plugs

Before cargo handling commences, all deck scuppers and open drains on the jetty (where applicable) must be effectively plugged to prevent spilled oil escaping into the water around the tanker or terminal. Accumulations of water should be drained periodically and scupper plugs replaced immediately after the water has been run off. Oily water should be transferred to a slop tank or other suitable receptacle.

6.9.4   Spill Containment

A permanently fitted spill tank, provided with suitable means of draining, should be fitted under all ship and shore manifold connections. Should no permanent means be provided, drip trays should be placed under each connection to retain any leakage.

6.9.5   Ship and Shore Cargo and Bunker Pipelines not in Use

The tightness of valves should not be relied upon to prevent the escape or seepage of oil. All shore pipelines, loading arms and hoses not in use at a berth must be securely blanked.

All ship's cargo and bunker pipelines not in use must be securely blanked at the manifold. The stern cargo pipelines should be isolated from the tanker's main pipeline system forward of the aft accommodation by blanking or by the removal of a spool piece.

6.10   SHIP/SHORE INSULATING, EARTHING AND BONDING

6.10.1   Ship/Shore Insulating and Earthing

In order to provide protection against arcing during connection and disconnection, the terminal operator should ensure that cargo hose strings and metal arms are fitted with an insulating flange or a single length of non-conducting hose to ensure electrical discontinuity between the ship and shore. All metal on the seaward side of the insulating section should be electrically continuous to the ship, and that on the landward side should be electrically continuous to the jetty earthing system.

The insulating flange or single length of non-conducting hose must not be short-circuited by contact with external metal; for example, an exposed metallic flange on the seaward side of the insulating flange or hose length should not make contact with the jetty structure either directly or through hose handling equipment.

Insulating flanges should be inspected and tested periodically to ensure that the insulation is clean and in good condition. The resistance should be measured between the metal pipe on the shore side of the flange and the end of the hose or metal arm when freely suspended. The measured value after installation should be not less than 1,000 ohms. A lower resistance may indicate damage to, or deterioration of, the insulation.

It should be noted that switching off a cathodic protection system is not a substitute for the installation of an insulating flange or a length of non-conducting hose.

See Appendix D for a typical insulating flange joint. Cargo hoses with internal bonding between the end flanges should be checked for electrical continuity before they are taken into service and periodically thereafter.

6.10.2 Ship/Shore Bonding Cables

As explained in Chapter 20, a ship/shore bonding cable is not effective as a safety device and may even be dangerous. A ship/shore bonding cable should therefore not be used.

> **Note: Although the potential dangers of using a ship/shore bonding cable are widely recognised, attention is drawn to the fact that some national and local regulations may still require a bonding cable to be connected. If a bonding cable is insisted upon, it should first be inspected to see that it is mechanically and electrically sound. The connection point for the cable should be well clear of the manifold area. There should always be a switch on the jetty in series with the bonding cable and of a type suitable for use in a Zone 1 hazardous area. It is important to ensure that the switch is always in the 'off' position before connecting or disconnecting the cable. Only when the cable is properly fixed and in good contact with the ship should the switch be closed. The cable should be attached before the cargo hoses are connected and removed only after the hoses have been disconnected.**

6.10.3 Application to Offshore Facilities (Sea Islands)

Offshore facilities which are used for tanker cargo handling operations should be treated in the same way as shore terminals for the purpose of earthing and bonding.

6.11 PROXIMITY TO OTHER VESSELS

6.11.1 Tankers at Adjacent Berths

Flammable concentrations of petroleum gas may be encountered if cargo or ballast handling, purging, tank cleaning or gas freeing operations are being conducted by another tanker at an adjacent berth. In such circumstances appropriate precautions should be taken as described in Section 6.1.

6.11.2 General Cargo Ships at Adjacent Berths

It is unlikely that general cargo ships will be able to comply as fully as tankers with the safety requirements relating to possible sources of ignition such as smoking, naked lights, cooking and electrical equipment.

Accordingly, when a cargo vessel is at a berth in the vicinity of a tanker loading or discharging volatile petroleum, loading non-volatile petroleum into tanks containing hydrocarbon vapour, ballasting tanks containing hydrocarbon vapour, or purging or gas freeing after the discharge of volatile petroleum, it will be necessary for the terminal to evaluate any consequential safety hazards and to take precautions additional to those set out in this Chapter. Such precautions should include inspecting the cargo vessel involved and clearly defining the precautions to be taken on board that vessel.

6.11.3 Tanker Operations at General Cargo Berths

Where tanker operations are conducted at general cargo berths, it is unlikely that personnel on such berths will be familiar with safety requirements relating to possible sources of ignition, or that cranes or other equipment will comply with the requirements for the design and installation of electrical equipment in hazardous areas.

Accordingly, it will be necessary for the terminal to take precautions additional to those set out in this Chapter. These precautions should include restricted vehicular access, removable barriers, additional fire fighting equipment and control of sources of ignition, together with restrictions on the movement of goods and equipment and the lifting of loads.

6.11.4 Tugs and Other Craft Alongside

The number of craft which come alongside and the duration of their stay should be kept to a minimum. Subject also to any port authority regulations, only authorised craft having the permission of the responsible officer and, where applicable the terminal representative, should be permitted to come alongside or remain alongside a tanker while it is handling volatile petroleum or is ballasting tanks containing hydrocarbon vapour. The responsible officer should instruct personnel manning the craft that smoking, naked light and cooking appliance regulations must be observed on the craft. In the event of a breach of the regulations it will be necessary to cease operations.

Terminals should issue appropriate instructions to the operators of authorised craft on the use of engines and other apparatus and equipment so as to avoid sources of ignition when going alongside a tanker or a jetty. These will include advice on spark arresters for engine exhausts, where applicable, and on proper fendering. Terminals should also ask for suitable notices to be prominently posted on the craft informing personnel and passengers of the safety precautions to be observed.

If any unauthorised craft come alongside or secure in a position which may endanger the operations, they should be reported to the port authority and, if necessary, operations should cease.

6.12 HELICOPTER OPERATIONS

Helicopter operations must not be permitted over the tank deck unless all other operations have been suspended and all cargo tank openings closed.

Helicopter operations should only be conducted in accordance with the ICS 'Guide to Helicopter/Ship Operations'.

Chapter 7

Handling of Cargo and Ballast

This Chapter covers the precautions to be taken and the procedures that should be observed on all occasions when handling cargo or ballast, whether at terminals or during transfers between vessels. These precautions are additional to those given in Chapters 2, 4 and 6.

7.1 SUPERVISION AND CONTROL

7.1.1 General

The responsibility for safe cargo handling operations is shared between the ship and the terminal and rests jointly with the master and the responsible terminal representative. The manner in which the responsibility is shared should therefore be agreed between them so as to ensure that all aspects of the operations are covered.

7.1.2 Joint Agreement on Readiness to Load or Discharge

Before starting to load or discharge cargo or ballast, the responsible officer and the terminal representative must formally agree that both the tanker and the terminal are ready to do so safely.

7.1.3 Supervision

The following safeguards must be maintained throughout loading and discharging:

- A responsible officer must be on watch and sufficient crew on board to deal with the operation and security of the tanker. A continuous watch of the tank deck must be maintained. If a ship's cargo control room, from which all operations can be controlled, does not have an overall view of the tank deck, then a competent member of the ship's crew must be continuously on watch on the tank deck.

- A senior terminal representative must be on duty and communications between him and the responsible officer continuously maintained (see Section 4.5).

- A competent member of the terminal organisation should be on continuous duty in the vicinity of the ship to shore connections. Supervision should be aimed at preventing the development of hazardous situations. If, however, such a situation arises, the controlling personnel should have adequate means available to take corrective action. Supervision by systems incorporating television should only be used where they give effective control over the cargo operations and cannot be regarded as satisfactory when cargo operations are at a critical phase or during adverse weather conditions.

- The agreed ship to shore communications system must be maintained in good working order.

- At the commencement of loading or discharging, and at each change of watch or shift, the responsible officer and the terminal representative must each confirm that the communications system for the control of loading and discharging is understood by them and by personnel on watch and on duty.

- The stand-by requirements for the normal stopping of shore pumps on completion of loading and the emergency stop system for both the tanker and terminal must be fully understood by all personnel concerned.

7.1.4 Checks During Cargo Handling

At the start of and during cargo handling frequent checks should be made by the responsible officer to confirm that cargo is only entering or leaving the designated cargo tanks and that there is no escape of cargo into pumprooms or cofferdams, or through sea and overboard discharge valves.

Tanker and terminal personnel should regularly check the pipeline and hose or metal arm pressures in addition to the estimated quantity of cargo loaded or discharged. Any drop in pressures or any marked discrepancy between tanker and terminal estimates of quantities could indicate pipeline or hose leaks, particularly in submarine pipelines, and require that cargo operations be stopped until investigations have been made.

7.2 MEASURING AND SAMPLING

7.2.1 General

Depending on the toxicity and/or volatility of the cargo, it may be necessary to prevent or minimise the release of vapour from the cargo tank headspace during measurement and sampling operations. Wherever possible, this should be achieved by use of closed gauging and sampling equipment. Equipment required for the measurement of ullage and temperature within cargo tanks may be either fixed (permanently installed) or portable and samples will normally be drawn using portable equipment. Closed gauging or sampling will be undertaken using the fixed gauging system or by using portable equipment passed through a vapour lock. Such equipment will enable ullages, temperatures, water cuts and interface measurements to be obtained with a minimum of cargo vapours being released. This portable equipment, passed through vapour locks, is sometimes referred to as 'restricted gauging equipment'.

When it is not possible to undertake closed gauging and/or sampling operations, open gauging will need to be employed. This will involve the use of equipment passed into the tank via an ullage or sampling port or a sounding pipe and personnel may therefore be exposed to greater concentrations of cargo vapour.

As cargo compartments may be in a pressurised condition, the opening of vapour lock valves, ullage ports or covers and the controlled release of any pressure should be undertaken by authorised personnel only.

When measuring or sampling, care must be taken to avoid inhaling gas. Personnel should therefore keep their heads well away from the issuing gas and stand at right angles to the direction of the wind. Standing immediately upwind of the ullage port might create a back eddy of vapour towards the operator. In addition, depending on the nature of the cargo being handled, consideration may have to be given to the use of appropriate respiratory protective equipment (see Section 7.2.4).

When open gauging procedures are being employed, the tank opening should only be uncovered long enough to complete the operation.

7.2.2 Measuring and Sampling Non-inerted Tanks (Table 7-1 refers)

Static electricity hazards may be present when gauging and sampling non-inerted tanks. An electrostatic charge may be present on the surface of the liquid in the tank, either because it is being pumped or is subjected to agitation. A charge may also be generated on the gauging or sampling equipment or on the person using the equipment.

Reference should be made to Chapter 20 for a full explanation of static electrical hazards. Section 20.3 provides guidance on the safe handling of static accumulator oils and Section 20.5 addresses hazards associated with dipping, ullaging and sampling operations.

Electrostatic Charges:

- **Static charge accumulation on unearthed probes introduced into tanks:**

  Regardless of the volatility of the cargo, in a non-inerted tank there is always the possibility that the atmosphere may be within the flammable range.

  When ullaging, dipping, gauging or sampling all cargoes in non-inerted tanks, irrespective of the volatility classification of the cargo, the following precautions must be observed in order to avoid hazards associated with the possible accumulation of electrical charges on probes, such as metal tapes, lowered into the tank:

  - Metal tapes or other gauging/sampling devices which could act as electrical conductors throughout their length must be effectively earthed or bonded before introduction into the tank until after removal.

  - No synthetic tapes or ropes should be used.

  (Reference should also be made to Section 7.4.3(c) regarding operations conducted through full depth sounding pipes).

- **Static accumulation properties of the cargo:**

  The precautions to be taken against static electricity during the ullaging, dipping, gauging or sampling of static accumulator oils are to be found in Section 7.4.3 and must be rigidly adhered to in order to avoid hazards associated with the accumulation of electrical charge on the cargo.

7.2.3 Measuring and Sampling Inerted Tanks

Ships fitted with inert gas systems will have closed gauging systems for taking measurements during cargo operations. In addition, many vessels will be provided with vapour locks to enable closed gauging and sampling to be undertaken for custody transfer purposes.

Ships equipped with a vapour lock on each cargo tank can measure and sample cargo without reducing the inert gas pressure. The vapour locks are in many cases accompanied by specially adapted measurement devices, including sonic tapes, samplers and temperature tapes. The valves of the vapour lock should not be opened until the instrument is properly attached to the standpipe. Care should be taken to ensure that there is no blow-back of vapour.

Sonic tapes, temperature tapes etc. must be used in accordance with good safety practices and the manufacturers' instructions. The requirements for portable electrical equipment apply to these measurement devices (see Section 2.4).

On ships which are not equipped with vapour locks, special precautions need to be taken for the open measuring and sampling of cargo carried in tanks which are inerted (for inspection of inerted tanks prior to loading, see Section 5.4). When it is necessary to reduce the pressure in any tank for the purposes of measuring and sampling, the following precautions should be taken:

- A minimum positive inert gas pressure should be maintained during measuring and sampling. The low oxygen content of inert gas can rapidly cause asphyxiation and care should therefore be taken to avoid standing in the path of vented gas during measuring and sampling (see Section 7.2.1). No cargo or ballast operations are to be permitted in cargo compartments while the inert gas pressure is reduced to allow measuring and sampling.

- Only one access point should be opened at a time and for as short a period as possible. In the intervals between the different stages of cargo measurement (e.g. between ullaging and taking temperatures) the relevant access point should be kept firmly closed.

- After completing the operation and before commencing the discharge of cargo, all openings should be secured and the cargo tanks re-pressurised with inert gas. (See Chapter 10 for the operation of ship's inert gas system during cargo and ballast handling).

- Measuring and sampling which require the inert gas pressure to be reduced and cargo tank access points opened should not be conducted during mooring and unmooring operations or while tugs are alongside. It should be noted that if access points are opened while a vessel is at anchor or moored in an open roadstead any movement of the vessel may result in the tanks breathing. To minimise this risk in such circumstances, care should be taken to maintain sufficient positive pressure within the tank being measured or sampled.

If it is necessary to sound the tanks when approaching the completion of discharge, the inert gas pressure can again be reduced to minimum safe operational level to permit sounding through sighting ports or sounding pipes. In order to avoid the ingress of air or an excessive release of inert gas it is essential that during this operation tanks which are still being discharged are not opened.

7.2.4 Measuring and Sampling Cargoes Containing Toxic Substances

Special precautions need to be taken when vessels carry cargoes containing toxic substances in concentrations sufficient to be hazardous.

Loading terminals have a responsibility to advise the Master if the cargo to be loaded contains hazardous concentrations of toxic substances. Similarly, it is the responsibility of the Master to advise the receiving facility that the cargo to be discharged contains toxic substances. This information is required to be exchanged by the Ship/Shore Safety Check List (see Appendix A).

The ship must also advise the terminal and any other tank inspectors or surveyors if the previous cargo contained toxic substances.

Ships carrying cargoes containing toxic substances should adopt closed sampling and gauging procedures or require all personnel undertaking these activities to wear personal protective equipment (see Sections 16.4 and 16.5).

When closed gauging or sampling cannot be undertaken, tests should be made to assess the vapour concentrations in the vicinity of each access point when open in order to ensure that concentrations of vapour do not exceed the Permissible Exposure Limits (PELs) of the toxic substances that may be present. If monitoring indicates the limit could be exceeded, suitable respiratory protection should be worn (see Section 16.4). Access points should be opened only for the shortest possible time.

If effective closed operations cannot be maintained, or if concentrations of vapour are rising because of defective equipment or due to still air conditions, consideration should be given to suspending operations and closing all venting points until defects in equipment are corrected or weather conditions change and improve gas dispersion.

Reference should be made to Chapter 16 for a description of the toxicity hazards of petroleum and its products.

7.2.5 Closed Gauging for Custody Transfer

The gauging of tanks for custody transfer purposes should be effected by use of a closed gauging system or via vapour locks. For the ullaging system to be acceptable for this purpose, the gauging system should be described in the vessel's tank calibration documentation. Corrections for datum levels, and for list and trim should be checked and approved by the vessel's classification society.

Temperatures can be taken using electronic thermometers deployed into the tank through vapour locks. Such instruments should have the appropriate approval certificates and should also be calibrated.

Samples should be obtained by the use of special sampling devices using the vapour locks.

7.3 OPERATION OF PUMPS AND VALVES

7.3.1 Pressure Surges

The incorrect operation of pumps and valves can produce pressure surges in a pipeline system. These surges may be sufficiently severe to damage the pipeline, hoses or metal arms. One of the most vulnerable parts of the system is the ship to shore connection. Pressure surges are produced upstream of a closing valve and may become excessive if the valve is closed too quickly. They are more likely to be severe where long pipelines and high flow rates are involved.

Where the risk of pressure surges exists, information should be exchanged and written agreement reached between the tanker and the terminal concerning the control of flow rates, the rate of valve closure, and pump speeds. This should include the closure period of remote controlled and automatic shutdown valves. These arrangements should be included in the operational plan (see Sections 5.3 and 5.4).

7.3.2 Butterfly and Non-Return (Check) Valves

Butterfly and pinned back non-return valves in ship and shore cargo systems have been known to slam shut when cargo is flowing through them at high rates, thereby setting up very large surge pressures which can cause line, hose, or metal arm failures and even structural damage to jetties. These failures are usually due to the valve disc not being completely parallel to, or fully withdrawn from, the flow when in the open position. This can create a closing force which may shear either the valve spindle in the case of butterfly valves, or the hold open pin in the case of pinned back non-return valves. It is therefore important to check that all such valves are fully open when they are passing cargo or ballast.

7.3.3 Valve Operation

To avoid pressure surges, valves at the downstream end of a pipeline system should as a general rule, not be closed against the flow of liquid except in an emergency. This should be stressed to all personnel responsible for cargo handling operations both on the tanker and at the terminal.

In general, where pumps are used for cargo transfer, all valves in the transfer system (both ship and shore) should be open before pumping begins, although the discharge valve of a centrifugal pump may be kept closed until the pump is up to speed and the valve then opened slowly. In the case of ships loading by gravity, the final valve to be opened should be that at the shore tank end of the system.

If the flow is to be diverted from one tank to another, either the valve on the second tank must be opened before the valve on the first tank is closed, or pumping should be stopped while the change is being made.

Valves which control liquid flow should be closed slowly. The time taken for power operated valves to move from open to shut and from shut to open should be checked regularly at their normal operating temperatures.

7.3.4 Control of Pumping

Throughout pumping operations no abrupt changes in the rate of flow should be made.

Reciprocating main cargo pumps can set up excessive vibration in metal loading/discharging arms which in turn can cause leaks in couplers and swivel joints, and even mechanical damage to the support structure. Where possible such pumps should not be used. If they are, care must be taken to select the least critical pump speed or, if more than one pump is used, a combination of pump speeds to achieve an acceptable level of vibration. A close watch should be kept on the vibration level throughout the cargo discharge.

Centrifugal pumps should be operated at speeds which do not cause cavitation. This effect may damage the pump and other equipment on the ship or at the terminal.

7.4 HANDLING STATIC ACCUMULATOR CARGOES

7.4.1 General

Precautions against static electricity may be necessary when the cargo being handled is an accumulator of static electricity. Reference should be made to Chapter 20 for a full explanation of the hazards of static electricity.

7.4.2 Static Accumulation

a) Clean oils are, in general, accumulators of static electricity because of their low conductivity. Static accumulator oils include:

- Natural gasolines
- Kerosenes
- White spirits
- Motor and aviation gasolines
- Jet fuels
- Naphthas
- Heating oils
- Heavy gas oils
- Clean diesel oils
- Lubricating oils

Under certain conditions, cargo handling operations involving static accumulator oils will require adherence to the anti-static precautions described in Section 7.4.3.

Other hazards associated with static electricity may occur during cargo handling operations. It is essential that the precautions detailed in Section 7.2.2 are also rigorously followed to prevent hazards associated with the accumulation of static electricity on measurement and sampling equipment.

(b) As explained in Chapter 20, black oils have sufficient conductivity to prevent the accumulation of static electricity. Consequently, black oil cargoes such as:

- Crude oils
- Black diesel oils
- Residual fuel oils
- Asphalts (bitumens)

are not classed as static accumulators and the anti-static precautions described in Section 7.4.3 will not necessarily be required when handling such oils.

Hazards associated with static electricity may still occur with such black oil cargoes. It is important that the precautions detailed in Section 7.2.2 are followed to prevent the accumulation of static electricity on measurement and sampling equipment.

Cargo Tank Operation When hazard can occur:	Lowering of equipment with ropes or tapes of synthetic material	Loading clean oils	Tank washing
Electrostatic Hazard (Chapter 20)	Rubbing together of synthetic polymers (Chapter 20.5.2)	Flow of static accumulator liquids (Sections 20.3, 20.5.3)	Water mist droplets (Section 20.4.2, 20.5.5)
Precautions Necessary For dipping, ullaging and sampling with:	(Sections 7.4.3(b), 9.2.4(i))	(Section 7.4.3(b))	(Sections 9.2.3(b), 9.2.4(i))
(i) metallic equipment not earthed or bonded:	Use of ropes or tapes made of synthetic materials for lowering equipment into cargo tanks not permitted at any time	Not permitted at any time	Not permitted during washing and for 5 hours thereafter
(ii) metallic equipment which is earthed and bonded from before introduction until after removal:	,,	Not permitted during loading and for 30 minutes thereafter	No restrictions
(iii) non-conducting equipment with no metallic parts:	,,	No restrictions	No restrictions
Exceptions Permitted if:		Sounding pipe is used	(a) sounding pipe is used or (b) tank is continuously mechanically ventilated, when 5 hours can be reduced to 1 hour

Table 7-1 Non-Inerted Tanks

Summary of Precautions Against Electrostatic Hazards when Gauging and Sampling

7.4.3   Precautions Against Static Electricity Hazards

When a tank is maintained in an inert condition no anti-static precautions are necessary.

If the tank is in a non-inert condition, specific precautions will be required with regard to safe flow rates and ullaging, sampling and gauging procedures when handling static accumulator oils as follows:

(a) During the initial stages of loading into each individual tank the flow rate in its branch line should not exceed a linear velocity of 1 metre/second.

When the bottom structure is covered and after all splashing and surface turbulence has ceased, the rate can be increased to the lesser of the ship or shore pipeline and pumping system maximum flow rates, consistent with proper control of the system. Experience indicates that hazardous potentials do not occur if the velocity is below 7 m/s and some national codes of practice suggest this as the maximum velocity. However, where well documented experience indicates that higher velocities have been safely used, the limit of 7 m/s may be replaced by an appropriate higher value.

To assist in calculating the volumetric loading rate which corresponds to a linear velocity in a branch line of 1 metre/second, the following table can be used to relate the volumetric flow rate to the pipeline diameter:

Pipeline Diameter* mm	Approximate Flow Rate Cubic Metres/Hour
80	17
100	29
150	67
200	116
250	183
305	262
360	320
410	424
460	542
510	676
610	987
710	1354
810	1782

Table 7.2 *Rates Corresponding to 1 Metre/Second*

*Note that the diameters given are nominal diameters which are not necessarily the same as the actual internal diameters.

(b) During loading, and for 30 minutes after the completion of loading, metallic equipment for dipping, ullaging or sampling must not be introduced into or remain in the tank. Examples of equipment include manual steel ullage tapes, portable gauging devices mounted on deck standpipes, metal sampling apparatus and metal sounding rods. Non-conducting equipment with no metal parts may, in general, be used at any time. However, ropes or tapes used for lowering equipment into tanks must not be made from synthetic materials (see Section 7.2.2).

After the 30 minutes waiting period, metallic equipment may also be used for dipping, ullaging and sampling but it is essential that it is effectively bonded and securely earthed to the structure of the ship before it is introduced into the tank and that it remains earthed until after it has been removed. (see also Section 20.5.3).

(c) Operations carried out through sounding pipes are permissible at any time because it is not possible for any significant charge to accumulate on the surface of the liquid within a correctly designed and installed sounding pipe. A sounding pipe is defined as a conducting pipe which extends the full depth of the tank and which is effectively bonded

Note: In all cases where there may be a toxicity hazard, refer to Section 7.2.4

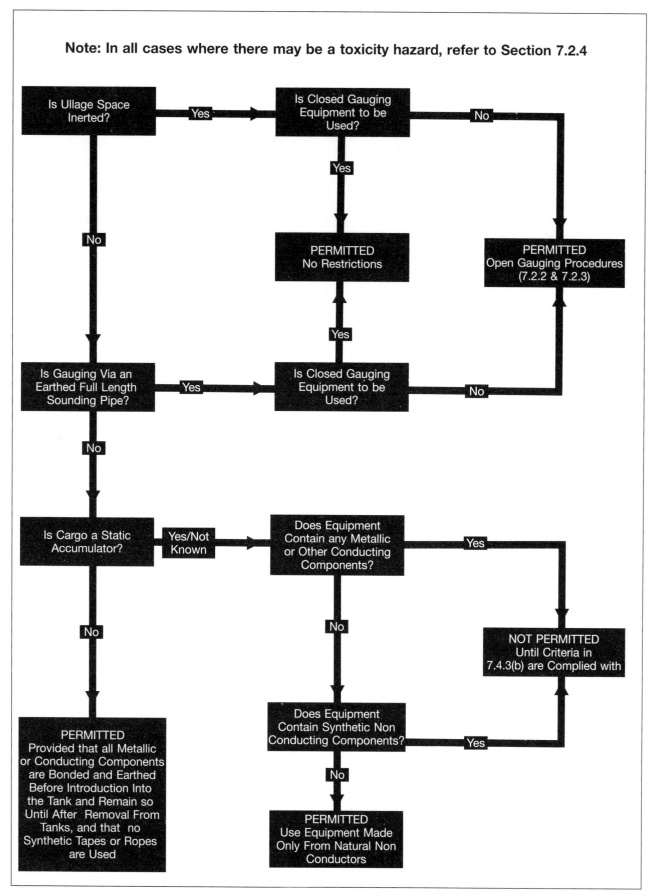

Figure 7-1. *Guide to Precautions Required When Using Portable Measuring and Sampling Equipment*

and earthed to the tank structure at its extremities. The pipe should be slotted in order to prevent any pressure differential between the inside of the pipe and the tank and to ensure that true level indications are obtained.

If the sounding facilities are provided, for example, through a deck standpipe that does not extend the full depth of the tank, all the static precautions detailed in Section 7.4.3 a) and b) above should be strictly adhered to.

A permanently fitted metal float level gauge does not present a static electricity hazard provided the metal float has electrical continuity through the tape to the structure of the ship and the metal guide wires are intact. Other wire guided gauging systems may be used provided the metal guide wires are intact.

(d) Micropore filters, usually made of paper, cellulose or glass fibre are known to be capable of generating high static charge levels. If a micropore filter is fitted in the shore pipeline system the loading rate should be adjusted to ensure that at least 30 seconds elapse between the time the cargo leaves the filter and the time it enters any cargo tank.

7.4.4 Discharge of Static Accumulator Oils

As air and/or gas bubbles in a liquid can generate static electricity, stripping pumps and eductors should be operated in order to avoid as far as possible the entrainment of air or gas.

7.4.5 Discharge into Shore Installations

In addition to the requirements set out in the preceding paragraphs, when discharging static accumulator oils into shore tanks the initial flow rate should be restricted to 1 metre/second unless or until the shore tank inlet is covered sufficiently to limit turbulence.

For a side entrance (horizontal entrance) the inlet is considered adequately covered if the distance between the top of the inlet and the free surface exceeds 0.6 metre. An inlet pointing downwards is considered sufficiently covered if the distance between the lower end of the pipe and the free surface exceeds twice the inlet diameter. An inlet pointing upward may require a considerably greater distance to limit turbulence. In floating roof tanks, the low initial flow rate should be maintained until the roof is floating. Similar requirements apply to fixed roof tanks with inner floats.

7.5 DEBALLASTING

7.5.1 Commencement of Deballasting

Deballasting to shore tanks must only be commenced with the agreement of the terminal and after it has signified that the shore system is ready to receive the ballast.

7.5.2 Allowance for Stress

Ballast must be discharged in such a way as to avoid the ship's hull being subjected to excessive stress.

7.5.3 Deballasting of a Ship Fitted with an Inert Gas System

Ships fitted with an inert gas system must replace the ballast discharged from cargo tanks with inert gas so as to maintain the oxygen content of the tank atmosphere at not more than 8% by volume.

7.5.4 Segregated Ballast

Ballast carried in segregated tanks may be retained on board in order to restrict the freeboard if this is necessary because of weather conditions or to keep within the envelope restrictions of the terminal metal loading arms or shore gangway. Care must be taken, however, not to exceed the maximum draught for the berth and to include the ballast weights in the hull stress calculations.

7.6　LOADING OF CARGO

7.6.1　Stability Considerations

The loading plan of combination carriers and double hull tankers must take into account the ship's stability instructions and the need to avoid excessive free surface with consequent loss of stability (see Sections 8.1 and 12.4.2).

7.6.2　Inert Gas Procedures

The inert gas plant should be closed down and the inert gas pressure in the tanks to be loaded reduced prior to the commencement of loading unless simultaneous loading of cargo and discharge of ballast from cargo tanks is to take place.

7.6.3　Closed Loading

For effective closed loading, cargo must be loaded with the ullage, sounding and sighting ports securely closed. The gas displaced by the incoming cargo must be vented to the atmosphere via the mast riser(s) or through high velocity or constant velocity valves, either of which will ensure that the gases are taken clear of the cargo deck. Devices fitted to mast risers or vent stacks to prevent the passage of flame must be regularly checked to confirm they are clean, in good condition and correctly installed.

To undertake closed loading, the vessel should be equipped with ullaging equipment and independent overfill alarms (see Section 7.7.3) which allow the tank contents to be monitored without opening tank apertures. On vessels without inert gas systems this equipment should comply with the precautions highlighted in Sections 7.4 and 20.5.

Vessels operating with inert gas are considered always to be capable of closed loading.

7.6.4　Commencement of Loading Alongside a Terminal

When all necessary terminal and tanker valves in the loading system are open, and the ship has signified its readiness, loading can commence. Whenever possible the initial flow should be by gravity, the shore pumps not being started until the system has been checked and the ship advises that cargo is being received in the correct tank(s). When the pumps have been started the ship/shore connections must be checked for tightness until the agreed flow rate or pressure has been reached.

7.6.5　Commencement of Loading at Buoy Berths

Before commencing to load at an offshore berth, the ship should confirm its full understanding of the communications system which will be used to control the operation. A secondary communications system should be provided ready to be brought into immediate action in the event of failure of the primary system.

After an initial slow loading rate to test the system, the flow rate may be brought up to the agreed maximum. A close watch should be kept on the sea in the vicinity of the seabed manifold so that leaks may be detected. During darkness, where safe and practical, a bright light should be shone on the water in the vicinity of the hoses.

7.6.6　Commencement of Loading Through a Stern Line

Before commencing loading through a stern loading line the dangerous area extending not less than 3 metres from the manifold valve should be clearly marked and no unauthorised personnel should be allowed within this area during the entire loading operation.

A close watch must be maintained for any leakage and all openings, air inlets and doors to enclosed spaces should be kept tightly closed.

Fire fighting equipment must be laid out and ready for use in the vicinity of the stern loading manifold.

7.6.7 Commencement of Loading Through a Bow Line

Vessels involved in bow loading will necessarily be designed for use at particular terminals (normally single point moorings) for which detailed operating and safety procedures will be specified.

In general, however, the following checks should be carried our prior to loading:

- The mooring system should be inspected for security of connection and to ensure that any wear is within acceptable operational limits.

- The cargo hose connection should be carefully inspected for correct alignment and security of coupling. Where possible, a water pressure test of the coupling seals should be made.

- Any emergency release systems provided for the mooring and cargo connection should be operational. Tests of these systems should take place prior to mooring.

- Mooring load monitoring systems should be activated and tested.

- All primary and secondary means of communication with the loading terminal should be tested, including any telemetry control system.

A continuous watch by a responsible crew member should be maintained on the bow throughout loading. During darkness the illumination on and around the vessel's bow should permit an effective visual watch to be maintained on the mooring point, mooring system, cargo hose connection, loading hoses and the area of water around the bow.

7.6.8 Emergency Shutdown Plan

An emergency shutdown procedure should be agreed between the ship and the terminal and recorded on an appropriate form.

The agreement should designate those circumstances in which operations must be stopped immediately.

Due regard should be given to the possible dangers associated with any emergency shutdown procedure (see Sections 6.5.5 and 7.3.1).

7.6.9 Fluctuation of Loading Rate

The loading rate should not be substantially changed without informing the ship.

7.6.10 Cessation of Loading by the Terminal

Many terminals require a 'standby' period for stopping pumps and this should be understood and noted as discussed in Section 8 of the Ship/Shore Safety Check List Guidelines before loading commences (see Appendix A).

7.6.11 Topping Off on Board the Tanker

The ship should advise the terminal when the final tanks are to be topped off and request the terminal, in adequate time, to reduce the loading rate sufficiently to permit effective control of the flow on board the ship. After topping off individual tanks, master valves should be shut, where possible, to provide two valve segregation of loaded tanks. Ullages should be checked from time to time to ensure that overflows do not occur as a result of leaking valves or incorrect operations.

The number of valves to be closed during the topping off period should be reduced to a minimum.

The tanker should not close all its valves against the flow of oil.

Before topping off operations commence at an offshore berth, the ship/shore communications system must be tested.

Where possible the completion of loading should be done by gravity. If pumps have to be used to the end, their delivery rate during the 'standby' time should be regulated so that shore control valves can be closed as soon as requested by the ship. Shore control valves should be closed before the ship's valves.

7.6.12 Checks After Loading

After the completion of loading, a responsible officer should check that all valves in the cargo system are closed, that all appropriate tank openings are closed and that pressure/vacuum relief valves are correctly set.

7.6.13 Loading Very High Vapour Pressure Cargoes

Consideration should be given to the need for special precautions during loading when the True Vapour Pressure (TVP) of the cargo is expected to exceed the following:

- For natural gasoline type cargoes (e.g. pentanes plus): 0.75 bar

- For crude oils, with or without added gas: 1.0 bar.

For some intermediate cargoes (for example flash stabilised condensates, some distillation overhead products, and crude oils with abnormally low methane and ethane contents) TVP limits may lie between these two values.

When cargo temperature, crude oil stabilization conditions and Reid Vapour Pressures are known, true vapour pressures can be calculated for checking with the above criteria. The necessary information should be supplied by the terminal.

Precautions which should be applied may include:

- Permitting only closed loading methods (see Section 7.6.3).

- Avoiding loading when the wind speed is less than 5 knots.

- The use of very low initial flow rates into tanks.

- The use of very low topping off rates.

- Avoiding a partial vacuum in the loading line.

- Avoiding loading hot oil which has been lying in shore lines exposed to the sun; if this is unavoidable, loading this oil in tanks which vent well clear of the superstructure (e.g. forward tanks).

- Providing additional supervision to see that gas dispersion is monitored and to ensure compliance with all safety requirements.

7.6.14 Loading Heated Products

Unless the ship is specially designed for carrying very hot cargoes (e.g. a bitumen carrier), cargo heated to a high temperature can damage a tanker's structure, protective coatings and equipment such as valves, pumps and gaskets.

Some classification societies have rules regarding the maximum temperature at which cargo may be loaded and masters should consult their owners whenever the cargo to be loaded has a temperature in excess of 60°C.

The following precautions may help to alleviate the effects of loading a hot cargo:

- Spreading the cargo throughout the ship as evenly as possible in order to dissipate excess heat and to avoid local heat stress.

- Adjusting the loading rate in an attempt to achieve a more reasonable temperature.

- Taking great care to ensure that tanks and pipelines are completely free of water before receiving any cargo that has a temperature above the boiling point of water.

7.6.15 Loading Overall (Loading from the Top)

There may be specific port or terminal regulations relating to loading overall.

Volatile petroleum, or non-volatile petroleum having a temperature higher than its flashpoint minus 10°C, must never be loaded or transferred overall into a non-gas free tank.

Non-volatile petroleum having a temperature lower than its flashpoint minus 10°C may be loaded overall in the following circumstances:

- If the tank concerned is gas free and provided no contamination by volatile petroleum can occur.

- If prior agreement is reached between the master and the terminal representative.

The free end of the hose should be lashed inside the tank coaming to prevent movement.

Ballast or slops must not be loaded or transferred overall into a tank which contains a flammable gas mixture.

7.7 LOADING AT TERMINALS HAVING VAPOUR EMISSION CONTROL SYSTEMS

7.7.1 General

The fundamental concept of a vapour emission control system is relatively simple. When tankers are loading at a terminal, the vapours are collected as they are displaced by the incoming cargo or ballast and are transferred ashore for treatment or disposal. However, the operational and safety implications are significant because the ship and terminal are connected by a common stream of vapours, thereby introducing into the operation a number of additional hazards which have to be effectively controlled. Detailed guidance on technical issues associated with vapour emission control and treatment systems are available from a number of sources. IMO has developed international standards for the design, construction and operation of vapour collection systems on tankers and vapour emission control systems at terminals and OCIMF has promulgated guidance on vapour manifold arrangements.

The primary hazards associated with the use of vapour emission control (VEC) systems are summarised below.

7.7.2 Misconnection of Liquid and Vapour Lines

To guard against the possible misconnection of the ship's vapour manifold to a terminal liquid loading line, the vapour connection should be clearly identified by painting the outboard 1 metre section with yellow and red bands and by stencilling the word "VAPOUR" in black letters upon it. In addition, a cylindrical stud should be permanently attached to each presentation flange face at the 12 o'clock position on the flange bolt circle. The stud should project 25.4mm (1 inch) perpendicular to the flange face, and should be 12.7mm (½ inch) in diameter, in order to prevent the connection of standard liquid transfer hoses. Blank flanges, inboard ends of reducers and hoses for the vapour line will have an extra hole to accommodate the lug on the presentation flange (see Figure 7-2).

Full details of vapour manifold arrangements, materials and fittings are contained in the OCIMF publication "Recommendations for Oil Tanker Manifolds and Associated Equipment".

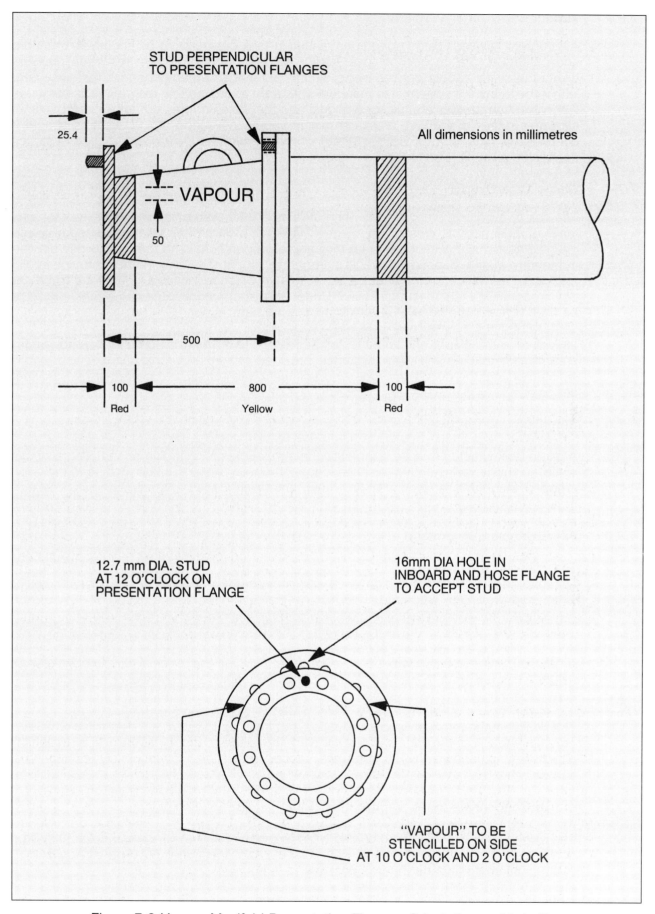

STUD PERPENDICULAR
TO PRESENTATION FLANGES

25.4

All dimensions in millimetres

VAPOUR

50

500

100
Red

800
Yellow

100
Red

12.7 mm DIA. STUD
AT 12 O'CLOCK ON
PRESENTATION FLANGE

16mm DIA HOLE IN
INBOARD AND HOSE FLANGE
TO ACCEPT STUD

"VAPOUR" TO BE
STENCILLED ON SIDE
AT 10 O'CLOCK AND 2 O'CLOCK

Figure 7-2 *Vapour Manifold Presentation Flanges, Orientation and Labelling*

7.7.3 Vapour Over/Under Pressure

Although all "closed" cargo operations require in-tank pressures to be effectively monitored and controlled, the connection to a vapour emission control system results in pressures within the ship's vapour spaces being directly influenced by any changes that may occur within the terminal's system. It is therefore important to ensure that the individual cargo tank P/V protection devices are fully operational and that loading rates do not exceed maximum allowable rates. In addition, pressures within vapour collection piping systems should be continuously monitored by sensors that incorporate high and low pressure alarm functions connected to audible and visual alarms.

7.7.4 Cargo Tank Overfill

The risk of overfilling a cargo tank when utilising a VEC system is no different to that when loading under normal "closed" conditions. However, owing to the reliance placed on closed gauging systems, it is important that they are fully operational and that back-up is provided in the form of an independent overfill alarm arrangement. The alarm should provide audible and visual indication and should be set at a level which will enable operations to be shut down prior to the tank being overfilled. Under normal operations, the cargo tank should not be filled higher than the level at which the overfill alarm is set.

Individual overfill alarms should be tested at the tank to ensure their proper operation prior to commencing loading unless the system is provided with an electronic self-testing capability which monitors the condition of the alarm circuitry and sensor and confirms the instrument set point.

7.7.5 Sampling and Gauging

A cargo tank should never be opened to the atmosphere for gauging or sampling purposes while the ship is connected to the shore vapour recovery system unless loading to the tank is stopped, the tank is isolated from any other tank being loaded and precautions are taken to reduce any pressure within the cargo tank vapour space.

7.7.6 Fire/Explosion/Detonation

The inter-connection of ship and shore vapour streams, which may or may not be within the flammable range, introduces significant additional hazards which are not normally present when loading. Unless adequate protective devices are installed and operational procedures are adhered to, a fire or explosion occurring in the vapour space of a cargo tank onboard could transfer rapidly to the terminal, and *vice versa*.

A detonation arrestor should be fitted in close proximity to the terminal vapour connection at the jetty head in order to provide primary protection against the transfer or propagation of a flame from ship to shore or from shore to the ship.

The design of the terminal vapour collection and treatment system will determine whether or not flammable vapours can be safely handled and, if they cannot, will include provisions for either inerting, enriching or diluting the vapour stream and continuously monitoring its composition.

7.7.7 Liquid Condensate in the Vapour Line

The ship's systems should be provided with means to effectively drain and collect any liquid condensate that may accumulate within vapour pipelines. Any build-up of liquid in the vapour line could impede the free passage of vapours and thus increase in-line pressures and also could result in the generation of significant electrostatic charges on the liquid's surface. It is important that drains are installed at the low points in the ship's piping system and that they are routinely checked to ensure that no liquid is present.

7.7.8 Electrostatic Discharge

The precautions contained in Section 7.4 with regard to initial loading rates and measuring and sampling procedures should be followed. In addition, to prevent the build up of electrostatic charges within the vapour collection system, all pipework should be electrically bonded to the hull and should be electrically continuous. The bonding arrangements should be inspected periodically to check their condition.

The terminal vapour connections should be electrically insulated from the tanker vapour connection by the use of an insulating flange or a single section of insulating hose.

7.7.9 Training

It is important that ship and shore personnel in charge of transfer operations complete a structured training programme covering the particular vapour emission control system installed either onboard their ship or within their terminal. Ship's personnel should be provided with general information on typical terminal arrangements and procedures and shore personnel should be made aware of typical tanker equipment and operating procedures.

7.7.10 Communications

The introduction of VEC's reinforces the importance of good cooperation and communications between the ship and shore. Pre-transfer discussions should provide both parties with an understanding of each others' operating parameters. Details such as maximum transfer rates, maximum allowable pressure drops in the vapour collection system and alarm and shut-down conditions and procedures, must be agreed before operations commence. (see Appendix A – Ship/Shore Safety Checklist).

A summary of the terminal's vapour emission control system should be included in the terminal information booklet.

7.8 MONITORING OF VOID AND BALLAST SPACES

Void and ballast spaces located within the cargo tank block should be routinely monitored to check that no leakage has occurred from adjacent cargo tanks. Monitoring should include regular atmosphere checks for hydrocarbon content and regular sounding/ullaging of the empty spaces.

The guidance given in Chapter 8 'Double Hull Operations' should be followed to the extent that it may apply to single hull tankers, particularly with regard to routine monitoring procedures (Section 8.2); actions to be taken in the event of cargo leakage being detected (Section 8.5) and the handling of ballast after a leak (Section 8.9).

7.9 DISCHARGE OF CARGO

7.9.1 Combination Carriers and Double Hull Tankers

The discharge plan of these ships must particularly take into account the ship's stability instructions and the need to avoid excessive free surface and consequent loss of stability (see Sections 8.1 and 12.4.2).

7.9.2 Inert Gas Procedures

Ships using an inert gas system must have the system fully operational and producing good quality (i.e. low oxygen content) inert gas at the commencement of discharge.

The inert gas system must be fully operational and working satisfactorily throughout the discharge of cargo or deballasting. Chapter 10 gives details on the operation of the IGS.

Cargo discharge must not be started until:

- All relevant cargo tanks, including slop tanks, are common with the IG main.

- All other cargo tank openings, including vent valves, are securely closed.

- The inert gas main is isolated from the atmosphere and, if a cross connection is fitted, also from the cargo main.

- The inert gas plant is operating.

- The deck isolating valve is open.

A low but positive inert gas pressure after completion of discharge will permit the draining of the manifold driptray into a tank and, if required, allow manual dipping of each tank.

7.9.3 Closed Discharging

Vessels correctly operating their inert gas systems may be considered to be conducting closed discharging operations.

Discharge should normally take place on non-inerted vessels with all ullage, sounding and sighting ports closed. Air should be admitted to the tanks by the dedicated venting system. Where the design of the vessel does not allow admittance of air via the vapour system at a satisfactory rate, air may be admitted via a sighting or ullage port providing it is fitted with a permanent flame screen.

When cargo is being run between tanks during discharge operations care should be taken to ensure that vapours are vented to deck via the deck apertures protected by flame screens.

7.9.4 Pressurising of Cargo Tanks

When high vapour pressure petroleum (e.g. natural gasoline and certain crude oils) reaches a low level in cargo tanks, the head of liquid is sometimes insufficient to keep cargo pumps primed. If an inert gas system is installed in the tanker this system can be used for pressurising cargo tanks in order to improve pump performance.

7.9.5 Crude Oil Washing

If the ship needs to crude oil wash all or some of its tanks during discharge, the responsible officer should incorporate a crude oil washing plan in the required discharge plan set out in Section 5.5.

A full description of the requirements relating to crude oil washing is given in Section 9.4.

7.9.6 Commencement of Discharge Alongside a Terminal

Shore valves must be fully open to receiving tanks before the tanker's manifold valves are opened. If there is a possibility that, owing to the elevation of the shore tanks above the level of the ship's manifold, pressure might exist in the shore line and no non-return (check) valves are fitted in the shore line, the ship must be informed and the tanker's manifold valves should not be opened until an adequate pressure has been developed by the pumps.

Discharge should start at a slow rate, and only be increased to the agreed rate once both parties are satisfied that the flow of oil to and from designated tanks is confirmed.

7.9.7 Commencement of Discharge at an Offshore Terminal

Before commencing discharge at an offshore terminal, communications between ship and shore should be tested and fully understood. The ship must not open its manifold valves or start its pumps until a clear signal has been received from the shore that the terminal is ready.

Discharge must be started slowly until the system has been tested and then gradually brought up to the maximum agreed flow rate or pressure. A close watch should be kept on the sea in the vicinity of the hoses to detect leaks. During darkness a bright light should, where safe and practicable, be shone on the water in the vicinity of the hoses.

7.9.8 Commencement of Discharge Through a Stern Discharge Line

Before commencing discharge through a stern discharge line, a dangerous area extending not less than 3 metres from the manifold valve should be clearly marked and no unauthorised personnel should be allowed within this area during the entire discharge operation.

A close watch must be maintained for any leakage and all openings, air inlets and doors to enclosed spaces should be kept tightly closed.

Fire fighting equipment must be laid out and ready for use in the vicinity of the stern discharge manifold.

7.9.9 Fluctuations in Discharge Rate

During discharge the flow of cargo should be controlled by the tanker in accordance with the agreement reached with the terminal.

The discharge rate should not be substantially changed without informing the terminal.

7.9.10 Stripping and Draining of Cargo Tanks

If, during the discharge of the main bulk of cargo, a slop tank or other selected tank is used to receive the drainings of tanks being stripped, personnel should be alert to the fact that the ullage in the receiving tank will be decreasing. In these circumstances great care should be taken to avoid an overflow and proper precautions taken in respect of any vapours emitted.

7.9.11 Simultaneous Ballast and Cargo Handling

If ballasting of cargo tanks is carried out simultaneously with the discharge of cargo, vapours may be emitted from the tanks being ballasted, in which case proper precautions should be taken. Crude oil washing ships should, if required, control atmospheric emissions by using the methods described in Section 9.4.8.

7.10 FAILURE OF THE INERT GAS SYSTEM DURING DISCHARGE

In the event of the failure of the inert gas system to deliver the required quality and quantity of inert gas, or to maintain a positive pressure in the cargo tanks and slop tanks, action must be taken immediately to prevent any air being drawn into the tanks. All cargo and/or ballast discharge must be stopped, the inert gas deck isolating valve closed, the vent valve between it and the gas pressure regulating valve (if provided) opened, and immediate action taken to repair the inert gas system.

Masters are reminded that national and local regulations may require the failure of an inert gas system to be reported to the harbour authority, terminal operator and to the port and flag state administrations.

Pyrophoric iron sulphide deposits, formed when hydrogen sulphide gas reacts with rusted surfaces in the absence of oxygen, may be present in the cargo tanks and these deposits can heat to incandescence when coming into contact with air. Therefore, in the case of tankers engaged in the carriage of crude oil, the failed inert gas system must be repaired and restarted, or an alternative source of inert gas provided, before discharge of cargo or ballast is resumed.

In the case of product carriers the formation of pyrophors is usually inhibited by tank coatings. If, therefore, it is considered totally impracticable to repair the inert gas system, discharge may be resumed with the written agreement of all interested parties, provided an external source of inert gas is provided or the following precautions are taken:

- Devices to prevent the passage of flame or flame screens (as appropriate) are in place and are checked to ensure that they are in a satisfactory condition.

- Valves on the vent mast risers are opened.

- No free fall of water or slops is permitted.

- No dipping, ullaging, sampling or other equipment is introduced into the tank unless essential for the safety of the operation. If it is necessary for such equipment to be introduced into the tank it should be done only after at least 30 minutes have elapsed since the injection of inert gas has ceased. All metal components of any equipment to be introduced into the tank should be securely earthed. This restriction should be applied until a period of five hours has elapsed since the injection of inert gas has ceased.

See also Section 10.12 and Chapter 23.

7.11   PIPELINE AND HOSE CLEARING

7.11.1   General

The procedure for clearing the pipelines and hoses or arms between the shore valve and ship's manifold will depend on the facilities available and whether these include a slop tank or other receptacle. The relative heights of the ship and shore manifolds may also influence procedures.

Some terminals require the ship to displace with water the contents of the hoses or arms, and perhaps also the shore pipelines, on completion of cargo operations. Prior to commencing the displacement the ship and terminal should reach agreement on the procedures to be adopted.

7.11.2   Line Draining

On completion of loading, the ship's cargo deck lines should be drained into appropriate cargo tanks to ensure that thermal expansion of the contents of the lines cannot cause leakage or distortion. The hoses or arms and perhaps a part of the pipeline system between the shore valve and the ship's manifold are also usually drained into the ship's tanks. Sufficient ullage must be left in the final tanks to accept the drainings of the hoses or arms and ship or shore lines.

On completion of discharge the ship's cargo deck lines should be drained into an appropriate tank and then be discharged ashore or into a slop tank.

When draining is complete and before hoses or arms are disconnected, the ship's manifold valves and shore valves should be shut and the drain cocks at the vessel's manifold should be opened to drain into fixed drain tanks or portable drip trays. Cargo manifolds and arms or hoses should be securely blanked after being disconnected. The contents of portable or fixed drip trays should be transferred to a slop tank or other safe receptacle.

7.11.3   Clearing of Hoses and Arms

If lines, hoses or arms have to be cleared to the shore using compressed air or inert gas, the following precautions should be strictly observed in order to avoid the possible creation of a hazardous static electrical charge or mechanical damage to tanks and equipment:

- The procedure to be adopted must be agreed between ship and terminal.

- There must be adequate ullage in the reception tank.

- To ensure that the amount of compressed air or inert gas is kept to a minimum the operation must be stopped when the line has been cleared.

- The inlet to the receiving tank should be located well above any water that may be in the bottom of the tank.

- The line clearing operation must be continuously supervised by a responsible person.

7.11.4 Ship's Cargo Pipelines

When compressed air or inert gas is used to clear ship's pipelines (e.g. when evacuating the liquid column above a deep well pump), similar hazards to those identified in Section 7.11.3 may arise. Therefore when compressed air or inert gas is to be used for such pipeline clearing the precautions detailed in Section 7.11.3 must be observed. Line clearing operations must be undertaken in accordance with the operating procedures previously established for the particular ship.

7.12 TRANSFERS BETWEEN VESSELS

7.12.1 Ship to Ship Transfers

In ship to ship transfers both tankers should comply fully with the safety precautions required for normal cargo operations. If the safety precautions are not being observed on either vessel, the operations must not be started or, if in progress, must be stopped.

Ship to ship transfers undertaken in port or at sea may be subject to approval by the port or local marine authority and certain conditions relating to the conduct of the operation may be attached to such approval.

A full description of the safety aspects of transfer operations is contained in the ICS/OCIMF "Ship to Ship Transfer Guide (Petroleum)", to which reference should be made before starting the transfer.

7.12.2 Ship to Barge Transfers

In tanker/barge transfers of petroleum, only authorised and properly equipped barges should be used. Precautions similar to those set out for ship to ship cargo transfers in the ICS/OCIMF "Ship to Ship Transfer Guide (Petroleum)" should be followed. If the safety precautions are not being observed on either the barge or the tanker the operations must not be started or, if in progress, must be stopped.

Masters of ships should be aware that barge crews may not be conversant with the "Ship to Ship Transfer Guide (Petroleum)".

The rate of pumping from ship to barge must be controlled according to the size and nature of the receiving barge. Well understood communications procedures must be established and maintained, particularly when the freeboard of the ship is high in relation to that of the barge.

If there is a large difference in freeboard between the ship and the barge, the barge crew must make allowance for the contents of the hose on completion of the transfer.

Arrangements should be made to release the barge in an emergency, having regard to other shipping or property in the vicinity. If the tanker is at anchor, it may be appropriate for the barge to drop anchor clear of the tanker, where it could remain secured to wait for assistance.

Barges should be cleared from the ship's side as soon as possible after they have completed the loading or discharging of volatile petroleum.

7.12.3 Ship to Ship Transfers Using Vapour Balancing

Specific operational guidance should be developed to address the particular hazards associated with vapour emission control activities during ship to ship transfer operations where vapour balancing techniques should only be undertaken between inerted vessels and, as a minimum, the following recommendations should be followed:

- Before commencing cargo transfer:

  - Equipment should be provided on at least one of the vessels to enable the oxygen content of the vapour stream to be monitored. This should draw samples continuously from a location close to the vapour manifold connection and should include the facility for audible and visual alarms should the oxygen content of the vapour stream exceed 8% by volume. The oxygen analyser and associated alarms should be tested for proper function prior to each cargo transfer operation.

  - The oxygen content of the vapour space of each tank connected to the IG main of both ships should be checked and confirmed to be less than 8% by volume.

  - The vapour transfer hose should be purged of air and inerted prior to commencing transfer of vapours.

  - The vapour manifold valves should not be opened until the pressure in the vapour system of the receiving vessel exceeds that of the vessel discharging cargo.

- During the cargo transfer:

  - Transfer operations should be terminated if the oxygen content of the vapour stream exceeds 8% by volume and should only be resumed once the oxygen content in the tanks of the receiving ship has been reduced to 8% or less by volume.

  - The IG pressure on both ships should be monitored and each ship advised of the other's pressure on a regular basis at the same time as transferred volumes are compared.

  - No air should be permitted to enter the cargo tanks of the discharging ship.

Reference should also be made to Section 7.7 which provides general guidance on vapour recovery operations.

7.12.4 Ship to Ship Transfers Using Terminal Facilities

Where a tanker at a berth is transferring cargo to a tanker at another berth through the shore manifolds and pipelines, the two tankers and the terminal should comply with all regulations relating to ship to shore transfers, including written operating arrangements and communications procedures. The co-operation of the terminal in establishing these details is essential.

7.13 BALLASTING

7.13.1 General

The ballasting operation should be discussed and agreed in writing between ship and terminal representatives. In drawing up this agreement, the following should be borne in mind:

- The responsible officer must calculate the hull stresses imposed by ballast weights to ensure that they do not exceed permitted limits.

- Before ballasting of tanks containing hydrocarbon vapour is carried out alongside a terminal, the responsible officer must consult with the terminal representative and all safety checks and precautions applicable to the loading of volatile petroleum observed. Closed loading procedures should be followed.

- During ballasting of cargo tanks which contain hydrocarbon vapour, gas is expelled which may be within the flammable range on mixing with air. This gas should therefore be vented through the recognized vent lines as during loading.

- When ballasting tanks that previously contained cargoes which required closed operations to be adopted, the ballast should also be loaded 'closed' by following the procedures in Section 7.6.3.

- Ballast must not be loaded overall into tanks containing hydrocarbon vapour.

- The agreement of the terminal representative must be obtained before the simultaneous handling of cargo and ballast, other than segregated ballast, takes place.

7.13.2 Operation of Cargo Pumps

When starting to ballast, cargo pumps should be operated so that no oil is allowed to escape overboard when the sea suction valve is opened. See the ICS/OCIMF publication "Prevention of Oil Spillages Through Cargo Pumproom Sea Valves".

7.13.3 Sequence of Valve Operations

The following procedures should be adopted when loading ballast into non-inerted tanks which contain hydrocarbon vapour:

- The tank valves should be the first valves opened.

- The initial flow of ballast should be restricted so that the entrance velocity is less than 1 metre/second until the longitudinals are covered or, if there are no longitudinals, until the depth of the ballast in the tank is at least 1.5 metres.

These precautions are required to avoid a geyser effect which may lead to the build up of an electrostatic charge in a mist or spray cloud near the point where the ballast enters the tank. When a sufficient charge exists the possibility of a discharge and ignition cannot be excluded.

7.14 TANK OVER PRESSURISATION AND UNDER PRESSURISATION

7.14.1 General

Over pressurisation of cargo and ballast tanks is caused by compression of the ullage space due to the inadequate release of vapour or by the overfilling of the tank. The consequences may result in serious deformation of the tank structure and its peripheral bulkheads or catastrophic failure which can seriously affect the structural integrity of the vessel and could lead to fire, explosion and pollution.

Structural damage can also be caused by not allowing inert gas, vapour or air into a tank whilst liquid is being discharged. The resulting under pressure caused in the tank can result in deformation of the ship's structure which could result in fire, explosion or pollution.

To guard against over and under pressurisation of tanks, owners/operators should give consideration to fitting:

- Individual pressure sensors with an alarm on each tank.

- Individual full flow pressure/release devices to each tank.

7.14.2 Tank Over Pressurisation – Causes

Over pressurisation usually occurs during ballasting, loading or internal transfer of cargo or ballast. It can be caused by one of the following reasons:

- Overfilling of the tank with liquid.

- Incorrect setting of the tank's vapour or inert gas isolating valve to the vapour line or inert gas line.

- Failure of the isolating valve to the vapour line or inert gas line.

- Failure or seizure of the venting valve.

- Choked flame arresters/screens

- Loading the tank at a rate which exceeds the maximum venting capacity.

- Ice forming on vents during cold weather conditions.

- Ice on the surface of the ballast.

- Restriction in the vapour lines caused by wax, residues or scale.

7.14.3 Tank Over Pressurisation – Precautions

The major safeguard against tank over pressurisation is the adherence to good operating procedures. These should include:

- On ships without an inert gas system, establishing a procedure to control the setting of the isolating valves on the vent lines. The procedure should include a method of recording the current position of the isolating valves and a method for preventing them from being incorrectly or casually operated.

- A method of recording the status of all valves in the system and preventing them from being incorrectly or casually operated.

- A system for setting the valves in the correct position for the operation and monitoring that they remain correctly set.

- Restricting the operation of the valves to authorised personnel only.

On vessels with inert gas systems where isolating valves are fitted to the branch line to each tank, SOLAS requires these valves be *"provided with locking arrangements which shall be under the control of the responsible ship's officer"*. This statement should be taken to mean that the valves must be locked to prevent any change in the valve setting being possible without application to the responsible officer to obtain the means of releasing the locking system on the valve.

Failure or seizure of isolating valves, pressure/vacuum valves or high velocity vents can be guarded against by regular maintenance procedures, pre-operational testing and by operator awareness to detect failure during operation.

To protect against over pressurisation through filling tanks too quickly, all ships should have maximum filling rates for each individual tank available for reference onboard by ship's personnel.

Tank vents should be checked to ensure that they are clear when the operation commences, and during freezing weather conditions they should be inspected at regular intervals throughout the operation.

7.14.4 Tank Under Pressurisation – Causes

The causes of under pressurisation are similar to those of over pressurisation, particularly:

- Incorrect setting of the tank isolating valve sited between the tank and the vapour line or inert gas line.

- Failure of an isolating valve on the vapour line or inert gas line.

- The inert gas fan not being run due to breakdown or failure to operate it.

- Failure in one of the inert gas supply valves.

- A choked flame screen on the vapour inlet line.

- Ice forming on the ballast vents during cold weather conditions.

7.14.5 Tank Under Pressurisation – Precautions

The precautions to guard against under pressurisation are the same as those relating to over pressurisation (see Section 7.14.3).

Where under pressurisation of a tank or tanks is suspected the situation requires corrective action.

The methods of reducing a partial vacuum in a tank are either to raise the liquid level in the tank by running or pumping cargo or ballast into the affected tank from another tank or to admit inert gas or air into the tank ullage space.

– Cautions

- On a ship with an inert gas system, there is a possibility that the quality of the inert gas may be compromised by air leaking past the seals in the tank access locations.

- Admitting inert gas at a high velocity to return the tank to a positive pressure could cause an electrostatic hazard, and the precautions identified in Section 20.5.6 should be observed.

- On ships without an inert gas system where it is not possible to reduce the partial vacuum other than by admitting air into the tank, care should be exercised to ensure that foreign objects with a possible ignition capability, such as rust scale, are not drawn into the tank.

Chapter 8

Double Hull Operations

The purpose of this Chapter is to address the safety aspects relating to the operation of double hull tankers. It does not address any design or structural criteria except where they impact upon operations. The guidelines contained in this Chapter were developed in response to a request from IMO after the introduction of MARPOL Annex I Regulation 13F. In some cases it may only be new ships, as defined in Regulation 13F, which are able to comply fully with these guidelines. However other ships should endeavour to comply in so far as is practicable.

8.1 STABILITY CONSIDERATIONS

Single hull oil tankers usually have such a high metacentric height in all conditions of loading and ballasting that they can be considered as being inherently stable. Whilst tanker personnel have always had to take account of longitudinal bending moments and vertical shear forces, the actual stability of the ship has seldom been a prime concern. However the introduction of double hulls into tanker design is likely to change that situation.

The main problem likely to be encountered is the effect on the transverse metacentric height of liquid free surface in the cargo and double bottom tanks.

Depending upon the design, type and number of these tanks, the free surface effect could result in the transverse metacentric height being significantly reduced. The situation will be most severe in the case of wide cargo tanks with no centreline bulkhead and the so called "U" ballast tanks which have no centreline bulkhead.

The most critical stages of any operation will be whilst filling the double bottom ballast tanks during discharge of cargo, and emptying the tanks during loading of cargo. If sufficient cargo tanks and double bottom tanks are slack simultaneously, the overall free surface effect could well be sufficient to reduce the transverse metacentric height to a point at which the transverse stability of the ship may be threatened. This could result in the ship suddenly developing a severe list. Large free surface area is especially likely to threaten stability at greater soundings (innages) with associated high vertical centre of gravity.

It is imperative that tanker and terminal personnel involved in cargo and ballast operations are aware of this potential problem, and that all cargo and ballast operations are conducted strictly in accordance with the ship's loading manual.

Where they are fitted, interlock devices to prevent too many cargo and ballast tanks from being operated simultaneously, thereby causing an excessive free surface effect, should always be maintained in full operational order, and should never be over-ridden.

Ships which operate with limited metacentric height should be equipped with a loading computer which calculates metacentric height.

It is imperative that masters and officers be aware that partially loading a cargo tank with heavy weather ballast may present a potential problem. The combination of free surface and the flat tank bottom can result in the generation of wave energy of sufficient power to severely damage internal structure and pipelines.

8.2   ROUTINE MONITORING OF DOUBLE HULL SPACES

Double hull spaces should be regularly monitored in order to check the integrity of the inner shell plating. This can be accomplished by monitoring the ballast tank atmosphere for hydrocarbon gas, and by regular sounding/ullaging of ballast tanks. The sampling referred to in this section is for leak detection purposes only, and should not be used as the criteria for tank entry. Section 8.3 refers to the procedures relating to tank entry for double hull spaces.

The atmosphere in each double hull tank and double bottom tank should be monitored for hydrocarbon content:

• Regularly during the loaded passage.

• Prior to ballasting the tank following a period of heavy weather.

• After any unusual event or occurrence eg. unexpected lists, unforeseen operational problems.

The atmosphere monitoring programme should ensure that each tank is monitored at least once per week during the loaded passage. However, where ships are engaged on short haul voyages which make this impractical, visual inspection of the tanks or the ballast water is considered to be a suitable alternative measure.

The hydrocarbon measurements should be taken with a portable gas detector at designated sampling points using installed fixed lines or a portable sampling hose, or with a fixed gas detection system where one is installed.

Where fixed gas detection systems are installed, operators should develop procedures to ensure that tank atmospheres are monitored on a regular basis. They should ensure that full operating, maintenance and fault detection instructions are readily available to ship's personnel, and that they are familiar with the use of the equipment.

Information as to the point of origin of each fixed sampling line should be readily available to ship's personnel.

Procedures should be developed for the regular clearing of all fixed sampling lines.

The ship should be provided with information relating to any restrictions on lowering a sampling hose into the tank which might be imposed as a result of normal operating trim or list.

During the loaded passage, ballast tanks should be sounded on a frequent and regular basis as a back up method of detecting any oil leakage into them.

After ballasting, tanks should be checked visually to ascertain if any oil is present. A similar procedure should be carried out prior to discharge of ballast.

During the ballast voyage, the ullage of each ballast tank should be checked at frequent and regular intervals. Consideration should also be given to the feasibility of routine monitoring to detect water ingress to the cargo tanks.

8.3 TANK ENTRY PROCEDURES FOR DOUBLE HULL SPACES

All tank entry must be strictly controlled, and it is strongly recommended that this control is exercised in accordance with the Tank Entry Permit procedures referred to in Chapter 11. It must however be appreciated that the compartmentalised structure in double hull and double bottom tanks makes them more difficult to gas free than conventional tanks and particular care should be taken to monitor the tank atmosphere.

Although entry into double hull or double bottom tanks should be kept to a minimum, tank entry will on occasion be required for such purposes as tank inspections and maintenance of ballast tank systems, gauging systems etc. In such cases, the recommendations in this section should be strictly enforced.

Measurements of hydrocarbon, oxygen and toxic gas (as appropriate) must be taken at every sampling point and in each case must meet the criteria specified in section 11.3.

The tank must be kept continuously ventilated throughout the period that people are inside it and during any breaks in the entry. If the ventilation is suspended for any significant period, the atmosphere must be re-verified as above and a new entry permit issued.

Once the tank atmosphere meets the entry criteria at each sampling point, actual entry by personnel should be undertaken in two stages. The first stage should be for the purpose of atmosphere verification and a general safety review.

In addition to the problems associated with gas freeing, the design and structure may add additional hazards to the entry process and therefore the following additional precautions should be considered during the initial entry. A strict radio reporting procedure should be established between those entering the tank and a monitor on deck.

One person should be assigned responsibility for atmosphere monitoring and communications. Personnel making the entry should be equipped with an emergency escape breathing set, a personal gas detector capable of monitoring at least hydrocarbon and oxygen, a portable radio, an emergency light source, a retrieval harness and an alternative means of attracting attention, eg. a whistle.

Only after this initial stage has verified that the atmosphere throughout the tanks is safe for the intended task should entry for other purposes be permitted. All such entry operations should be conducted in accordance with the procedures detailed in Chapter 11.

In order for people entering the tank to ascertain their position within the tank, and to facilitate position reporting, each tank bay should be identified by a simple number and/or letter system. This should be clearly marked in each bay and maintained in a visible condition throughout the life of the ship.

The tank entry route and the extent of penetration should be planned in advance. Any deviation from this plan should be agreed in advance with the person monitoring those inside the tank.

Consideration should be given to the laying out of hand lines to provide both an easy identification of the exit route and an aid to any rescue team.

8.4 VENTILATION PROCEDURES

The complexity of the structure in double hull and double bottom tanks makes them more difficult to gas free than conventional ballast tanks. It is strongly recommended that the operator develop guidelines and procedures relating to the ventilation of each tank.

Whenever possible, these guidelines and procedures should be developed in conjunction with the shipbuilder and should be based on actual tests/experiments as well as on calculation. They should give details of the configuration of each tank, the method of ventilation and the equipment to be used. Details should also include the time required for each method of ventilation to gas free the tank for entry. This should be the time to remove all contaminants rather than a simple volume/rate calculation.

Where portable fans are used for ventilation purposes, the above information should be provided for a range of drive pressures and different numbers of fans.

Where tanks are identical in structure and size, and where the method of venting is identical, the data can be obtained from tests on a representative tank. Otherwise the tests referred to above should be carried out for each tank.

8.5   ACTION TO BE TAKEN IN THE EVENT OF CARGO LEAKAGE

This section addresses the actions to be taken if the procedures in Section 8.2 identify a leak of hydrocarbons into a double hull or double bottom tank.

If a hydrocarbon leak is discovered the first step should be to check the atmosphere in the tank to establish the hydrocarbon level. It should be noted that the atmosphere in the tank could be above the UFL, within the flammable range, or below the LFL. Regardless of the number of samples taken, any or all of these conditions may exist in different locations within the tank, due to the complexity of the structure. It is thus essential that gas readings are taken at different levels at as many points as possible in order to establish the profile of the tank atmosphere.

If hydrocarbon gas is detected in a tank, there are a number of options which can be considered to maintain the tank atmosphere in a safe condition:

- Continuous ventilation of the tank.

- Inerting the tank.

- Filling, or partially filling the tank with ballast.

- Securing the tank with flame screens in place at the vents.

- A combination of the foregoing.

The option chosen will depend upon a number of factors, not least the degree of confidence in having established the hydrocarbon content of the atmosphere, bearing in mind the potential problems identified above.

It is strongly recommended that operators develop guidelines, taking into account the tank structure and any limitations of the available atmosphere monitoring system, which will assist ship's personnel to select the appropriate method of rendering the atmosphere safe.

Filling or partially filling the tank with ballast in order to render the atmosphere safe and/or stop any further leakage of cargo into the tank must take into account prevailing stress, trim, stability and loadline factors. It must also be borne in mind that the ballast may be classed as dirty ballast and may have to be processed in accordance with the MARPOL regulations (see Section 8.9).

If the tank is ventilated or inerted in lieu of filling, it should be regularly sounded to ascertain the rate of liquid build up and thus of leakage.

If the quantity of cargo leaking into the space is determined to be pumpable, it should be transferred to another cargo tank via the emergency ballast/cargo spool piece connection (see Section 8.9), or other emergency transfer method, in order to minimise contamination of the space and to facilitate subsequent cleaning and gas freeing operations. Ships should have written procedures available on board which indicate the actions to be taken and the operations necessary for the safe transfer of the cargo.

So far as is possible entry into the tank should be prohibited until it is safe for entry and there is no further possibility of oil ingress. However, if it is deemed essential to enter the tank for any reason, such entry must be carried out in accordance with Section 11.4.4. The entry, which must be carefully planned and controlled, should be made by people trained and experienced in the use of self-contained breathing apparatus, who should have two independent sources of air available to them.

8.6   INERTING DOUBLE HULL SPACES

If the decision is taken to inert a leaking double hull tank, the operation should be carried out in accordance with the guidelines contained in this section.

The complexity of the structure in double hull and double bottom tanks makes them more difficult to inert than conventional tanks. It is strongly recommended that the operator use these guidelines as a basis for developing procedures relating to the inerting of such tanks.

Whenever possible these procedures should be developed in conjunction with the shipbuilder and should be based on actual tests/experiments as well as on calculation. They should give details for each tank :

- The procedures to be followed.

- The equipment to be used and its configuration.

- The time required to reduce the oxgyen level in the tank to less than 8% by volume.

Where tanks are identical in structure and size, and where the method of inerting is identical, the data can be obtained from tests on a representative tank. Otherwise the tests referred to above should be carried out for each tank.

The introduction of inert gas into a tank may give rise to electrostatic charging. The compartmentalised structure of the tanks means that this charge is unlikely to reach incendive levels. However, because there may be a flammable atmosphere in certain areas within the tank (see Section 8.5) it is essential that all electrostatic precautions detailed in Sections 7.4 and 10.6.7 are complied with throughout the inerting process and for 30 minutes thereafter.

Flexible hoses used for inerting double hull tanks should be clearly identified, be dedicated solely to this use, and stowed safely and correctly. The hose string should be electrically continuous, and this should be verified prior to putting hoses into service. It should be confirmed that the string is properly earthed before inerting commences.

In order to minimise the transfer of hydrocarbon vapour from cargo tanks all cargo tank inert gas supply valves, where fitted, should be temporarily closed. Prior to connecting the hoses the inert gas line should be purged with inert gas. The hoses should not be connected until required.

Once the tank has been inerted, consideration should be given to the benefits of keeping it permanently connected to the inert gas system – constant pressure monitoring, over pressure protection via the deck water breaker, ease of topping up – against any potential problems of vapour transfer, vulnerability of the hose to heavy seas etc. If the hoses remain connected then all the cargo tank inert gas inlet valves must be re-opened. If the hoses are disconnected the inert gas system must be returned to its original status.

If cargo is to be transferred from a space which has been inerted, it is important to ensure that further inerting is carried out during the operation in order to avoid the introduction of oxygen into the tank.

Once inerted the tank should be kept topped up as necessary to ensure that a positive pressure is maintained and the oxygen content does not exceed 8% by volume.

The exhaust vapour from the tank during inerting should be ventilated through an opening at least 2metres above the deck. Portable stand pipes should be used where necessary.

Double hull tanks are not usually fitted with devices such as P/V valves which allow a positive pressure to be maintained in the tank. The guidelines referred to in Section 8.4 for venting tanks should address the sealing of openings which might let air into the tank and the method for ensuring that the tank cannot be over-pressurised.

The progress of inerting can be monitored by measuring the oxygen content of the exhaust vapour. However, atmosphere measurements to determine when the tank is fully inert, and subsequent monitoring measurements, must be taken at all designated sampling points with the inert gas supply secured.

8.7   GAS FREEING AND TANK ENTRY AFTER INERTING

The complex internal structure of the double hull tanks means that, before the entry of personnel can be considered, particular care must be taken when gas freeing the tanks after they have been inerted, in order to ensure that there are no pockets of inert gas or hydrocarbon gas anywhere within the tank.

Where the tank ventilation system may have been modified (see Section 8.6) it must be returned to its original status before commencing any operations.

A method of removing all inert gas vapours from the tanks is to fill the tank with ballast and then empty it, but this should not be relied on to produce a gas free atmosphere. Every effort should be made, taking account of stress, trim and loadline factors, to carry out this operation as the initial stage of the gas freeing operation. However it must always be borne in mind that this ballast may be dirty ballast which must be handled in accordance with the MARPOL regulations (see Section 8.9). When ballasting the tank it should not be allowed to overflow on to the deck.

(Note: Although filling the tank with water is an efficient method of gas freeing, consideration should be given to the fact that the operation may result in spreading oil onto the tank structure, thereby making the subsequent cleaning operation more difficult.)

Prior to any venting operation, in order to ensure that the atmosphere in the tank will not enter the flammable range, the tank should be purged with inert gas to reduce the average hydrocarbon content to less than 2% by volume. Readings should be taken at all sampling points. The purging operation should be carried out in accordance with the procedures referred to in Section 8.6.

After this has been completed, the tank should be ventilated in accordance with procedures referred to in Section 8.4 until readings at each sampling point indicate that the atmosphere meets the "safe for entry" criteria in Section 11.3.

In the unlikely event that it is not possible to ballast and deballast the tank, it should be ventilated in accordance with the procedures referred to in Section 8.4 until readings at each sampling point indicate that the atmosphere meets the "safe for entry" criteria in Section 11.3.

Entry into the tank after gas freeing should be carried out in accordance with the procedures in Section 8.3. Because of the additional hazard posed by the possible presence of inert gas the initial entry for atmosphere verification must be carefully planned in advance and should be the subject of its own specific entry permit. Those making the entry should be equipped with emergency escape respiratory protection or self-contained breathing apparatus as appropriate, and personal gas detectors. They should proceed through the tank compartments in accordance with the pre-planned sequence, verifying and reporting the atmosphere in each compartment prior to proceeding to the next compartment. Only when the entire tank has been systematically examined and verified to be free of inert gas should general entry be permitted. Such general entry should always be controlled in accordance with the procedures in Chapter 11.

The cargo tank from which the leak originated must also be gas freed prior to entry into the double hull space.

8.8   TANK CLEANING

So far as possible tank cleaning, particularly in the initial stages, should be carried out by methods other than hand hosing. Such methods may include, but not be limited to, using portable machines, the use of detergents, or washing the bottom of the tank with water and detergent. Hand hosing should only be permitted for small areas of contamination, or for final cleaning. Whichever method is used the tank washings must always be handled in accordance with the MARPOL regulations.

After a machine or detergent wash, prior to entry for final hand hosing, the tank must be ventilated in accordance with the procedures referred to in Section 8.4 until readings at each sampling point indicate that the atmosphere meets the "safe for entry" criteria in Chapter 11. A new entry permit should then be issued.

8.9   HANDLING BALLAST AFTER A LEAK

All ballast loaded into a tank after a leak has been found and all tank washings associated with cleaning the tank are "dirty ballast" as defined by the MARPOL regulations and must be processed in accordance with those regulations. This means that they must either be transferred directly to a cargo or slop tank for further processing in accordance with the requirements or, if discharged directly to sea, passed via the oil content monitor.

It is recommended that written procedures giving details as to how such an operation be carried out be developed by the operator in conjunction with the shipbuilder.

The spool piece used to connect the ballast system to the cargo system should be clearly identified and stowed close to its working position. It should not be used for any other purpose.

Chapter 9

Tank Cleaning and Gas Freeing

This Chapter deals with the procedures for cleaning and gas freeing cargo tanks and other enclosed spaces after the discharge of volatile petroleum or of non-volatile petroleum carried in a non-gas free tank, or when there is a possibility of flammable gas entering the tank or space. Safety precautions to be taken are set out, including those related to crude oil washing of cargo tanks.

9.1 SUPERVISION AND PREPARATIONS

9.1.1 Supervision

A responsible officer must supervise all tank cleaning and gas freeing operations.

9.1.2 Preparations

Both before and during tank cleaning and gas freeing operations, the responsible officer should be satisfied that all the appropriate precautions set out in Chapters 2 and 6 are being observed. All personnel on board should be notified that tank cleaning or gas freeing is about to begin.

If craft are alongside the tanker, their personnel should also be notified and their compliance with all appropriate safety measures should be checked.

Before starting to gas free or tank clean alongside a terminal, the following additional measures should be taken:

- The precautions in Chapter 4 should be observed as appropriate.

- The appropriate personnel ashore should be consulted to ascertain that conditions on the jetty do not present a hazard and to obtain agreement that operations can start.

9.1.3 Gas Freeing and Tank Cleaning Concurrently with Cargo Handling

As a general rule tank cleaning and gas freeing should not take place concurrently with cargo handling. If for any reason this is necessary, there should be close consultation with, and agreement by, both the terminal representative and the port authority.

Crude oil washing and cargo discharge may take place concurrently, but the terminal representative should be advised (see Section 9.4).

9.1.4 Testing of Tank Cleaning Hoses

All hoses should be tested for electrical continuity in a dry condition prior to use and in no case should the resistance exceed 6 ohms per metre length.

9.1.5 Entry into Cargo Tanks

No one should enter any cargo tank unless permission to do so has been received from the responsible officer and all appropriate precautions have been taken, including the issue of an entry permit (see Chapter 11).

9.1.6 Gas Measuring Equipment

In order to maintain a proper control of the tank atmosphere and to check the effectiveness of gas freeing, a number of gas measuring instruments should be available on the ship.

Depending upon the type of atmosphere being measured, at least two of each of the following portable instruments should be available:

- With a too lean tank atmosphere.

  - Flammable gas indicator capable of measuring gas to the lower flammable limit and with the scale graduated as a percentage of this limit.

- With an inerted tank atmosphere.

  - Gas indicator capable of measuring percentage volume of hydrocarbon gas in an inerted atmosphere.

  - Oxygen analyser.

- With an over rich tank atmosphere.

  - Gas indicator capable of measuring hydrocarbon gas concentrations above 15% volume in air.

In order to be able to check the effectiveness of gas freeing for tank entry the following instruments should be provided:

- A flammable gas indicator capable of measuring gas to the lower flammable limit and with the scale graduated as a percentage of this limit.

- An oxygen analyser.

- An instrument capable of measuring concentrations in the human toxicity range of toxic gases and calibrated in parts per million.

The instruments to be used for gas measurement should be calibrated and tested in accordance with the manufacturer's instructions before starting to tank clean or gas free.

Tank atmosphere sampling lines should be, in all respects, suitable for and impervious to, the gases present and should be resistant to the effects of hot wash water.

9.2 CARGO TANK WASHING AND CLEANING

9.2.1 Tank Atmospheres

Tank atmospheres can be any of the following:

Inerted • An atmosphere made incapable of burning by the introduction of inert gas and the resultant reduction of the overall oxygen content. For the purposes of this guide the oxygen content of the tank atmosphere should not exceed 8% by volume.

Too lean • An atmosphere made incapable of burning by the deliberate reduction of the hydrocarbon content to below the lower flammable limit.

Over rich • An atmosphere which is above the flammable range (see Section 9.2.5).

Undefined • An atmosphere which may be above, below or within the flammable range.

9.2.2 Washing in an Inert Atmosphere

The requirements for the maintenance of an inert atmosphere and precautions to be observed during washing are set out in Section 10.6.8.

9.2.3 Washing in a too Lean Atmosphere

The following precautions must be observed:

(a) Before washing, the tank bottom should be flushed with water and stripped. The piping system including cargo pumps, crossovers and discharge lines, should also be flushed with water. The flushing water should be drained to the tank designed or designated to receive slops.

(b) Before washing, the tank should be ventilated to reduce the gas concentration of the atmosphere to 10% or less of the lower flammable limit. Gas tests must be made at various levels and due consideration given to the possible existence of local pockets of flammable gas. Mechanical ventilation and gas testing should continue during washing. Ventilation should, as far as possible, provide a free flow of air from one end of the tank to the other.

(c) If the tank has a venting system which is common to other tanks, the tank must be isolated to prevent an ingress of gas from other tanks.

(d) If portable washing machines are used, all hose connections should be made up and tested for electrical continuity before the washing machine is introduced into the tank. Connections should not be broken until after the machine has been removed from the tank. To drain the hose a coupling may be partially opened and then re-tightened before the machine is removed.

(e) During tank washing regular gas tests must be made at various levels. Consideration should be given to the possible effect of water on the efficiency of the gas measuring equipment. Washing should be discontinued if the gas concentration rises to 50% of the LFL. Washing may be resumed when continued ventilation has reduced the gas concentration to 20% of the LFL and has maintained it at or below that level for a short period.

(f) The tank should be kept drained during washing. Washing should be stopped to clear any build-up of wash water.

(g) Recirculated wash water should not be used for tank washing.

(h) Steam should not be injected into the tank.

(i) The same precautions relating to sounding and the introduction of other similar equipment should be taken as when washing in an undefined atmosphere (see Section 9.2.4(i)).

(j) Chemical additives may be employed provided the temperature of the wash water does not exceed 60°C.

(k) Wash water may be heated. If the wash water temperature is 60°C or less, washing should be discontinued if the gas concentration reaches 50% of the LFL. If the wash water temperature is above 60°C, washing should be discontinued if the gas concentration reaches 35% of the LFL.

9.2.4 Control of Washing in an Undefined Atmosphere

In an undefined atmosphere, the vapours in the tank may be in the flammable range. The only way to guarantee that an explosion cannot occur during washing in an undefined atmosphere is to make certain that there can be no source of ignition.

The following precautions must be taken if the risk from static electricity is to be eliminated:

(a) No machine may have a throughput greater than $60m^3/h$.

(b) The total water throughput per cargo tank should be kept as low as practicable and must in no case exceed $180m^3/h$.

(c) Recirculated wash water must not be used.

(d) Chemical additives must not be used.

(e) Wash water may be heated, but must not be above $60°C$.

(f) Steam must never be injected into the tank.

(g) The tank should be kept drained during washing. Washing should be stopped to clear any build-up of wash water.

(h) All hose connections must be made up and tested for electrical continuity before the washing machine is introduced into the tank. Connections should not be broken until after the machine has been removed from the tank. To drain the hose a coupling may be partially opened and then retightened before the machine is removed.

(i) Sounding and the introduction of other equipment must be done through a sounding pipe if fitted. If a sounding pipe is not fitted, it is essential that any metallic components of the sounding or other equipment are bonded and securely earthed to the ship before introduction into the tank and remain so earthed until removed. This precaution should be observed during washing and for five hours thereafter. If, however, the tank is continuously mechanically ventilated after washing, this period can be reduced to one hour. During this period:

- An interface detector of metallic construction may be used if earthed to the ship by means of a clamp or bolted metal lug.

- A metal rod may be used on the end of a metal tape which is earthed to the ship.

- A metal sounding rod suspended on a fibre rope should not be used even if the end at deck level is fastened to the ship because the rope cannot be completely relied upon as an earthing path.

- Equipment made entirely of non-metallic materials may, in general, be used: e.g. a wooden sounding rod may be suspended on a rope without earthing.

- Ropes made of synthetic polymers should not be used for lowering equipment into cargo tanks.

Further information on electrostatic precautions during tank washing is given in Chapter 20.

9.2.5 Washing in an Over Rich Atmosphere

The procedures for making a tank atmosphere over rich and thereafter water washing the tank involve special measures intended to prevent the ingress of air. This method of tank washing should only be carried out when authorised by the operator and under the supervision of a person who has received special training in these procedures.

Water washing must not be started, or if in progress must be discontinued and not re-started, if the hydrocarbon content of the tank atmosphere is less than 15% by volume.

9.2.6 Portable Tank Washing Machines and Hoses

The outer casing of portable machines should be of a material which on contact with the internal structure of a cargo tank will not give rise to an incendive spark.

Bonding wires should be incorporated within all water hoses. Couplings should be connected to the hose in such a way that effective bonding is ensured between them.

The coupling arrangement for the hose should be such that effective bonding can be established between the tank washing machine, the hoses and the fixed tank cleaning water supply line.

Hoses should be indelibly marked to allow identification. A record should be kept showing the date and the result of electrical continuity testing.

Washing machines should be electrically bonded to the water hose by means of a suitable connection or external bonding wire.

When suspended within a cargo tank, machines should be supported by means of a rope and not by means of the water supply hose.

9.2.7 Free Fall

It is essential to avoid the free fall of water or slops into a tank. The liquid level should always be such that the discharge inlets in the slop tank are covered to a depth of at least one metre to avoid splashing. This is not necessary when the slop and cargo tanks are fully inerted.

9.2.8 Spraying of Water

The spraying of water into a tank containing a substantial quantity of static accumulator oil could result in the generation of static electricity at the liquid surface, either by agitation or by water settling. Tanks which contain a static accumulator oil should always be pumped out before they are washed with water unless the tank is kept in an inert condition (see Section 7.4).

9.2.9 Steaming of Tanks

Because of the hazard from static electricity, the introduction of steam into cargo tanks should not be permitted where there is a risk of the presence of a flammable atmosphere. It should be borne in mind that a non-flammable atmosphere cannot be guaranteed in all cases where steaming might be thought to be useful (see Section 20.4.3).

9.2.10 Leaded Gasoline

Whereas shore tanks may contain leaded gasoline for long periods and therefore present a hazard from tetraethyl lead (TEL) and tetramethyl lead (TML), ships' tanks normally alternate between different products and ballast and thus present very little risk. Ships employed in the regular carriage of leaded gasoline should flush the bottom of the tanks with water after every cargo discharge unless the tank is to be ballasted.

Entry into ships' tanks used regularly for the carriage of leaded gasoline should not be permitted unless absolutely essential.

9.2.11 Removal of Sludge, Scale and Sediment

Before the removal by hand of sludge, scale and sediment, the tank atmosphere must be safe for entry and an entry permit issued. The precautions described in Section 11.6.5 should be maintained throughout the period of work.

Equipment to be used for further tank cleaning operations, such as the removal of solid residues or products, in tanks which have been gas freed should be so designed and constructed, and the construction materials so chosen, that no risk of ignition is introduced.

9.3   GAS FREEING

9.3.1   General

It is generally recognised that tank cleaning and gas freeing is the most hazardous period of tanker operations. This is true whether washing for clean ballast, gas freeing for entry, or gas freeing for hot work. The additional risk from the toxic effect of petroleum gas during this period cannot be over-emphasised and must be impressed on all concerned. It is therefore essential that the greatest possible care is exercised in all operations connected with tank cleaning and gas freeing.

9.3.2   General Procedures

The following recommendations apply to cargo tank gas freeing generally. Additional considerations which apply when the tank has been inerted are given in Chapter 10.

(a) The covers of all tank openings should be kept closed until actual ventilation of the individual tank is about to commence.

(b) Portable fans or blowers should only be used if they are hydraulically, pneumatically or steam driven. Their construction materials should be such that no hazard of incendiary sparking arises if, for any reason, the impeller touches the inside of the casing.

   The capacity and penetration of portable fans should be such that the entire atmosphere of the tank on which the fan is employed can be made non-flammable in the shortest possible time.

(c) The venting of flammable gas during gas freeing should be by the vessel's approved method, and where gas freeing involves the escape of gas at deck level or through tank hatch openings the degree of ventilation and number of openings should be controlled to produce an exit velocity sufficient to carry the gas clear of the deck (see Section 6.8.2).

(d) Intakes of central air conditioning or mechanical ventilating systems should be adjusted to prevent the entry of petroleum gas, if possible by recirculation of air within the spaces.

(e) If at any time it is suspected that gas is being drawn into the accommodation, central air conditioning and mechanical ventilating systems should be stopped and the intakes covered or closed.

   Window type air conditioning units which are not certified as safe for use in the presence of flammable gas or which draw in air from outside the superstructure must be electrically disconnected and any external vents or intakes closed.

(f) Where cargo tanks are gas freed by means of one or more permanently installed blowers, all connections between the cargo tank system and the blowers should be blanked except when the blowers are in use.

   Before putting such a system into service, the cargo piping system, including crossovers and discharge lines, should be flushed through with sea water and the tanks stripped. Valves on the systems, other than those required for ventilation, should be closed and secured.

(g) Tank openings within enclosed or partially enclosed spaces should not be opened until the tank has been sufficiently ventilated by means of openings in the tank which are outside these spaces. When the gas level within the tank has fallen to 25% of the LFL or less, openings in enclosed or partially enclosed spaces may be opened to complete the ventilation. Such enclosed or partially enclosed spaces should also be tested for gas during this subsequent ventilation.

(h) If the tanks are connected by a common venting system, each tank should be isolated to prevent the transfer of gas to or from other tanks.

(i) Portable fans, where used, should be placed in such positions and the ventilation openings so arranged that all parts of the tank being ventilated are equally and effectively gas freed. Ventilation outlets should generally be as remote as possible from the fans.

(j) Portable fans, where used, should be so connected to the deck that an effective electrical bond exists between the fan and the deck.

(k) Fixed gas freeing equipment may be used to gas free more than one tank simultaneously but must not be used for this purpose if the system is being used to ventilate another tank in which washing is in progress.

(l) On the apparent completion of gas freeing any tank, a period of about 10 minutes should elapse before taking final gas measurements. This allows relatively stable conditions to develop within the tank space. Tests should be made at several levels and, where the tank is sub-divided by a wash bulkhead, in each compartment of the tank. In large compartments such tests should be made at widely separate positions.

If satisfactory gas readings are not obtained, ventilation must be resumed.

(m) On completion of gas freeing, all openings except the tank hatch should be closed.

(n) On completion of all gas freeing and tank washing the gas venting system should be carefully checked, particular attention being paid to the efficient working of the pressure/vacuum valves and any high velocity vent valves. If the valves or vent risers are fitted with devices designed to prevent the passage of flame, these should also be checked and cleaned.

Gas vent riser drains should be cleared of water, rust and sediment, and any steam smothering connections tested and proved satisfactory.

9.3.3 Gas Free for the Reception of Cargo

A tank which is required to be gas free for receiving cargo should be ventilated until tests confirm that the hydrocarbon gas concentration throughout that tank does not exceed 40% of the LFL.

9.3.4 Gas Free for Entry and Cold Work Without Breathing Apparatus

In order to be gas free for entry without breathing apparatus a tank or space must be ventilated until tests confirm that the hydrocarbon gas concentration through the compartment is not more than 1% of the LFL and additional tests have been made to check for oxygen content, the presence of hydrogen sulphide, benzene and other toxic gases as appropriate (see Section 11.3).

9.3.5 Gas Free in Preparation for Hot Work

In addition to meeting the requirements of Section 9.3.4, the requirements of Section 2.8 must also be complied with.

9.4 CRUDE OIL WASHING

9.4.1 General

A crude oil tanker fitted with an inert gas system and approved fixed washing equipment in its cargo tanks can use crude oil from the cargo as the washing medium. This operation may take place either in port or at sea between discharge ports. It is most frequently carried out while the tanker is discharging cargo and permits the removal of oil fractions adhering to or deposited on tank surfaces. These deposits, which would normally remain on board after discharge, are then discharged with the cargo.

As a consequence, the need to water wash the discharged tanks during the ballast voyage for the removal of residues is much reduced and, in some cases, entirely eliminated.

Water rinsing will be necessary if the tank is to be used for clean ballast.

Reference should be made to the IMO publication "Crude Oil Washing Systems" and the vessel's approved Operations and Equipment Manual for further detailed guidance on the procedures involved.

9.4.2 Advance Notice

When it is required to carry out crude oil washing during cargo discharge, the master should inform the competent authority and the terminal (or vessel when ship to ship transfer is involved) at least 24 hours in advance, or in such time as is required. Crude oil washing should only proceed when their approval is received.

9.4.3 Tank Washing Machines

Only fixed tank washing machines may be used for crude oil washing.

9.4.4 Control of Tank Atmosphere

The oxygen content of the tank must not exceed 8% by volume as described in Section 10.6.8.

9.4.5 Precautions Against Leakage from the Washing System

Before arriving in a port where it is intended to crude oil wash, the tank washing system should be pressure tested to normal working pressure and examined for leaks.

All machines which are to be used should be operated briefly to check for leaks beyond the shut-off valve. Any leaks found should be made good.

During crude oil washing, the system must be kept under constant observation so that any leak can be detected immediately and action taken to deal with it.

9.4.6 Avoidance of Oil/Water Mixtures

Mixtures of crude oil and water can produce an electrically charged mist during washing much in excess of that produced by "dry" crude oil. The use of "dry" crude oil is therefore important, and before washing begins any tank which is to be used as a source of crude oil washing fluid should be partly discharged to remove any water which has settled out during the voyage. The discharge of a layer at least one metre in depth is necessary for this purpose.

For the same reason, if the slop tank is to be used as a source of oil for washing, it should first be completely discharged ashore and refilled with "dry" crude oil.

9.4.7 Exclusion of Cargo Oil from the Engine Room

If any part of the tank washing system extends into the engine room it must be blanked-off to prevent cargo oil from entering the engine room.

If the tank wash water heater is fitted outside the engine room, it must be blanked-off during crude oil washing to prevent oil from flowing through it.

9.4.8 Control of Vapour Emissions

During crude oil washing, hydrocarbon gas is generated within the cargo tanks beyond normally existing levels. Subsequent ballasting of such cargo tanks could lead to considerable hydrocarbon gas being expelled to the atmosphere. Some port authorities prohibit such discharges.

The emission of hydrocarbon gas from ballasted tanks can be avoided in one of four ways:

(a) By the use of permanent ballast tanks of sufficient capacity to provide the minimum departure draught.

(b) By containing gas in empty cargo tanks by simultaneous ballasting and cargo discharge where the ullage spaces of the tanks being ballasted are directly connected to those of the tanks being discharged.

(c) By the gas compression method which requires that, on completion of the discharge, the tank pressure is at a minimum and all cargo tanks are made common via the inert gas line. While ballasting, the gases from the ballasted cargo tanks are transferred through the inert gas lines into all available cargo tank space and, with all vent valves, ullage ports, etc. closed, the gases are compressed within the vessel up to a safe margin below p/v valve and breaker settings. The P/V valves, deck water seal and filled liquid breaker must be in good operational condition. All non-return devices must be closed to prevent the backflow of inert gas into the inert gas plant.

(d) By a suitable combination of any of these methods.

Generally, the ullage spaces of all cargo tanks are connected by the inert gas main line. If the ballasting of dirty tanks can be connected while discharge continues from other tanks, judicious adjustments of ballast and discharge rates can prevent the gas pressure rising sufficiently to cause a discharge to the atmosphere. Where the ballast rate exceeds the discharge rate it may be necessary to reduce or even temporarily stop the flow of inert gas to the tank system.

9.4.9   Supervision

The person in charge of crude oil washing operations must be suitably qualified in accordance with the requirements laid down by the flag administration of the vessel and any port regulations in force locally.

9.4.10   Cautionary Notice

A notice should be prominently displayed in the cargo and engine control rooms, on the bridge and on the notice boards of ships which have crude oil washing systems fitted. The following text is suggested

> **THE TANK WASHING LINES ON THIS SHIP MAY CONTAIN CRUDE OIL.**
>
> **VALVES MUST NOT BE OPERATED BY UNAUTHORISED PERSONNEL**

9.5   SPECIAL TANK CLEANING PROCEDURES

After the carriage of certain products, tanks can only be adequately cleaned by steaming, or by the addition of certain tank cleaning chemicals or additives to the wash water.

Steaming may only be carried out in tanks which have been either inerted or water washed and gas freed. The concentration of flammable gas should not exceed 10% of the LFL prior to steaming. Precautions should be taken to avoid the build-up of steam pressure within the tank.

If tank cleaning chemicals are to be used, it is important to understand that certain products may introduce a toxicity hazard. Personnel should be made aware of the TLV (Threshold Limit Value) of the product. Personnel entering tanks should wear breathing apparatus and appropriate protective clothing. All other tank entry precautions must be observed (see Section 11.4). Detector tubes are particularly useful for detecting the presence of specific gases and vapours in tanks.

Tank cleaning chemicals capable of producing a flammable atmosphere should normally only be used when the tank has been inerted. However, such products may be used to clean tank walls in a localised area (e.g. wiping down) in vessels not fitted with an inert gas system provided the amount of tank cleaning chemical used is small and the personnel entering the tank observe all enclosed space entry requirements.

In addition to the above, any manufacturers' instructions or recommendations for the use of these products should be observed.

Where these operations take place in port, additional requirements may be imposed by local authorities.

Chapter 10

Fixed Inert Gas Systems

This Chapter describes, in general terms, the operation of a fixed inert gas system in order to maintain a safe tank atmosphere. It also covers the precautions to be taken to avoid hazards to health. Reference should be made to the ship's operations manual, the manufacturer's instructions and installation drawings as appropriate for details on the operation of the system. The IMO publication "Guidelines for Inert Gas Systems" should be consulted for a more detailed explanation of the design and the operating principles and practices of typical inert gas systems.

10.1   GENERAL

Hydrocarbon gas normally encountered in petroleum tankers cannot burn in an atmosphere containing less than approximately 11% oxygen by volume. Accordingly one way to provide protection against fire or explosion in the vapour space of cargo tanks is to keep the oxygen level below that figure. This is usually achieved by using a fixed piping arrangement to blow inert gas into each cargo tank in order to reduce the air content, and hence the oxygen content, and render the tank atmosphere non-flammable.

This can be explained by reference to Figure 10-1 which shows the relationship between hydrocarbon gas and oxygen in a hydrocarbon gas/air mixture.

The flammable limits vary for different pure hydrocarbon gases and for mixtures derived from different petroleum liquids. For practical purposes the lower and upper flammable limits (LFL and UFL) of crude oil vapours are taken to be 1% and 10% respectively by volume.

These values are indicated by points C and D on the line A B in Figure 10-1.

Any point on the diagram represents mixtures of hydrocarbon gas, air and inert gas, specified in terms of hydrocarbon gas and oxygen contents.

For example, hydrocarbon gas/air mixtures without any inert gas lie on the line A B, the slope of which represents the reduction in oxygen as the hydrocarbon content increases.

Points to the left of line A B represent mixtures with their oxygen content reduced by the addition of inert gas. The further left these points lie the greater the proportion of inert gas and the smaller the percentage of oxygen.

As inert gas is added to the hydrocarbon gas/air mixture, the flammable range decreases until a point, represented by E, is reached where the LFL and UFL coincide. This point corresponds to an oxygen content of approximately 11%. No hydrocarbon gas/air mixture can burn at this oxygen level. For practical purposes and to allow a safety margin, 8% is taken as the level of oxygen at which no hydrocarbon gas/air mixture can burn under any circumstances. To prevent fire or explosion in a tank containing a hydrocarbon gas/air mixture it is therefore necessary to produce and supply inert gas having an oxygen content

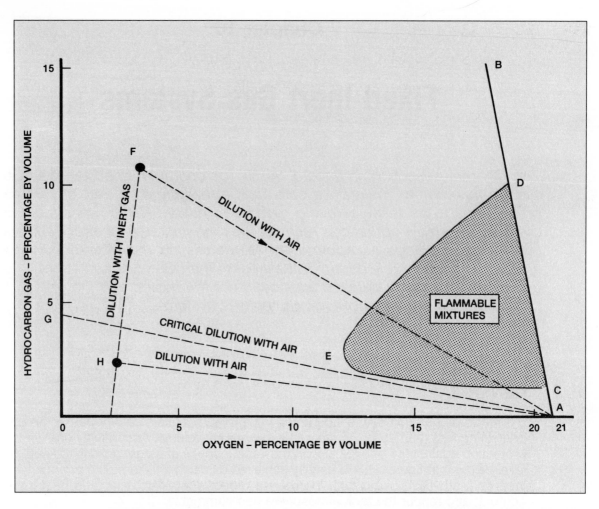

Figure 10-1. *Flammability Composition Diagram – Hydrocarbon Gas/Air/Inert Gas Mixture.*

This diagram is illustrative only and should not be used for deciding upon acceptable gas compositions in practical cases.

not normally exceeding 5% and to displace the existing air in the tank until the resultant oxygen level throughout the tank does not exceed 8% by volume.

The International Convention for the Safety of Life at Sea (SOLAS 1974), as amended, requires that inert gas systems be capable of delivering inert gas with an oxygen content in the inert gas main of not more than 5% by volume at any required rate of flow; and of maintaining a positive pressure in the cargo tanks at all times with an atmosphere having an oxygen content of not more than 8% by volume except when it is necessary for the tank to be gas free. Existing systems are only required to be capable of producing inert gas with an oxygen content not normally exceeding 5% by volume, and of maintaining the tank inerted at all times except when it is necessary for the tank to be gas free.

When air is introduced into an inert mixture, such as that represented by point F, its composition moves along the line FA and therefore enters the shaded area of flammable mixtures. This means that all inert mixtures in the region above the line GA (critical dilution line) pass through a flammable condition as they are mixed with air – for example, during a gas-freeing operation. Those below the line GA, such as that represented by point H, do not become flammable when air is mixed with them. It will be noted that it is possible to move from a mixture such as that represented by F to one such as that represented by H by the introduction of additional inert gas, i.e. by purging.

(See also Section 15.2 on flammability.)

10.2 SOURCES

Possible sources of inert gas on tankers and combination carriers are:

- Uptake gas from the ship's main or auxiliary boilers.

- An independent inert gas generator.

- A gas turbine fitted with an afterburner.

10.3 QUALITY

A final oxygen level of 8% or less will be more easily achieved if the oxygen content of the inert gas in the inert gas main is considerably less than 8%. Ideally the inert gas should not contain oxygen but this is not possible in practice.

When using flue gas from a main or auxiliary boiler, an oxygen level of less than 5% can generally be obtained, depending on the quality of combustion control and the load on the boiler.

When an independent inert gas generator or a gas turbine plant with afterburner is fitted, the oxygen content can be automatically controlled within finer limits, usually within the range 1.5% to 2.5% by volume and not normally exceeding 5%.

Whatever the source, the gas must be cooled and scrubbed with water to remove soot and sulphur acids before being supplied to the cargo tanks.

10.4 METHOD OF REPLACING TANK ATMOSPHERES

If the entire tank atmosphere could be replaced by an equal volume of inert gas the resulting tank atmosphere would have the same oxygen level as the incoming inert gas. In practice this is not the case and a volume of inert gas equal to several tank volumes must be introduced into the tank before the desired result can be achieved.

The replacement of a tank atmosphere by inert gas can be achieved by either inerting or purging. In each of these methods one of two distinct processes, dilution or displacement, will predominate.

Dilution takes place when the incoming inert gas mixes with the original tank atmosphere to form a homogeneous mixture through the tank so that, as the process continues, the concentration of the original gas decreases progressively. It is important that the incoming inert gas has sufficient entry velocity to penetrate to the bottom of the tank. To ensure this a limit must be placed on the number of tanks which can be inerted simultaneously. Where this is not clearly stipulated in the operations manual, only one tank should be inerted or purged at a time.

Displacement depends on the fact that inert gas is slightly lighter than hydrocarbon gas so that, while the inert gas enters at the top of the tank, the heavier hydrocarbon gas escapes from the bottom through suitable piping. When using this method it is important that the inert gas has a very low velocity to enable a stable horizontal interface to be developed between the incoming and escaping gas although, in practice, some dilution inevitably takes place owing to the turbulence caused in the inert gas flow. This system generally allows several tanks to be inerted or purged simultaneously.

Whatever method is employed, and whether inerting or purging, it is vital that oxygen or gas measurements are taken at several heights and horizontal positions within the tank to check the efficiency of the operation.

A mixture of inert gas and petroleum gas when vented and mixed with air can become flammable. The normal safety precautions taken when petroleum gas is vented from a tank should therefore not be relaxed.

10.5 CARGO TANK ATMOSPHERE CONTROL

Tankers using an inert gas system should maintain their cargo tanks in a non-flammable condition at all times.

It follows that:

- Tanks should be kept in an inert condition at all times except when it is necessary for them to be gas free for inspection or work, i.e. the oxygen content should be not more than 8% by volume and the atmosphere should be maintained at a positive pressure.

- The atmosphere within the tank should make the transition from the inert condition to the gas free condition without passing through the flammable condition. In practice this means that before any tank is gas freed it should be purged with inert gas until the hydrocarbon content of the tank atmosphere is below the critical dilution line (line GA in Figure 10-1).

- When a ship is in a gas free condition before arrival at a loading port the tanks must be inerted prior to loading.

In order to maintain cargo tanks in a non-flammable condition the inert gas plant will be required to:

- Inert empty cargo tanks (see Section 10.6.1).

- Be in operation during cargo discharge, deballasting, crude oil washing and tank cleaning (see Sections 10.6.5 and 10.6.8).

- Purge tanks prior to gas freeing (see Section 10.6.9).

- Top-up the pressure in the cargo tanks when necessary during other stages of the voyage (see Sections 10.6.4 and 10.6.6).

It must be emphasised that the protection provided by an inert gas system depends on the proper operation and maintenance of the entire system. Where an inert gas system is installed, it is essential that there is close co-operation between the deck and engine departments to ensure its proper maintenance and operation. It is particularly important to ensure that non-return barriers function correctly, especially the deck water seal and the non-return valves, so that there is no possibility of petroleum gas or liquid petroleum passing back to the machinery spaces.

To demonstrate that the inert gas plant is fully operational and in good working order, a record of inspection of the inert gas plant, including defects and their rectification, should be maintained on board.

10.6 APPLICATION TO CARGO TANK OPERATIONS

10.6.1 Inerting of Empty Tanks

Before the inert gas system is put into service the tests required by the operations manual or manufacturer's instructions should be carried out. The fixed oxygen analyser and recorder should be tested and proved in good order. Portable oxygen and hydrocarbon meters should also be prepared and tested.

When inerting empty tanks which are gas free, for example following a dry-docking or tank entry, inert gas should be introduced through the distribution system while venting the air in the tank to the atmosphere.

This operation should continue until the oxygen content throughout the tank is not more than 8% by volume. The oxygen level will not thereafter increase if a positive pressure is maintained by using the inert gas system to introduce additional inert gas when necessary.

If the tank is not gas free, the precautions against static electricity given in Section 10.6.7 should be taken.

When all tanks have been inerted they should be kept common with the inert gas main and the system pressurised with a minimum positive pressure of at least 100mm water gauge.

10.6.2   Loading Cargo or Ballast into Tanks in an Inert Condition

When loading cargo or ballast, the inert gas plant should be shut down and the tanks vented through the appropriate venting system. On completion of loading or ballasting, and when all ullaging is completed, the tanks should be closed and the inert gas system restarted and repressurised. The system should then be shut down and all safety isolating valves secured. Local regulations may prohibit venting after crude oil washing (see Section 9.4.8).

10.6.3   Simultaneous Cargo/Ballast Operations

In the case of simultaneous loading and discharge operations involving cargo or ballast, venting to the atmosphere can be minimised or possibly completely avoided by interconnecting the tanks concerned through the inert gas main. Depending on the relative pumping rates, pressure in the tanks may be increased or a vacuum drawn, and it may therefore be necessary to adjust the inert gas flow accordingly so as to maintain tank pressure within normal limits.

10.6.4   Loaded Passage

A positive pressure of inert gas should be maintained in the ullage space at all times in order to prevent the possible ingress of air. If the pressure falls below the low pressure alarm level, it will be necessary to start the inert gas plant to restore an adequate pressure in the system.

Loss of pressure is normally associated with leakages from tank openings and falling air and sea temperatures. In these cases it is all the more important to ensure that the tanks are gas tight. Gas leaks are usually easily detected by their noise and every effort must be made to eliminate leaks at tank hatches, ullage lids, tank cleaning machine openings, valves etc.

Leaks which cannot be eliminated should be marked and recorded for sealing during the next ballast passage or at another suitable opportunity.

Certain oil products, principally aviation turbine kerosenes and diesel oil, can absorb oxygen during the refining and storage process. This oxygen can later be liberated into an oxygen deficient atmosphere such as the ullage space of an inerted cargo tank. Although the recorded incidence of oxygen liberation is low, cargo tank oxygen levels should be monitored so that any necessary precautionary measures can be taken prior to the commencement of discharge.

10.6.5   Discharge of Cargo or Ballast from Tanks in an Inert Condition

The inert gas supply must be maintained through cargo or ballast discharge operations to prevent air entering the tanks. If on arrival in port the inert gas has to be depressurised in order to measure or sample the cargo, it may be difficult, because of the low boiler load, to repressurise with inert gas with a sufficiently low oxygen content. In this event it may be necessary to create a load on the boiler by using the main cargo pumps to circulate the cargo around the ship's pipelines until the inert gas quality is satisfactory. Great care is necessary to ensure that the pumping arrangements chosen for circulating cargo do not give rise to an overflow.

Throughout the discharge of cargo, particularly when the boiler load is low or fluctuating, the oxygen content of the inert gas supply must be carefully monitored.

If hand dipping of a tank is necessary, pressure may be reduced while dipping ports are open but care must be taken not to allow a vacuum to develop since this would pull air into the tank. To prevent this it may be necessary to reduce the cargo pumping rate, and discharge should be stopped immediately if there is a danger of the tanks coming under vacuum.

Both the oxygen content and pressure of the inert gas main should be continuously recorded during discharge.

If the inert gas plant fails during discharge, the positive pressure on the system should be rapidly lost. Discharge should be stopped immediately to avoid the tanks coming under vacuum. Crude oil tankers should not resume discharge until the operation of the inert gas plant is restored or an alternative source of inert gas is provided (see Sections 7.10 and 10.12.1).

In the case of product carriers, discharge should not be resumed until all interested parties have so agreed in writing and the necessary precautions have been taken (see Sections 7.10 and 10.12.2). If it is then decided to continue the discharge without an inert gas supply, air will be drawn into the tanks and the overall protection provided by the inert gas will be reduced or lost. It will be necessary to apply all the precautions needed in the absence of inert gas, including the precautions against static electricity set out in Section 10.6.7.

10.6.6   Ballast Passage

During the ballast passage tanks other than those required to be gas free should remain in the inert condition and under positive pressure to prevent an ingress of air. Whenever pressure falls to the low pressure alarm level the inert gas plant should be restarted to restore the pressure, care being taken to monitor the oxygen content of the inert gas delivered.

10.6.7   Static Electricity Precautions

In normal operations, the presence of inert gas prevents the existence of flammable gas mixtures inside cargo tanks. Hazards due to static electricity may arise, however, mainly in the case of a failure of the inert gas system. To avoid these hazards the following procedures are recommended:

- If the inert gas plant breaks down during discharge, operations should be suspended; if air has entered the tank, no dipping, ullaging, sampling or other equipment should be introduced into the tank until at least 30 minutes have elapsed since the injection of inert gas ceased. After this period equipment may be introduced provided that all metallic components are securely earthed. This restriction should be applied until a period of five hours has elapsed since the injection of inert gas ceased.

- During any necessary re-inerting of a tank following a failure and repair of the inert gas system, or during initial inerting of a non-gas free tank, no dipping, ullaging, sampling or other equipment should be inserted until it has been established that the tank is in an inert condition. This should be done by monitoring the gas vented from the tank being inerted. Should it be necessary, however, to introduce a gas sampling system into the tank for this purpose, at least 30 minutes should elapse after stopping the injection of inert gas before inserting the sampling system. Metallic components of the sampling system should be electrically continuous and securely earthed.

10.6.8 Tank Washing Including Crude Oil Washing

Before each tank is washed, the oxygen level must be determined, both at a point 1 metre below the deck and at the middle level of the ullage space. At neither of these locations should it exceed 8% by volume. Where tanks have a complete or partial swash bulkhead, the measurement should be taken from similar levels in each section of the tank. The oxygen content and pressure of the inert gas being delivered during the washing process should be continuously recorded.

If during washing:

* the oxygen level in the tank exceeds 8% by volume, or

* the pressure of the atmosphere in the tanks is no longer positive,

washing must be stopped until satisfactory conditions are restored. Operators should also be guided by Section 10.12.

10.6.9 Purging

When it is required to gas free a tank after washing, it should first be purged with inert gas to reduce the hydrocarbon content to 2% or less by volume so that during the subsequent gas freeing no portion of the tank atmosphere is brought within the flammable range. The tank may then be gas freed.

The hydrocarbon content must be measured with an appropriate meter designed to measure the percentage of hydrocarbon gas in an oxygen deficient atmosphere. The usual flammable gas indicator is not suitable for this purpose.

If the dilution method of purging is used, it should be carried out with the inert gas system set for maximum capacity to give maximum turbulence within the tank. If the displacement method is used, the gas inlet velocity should be lower to prevent undue turbulence.

10.6.10 Gas Freeing

Before starting to gas free, the tank should be isolated from other tanks. When either portable fans or fixed fans connected to the cargo pipeline system are used to introduce air into the tank, the inert gas inlet should be isolated. If the inert gas system fan, drawing fresh air, is employed, both the line back to the inert gas source and the inert gas inlet into each tank being kept inerted should be isolated.

10.6.11 Preparation for Tank Entry

To ensure the dilution of the toxic components of inert gas to below their Threshold Limit Values (TLV), gas freeing should continue until tests with an oxygen analyser show a steady oxygen reading of 21% by volume and tests with a flammable gas indicator show not more than 1% LFL.

If the presence of a toxic gas such as benzene or hydrogen sulphide is suspected, gas freeing should be continued until tests indicate that its concentration is below its TLV.

Positive fresh air ventilation should be maintained throughout the period that personnel are in a tank, and frequent tests should be made of both oxygen and hydrocarbon content of the tank atmosphere.

When other tanks in an inert condition are either adjacent or interconnected (e.g. by a pipeline) to the tank being entered, personnel should be alert to the possibility of inert gas leaking into the gas free tank through, for example, bulkhead fractures or defective valves. The risk of this occurring can be minimised by maintaining a small but positive inert gas pressure.

When a gas free tank is re-connected to the inert gas main it should immediately be re-inerted.

For general advice on entry into enclosed spaces see Chapter 11.

10.7 PRECAUTIONS TO BE TAKEN TO AVOID HEALTH HAZARDS

10.7.1 Inert Gas on Deck

Certain wind conditions may bring vented gases back down onto the deck, even from specially designed vent outlets. Also, if gases are vented at low level and the cargo hatches, ullage ports or other tank vents are used as outlets, the surrounding areas can contain levels of gases in harmful concentrations, and may be oxygen deficient. In these conditions all non-essential work should cease and only essential personnel should remain on deck, taking all appropriate precautions.

In addition, when the last cargo carried was a sour crude, tests should be made for hydrogen sulphide. If a level in excess of 10 ppm is detected, no personnel should be allowed to work on deck unless wearing suitable respiratory protection (see Section 16.5).

10.7.2 Ullaging and Inspection of Tanks from Cargo Hatches

The low oxygen content of inert gas can cause rapid asphyxiation. Care should therefore be taken to avoid standing in the path of vented gas (see Section 7.2.1).

10.7.3 Entry into Cargo Tanks

Entry into cargo tanks should be permitted only after they have been gas freed as described in Sections 10.6.9 and 10.6.10. The safety precautions set out in Section 11.4.2 should be observed and consideration given to the carriage of a personal oxygen deficiency alarm. If the hydrocarbon and oxygen levels specified in Section 10.6.11 cannot be achieved, entry should be permitted only in exceptional circumstances and when there is no practicable alternative. Personnel must wear breathing apparatus under such circumstances (see Section 11.4.4 for further details).

10.7.4 Scrubber and Condensate Water

Inert gas scrubber effluent water is acidic. Condensate water which tends to collect in the distribution pipes, particularly in the deck main, is often more acidic than the effluent and is highly corrosive.

Care should be taken to avoid unnecessary skin contact with either effluent or condensate water. Particular care should also be taken to avoid all contact with the eyes and protective goggles should be worn whenever there is a risk of such contact.

10.8 CARGO TANK PROTECTION

10.8.1 Pressure/Vacuum Breakers

Every inert gas system is required to be fitted with one or more pressure/vacuum breakers or other approved devices. These are designed to protect the cargo tanks against excessive pressure or vacuum and must therefore be kept in good working order by regular maintenance in accordance with the manufacturer's instructions.

When these are liquid filled, it is important to ensure that the correct fluid is used and the correct level is maintained. The level can normally only be checked when there is no pressure in the inert gas main line. Evaporation, condensation and possible ingress of sea water should be taken into consideration when checking the liquid condition and level. In heavy weather, the pressure surge caused by the motion of liquid in the cargo tanks may cause the liquid in the pressure/vacuum breaker to be blown out. This may be more liable to happen on combination carriers than on tankers.

10.8.2 Pressure/Vacuum Valves

These are designed to provide for the flow of the small volumes of tank atmosphere caused by thermal variations in a cargo tank and should operate in advance of the pressure/vacuum breakers. To avoid unnecessary operation of the pressure/vacuum breaker the pressure/vacuum valves should be kept in good working order by regular inspection and cleaning.

10.9 EMERGENCY INERT GAS SUPPLY

The International Convention for the Safety of Life at Sea (SOLAS 1974), as amended, requires that suitable arrangements be provided to enable the inert gas system to be connected to an external supply of inert gas.

These arrangements should consist of a 250mm nominal pipe size bolted flange, isolated from the inert gas main by a valve and located forward of the non-return valve. The design of the flange should be compatible with the design of other external connections in the ship's cargo piping system.

10.10 PRODUCT CARRIERS REQUIRED TO BE FITTED WITH AN INERT GAS SYSTEM

10.10.1 General

The basic principles of inerting are exactly the same on product carriers as on crude carriers. There are, however, some differences in operational detail as outlined in the following sections.

10.10.2 Carriage of Products Having a Flashpoint Exceeding 60°C

The 1974 SOLAS Convention, as amended, implies that tankers may carry petroleum products having a flashpoint exceeding 60°C (i.e. bitumens, lubricating oils, heavy fuel oils, high flashpoint jet fuels and some diesel fuels, gas oils and special boiling point liquids) without inert gas systems having to be fitted or, if fitted, without tanks containing such cargoes having to be kept in the inert condition.

However, when cargoes with a flashpoint exceeding 60°C are carried at a cargo temperature higher than their flashpoint less 5°C, the tanks should be maintained in an inert condition because of the danger that a flammable condition may occur.

It is recommended that, if inert gas systems are fitted, cargo tanks are maintained in an inert condition whenever there is a possibility that the ullage space atmosphere could be within the flammable range. (See also Chapter 24 regarding the carriage of residual fuel oils).

When a non-volatile cargo is carried in a tank that has not been previously gas freed, the tank should be maintained in an inert condition.

10.10.3 Additional Purging and Gas Freeing

Gas freeing is required on product carriers more frequently than on crude carriers, because of the greater need both for tank entry and inspection, especially in port, and for venting the vapours of previous cargoes. On inerted product carriers, any gas freeing operation has to be preceded by a purging operation (see Section 10.6.9).

It should be recognised, however, that purging is not essential before gas freeing when the hydrocarbon gas content of a tank is already below 2% by volume.

10.11 COMBINATION CARRIERS

10.11.1 General

Combination carriers carrying oil must be treated as tankers and all precautions applicable to tankers observed.

The basic principles of inerting can be applied in exactly the same way for a combination carrier as for a tanker. However, differences in design and operation give rise to certain particular considerations for combination carriers, which are outlined in the following sections.

10.11.2 Slack Holds

It is particularly important for combination carriers to maintain their holds in an inert condition. These holds may extend to the full width of the ship and, even at small angles of roll, agitation of clean or dirty ballast in a slack hold (i.e. one in which the liquid level is not within the coaming) may result in the generation of static electricity. This agitation is sometimes referred to as 'sloshing' and can occur whenever the liquid level of the hold is not pressed up into the hatch coaming (see Section 12.4.3).

Slack holds should be avoided whenever possible.

10.11.3 Leakage

To ensure that leakage of gas, particularly through the hatch centre-line joints, is eliminated or minimised, it is essential that the hatch covers are inspected frequently to determine the condition of their seals, their alignment etc. When the hatch covers have been opened, particularly after the ship has been carrying a dry bulk cargo, the seals and trackways should be inspected and cleaned to remove any foreign matter.

10.11.4 Ballast and Void Spaces

The cargo holds of combination carriers are adjacent to ballast and void spaces. Leakages in pipelines or ducts in these spaces, or a fracture in the boundary plating, may cause oil, inert gas or hydrocarbon gas to leak into the ballast and void spaces. Consequently gas pockets may form which, because of the complex structure of these spaces, could be difficult to disperse. Personnel should be alerted to this hazard.

10.11.5 Inert Gas Distribution System

Because of the special construction of combination carriers, the vent line from the cargo hatchway coaming is situated very close to the level of the cargo surface. Also, in many cases the inert gas main line passing along the main deck may be below the oil level in the hold. During rough weather oil or water may enter these lines and thus prevent an adequate supply of inert gas during tank cleaning or discharge. Vent lines should therefore have drains fitted at their lowest point and these should always be checked before any operation takes place within the cargo hold (see Section 12.6.2).

10.11.6 Slop Tanks

If slops are retained on board because of the lack of reception facilities, the slop tank or tanks should be maintained in an inert condition and at a minimum pressure of 100mm water gauge at all times. These tanks should be checked at intervals of not more than 2 days to ensure that the oxygen level does not exceed 8% by volume. If any oxygen level in excess of this figure is detected, the tanks should be re-inerted until the oxygen level is less than 8%.

Except when the slop tanks are being purged or re-inerted, they should be isolated from the inert gas main.

Additionally, all cargo lines to and from the slop tanks should be isolated by means of blanks.

10.11.7 Holds/Cargo Tanks

Where holds are required to carry cargo other than oil, they should be isolated from the inert gas main and oil cargo pipelines by means of blanks, which should remain in position at all times when cargoes other than oil are being handled or carried (see Section 12.13).

10.12 INERT GAS SYSTEM FAILURE

10.12.1 General

The SOLAS Convention requires each ship fitted with an inert gas system to have a manual containing detailed guidance on the operation, safety and maintenance requirements, and the occupational health hazards relevant to the installed system. The manual must include guidance on procedures to be followed in the event of a fault or failure of the inert gas system.

10.12.2 Crude Oil Tankers

Inerted cargo tanks should not be allowed to become flammable because of the danger of ignition from pyrophoric deposits. In the event of a failure of the inert gas system prior to or during discharge of cargo or ballast, immediate actions should be taken to prevent any air from being drawn into the tanks. All tank operations should be stopped and the deck isolating valve closed.

Discharge or tank cleaning should not commence or continue until the operation of the inert gas system has been restored or an alternative source of inert gas provided.

10.12.3 Product Carriers

If, on an inerted product carrier which has not carried a cargo of crude oil since the tanks were previously washed, it is considered totally impracticable to repair the inert gas system, discharge should not be resumed until the agreement of all interested parties has been obtained and only then provided the precautions detailed in Sections 7.10 and 10.6.7 are taken.

If it becomes essential to clean tanks while an inert gas system is inoperative, the manual referred to in Section 10.12.1 above must be consulted.

10.13 INERT GAS PLANT REPAIRS

As inert gas causes asphyxiation, great care must be taken to avoid the escape of inert gas into any enclosed or partly enclosed space.

Before opening the system, it should if possible be gas freed and any enclosed space in which the system is opened up should be ventilated to avoid any risk of oxygen deficiency.

Continuous positive ventilation must be maintained before and during the work.

No one should be allowed inside the scrubber or deck water seal until the atmosphere has first been tested and an oxygen level of 21% by volume obtained (refer Chapter 11). In addition, while personnel are working inside a scrubber tower, the atmosphere must be continuously monitored for oxygen content and personnel should be under constant supervision.

Chapter 11

Enclosed Space Entry

This Chapter describes the tests to be carried out to determine whether or not an enclosed space is safe for entry. The conditions for entry are set out as well as the precautions to be taken while work is being carried out in enclosed spaces. The Chapter also covers the emergency use of breathing apparatus in unsafe atmospheres and rescue from enclosed spaces. Terminals are recommended to use these guidelines in the absence of any national requirements or guidance. However, Masters should be aware that terminal requirements for enclosed space entry may differ from this guidance as a result of national legislation.

11.1   GENERAL

An enclosed space is one with restricted access that is not subject to continuous ventilation and in which the atmosphere may be hazardous due to the presence of hydrocarbon gas, toxic gases, inert gas or oxygen deficiency. This definition includes cargo tanks, ballast tanks, fuel tanks, water tanks, lubricating oil tanks, slop and waste oil tanks, sewage tanks, cofferdams, duct keels, void spaces and trunkings, pipelines or fittings connected to any of these. It also includes inert gas scrubbers and water seals and any other item of machinery or equipment that is not routinely ventilated and entered, such as boilers and main engine crankcases.

Many of the fatalities in enclosed spaces on oil tankers have resulted from entering the space without proper supervision or adherence to agreed procedures. In almost every case the fatality would have been avoided if the simple guidance in this chapter had been followed. The rapid rescue of personnel who have collapsed in an enclosed space presents particular risk. It is a human reaction to go to the aid of a colleague in difficulties, but far too many additional and unnecessary deaths have occurred from impulsive and ill-prepared rescue attempts.

11.2   RESPIRATORY HAZARDS

Respiratory hazards from a number of sources could be present in an enclosed space. These could include one or more of the following:

- Respiratory contaminants associated with organic vapours including those from aromatic hydrocarbons, benzene, toluene, etc.; gases such as hydrogen sulphide; residues from inert gas and particulates such as those from asbestos, welding operations and paint mists.

- Oxygen deficiency caused by, for example, oxidation (rusting) of bare steel surfaces, the presence of inert gas or microbial activity.

11.2.1 Hydrocarbon Vapours

During the carriage and after the discharge of hydrocarbons, the presence of hydrocarbon vapour should always be suspected in enclosed spaces for the following reasons:

- Cargo may have leaked into compartments, including pumprooms (see Section 2.17), cofferdams, permanent ballast tanks and tanks adjacent to those that have carried cargo.

- Cargo residues may remain on the internal surfaces of tanks, even after cleaning and ventilation.

- Sludge and scale in a tank which has been declared gas free may give off further hydrocarbon vapour if disturbed or subjected to a rise in temperature.

- Residues may remain in cargo or ballast pipelines and pumps.

The presence of gas should also be suspected in empty tanks or compartments if non-volatile cargoes have been loaded into non-gas free tanks or if there is a common ventilation system which could allow the free passage of vapours from one tank to another.

11.2.2 Oxygen Deficiency

Lack of oxygen should always be suspected in all enclosed spaces, particularly if they have contained water, have been subjected to damp or humid conditions, have contained inert gas or are adjacent to, or connected with, other inerted tanks.

11.2.3 Other Atmospheric Hazards

These include toxic contaminants such as benzene or hydrogen sulphide which could remain in the space as residues from previous cargoes.

11.3 ATMOSPHERE TESTS PRIOR TO ENTRY

11.3.1 General

Any decision to enter an enclosed space should only be taken after the atmosphere within the space has been comprehensively tested from outside the space with test equipment that has recently been calibrated and checked for correct operation.

It is essential that all atmosphere testing equipment used is:

- Suitable for the test required;

- Of an approved type;

- Correctly maintained;

- Frequently checked against standard samples.

A record should be kept of all maintenance work and calibration tests carried out and of the period of their validity. Testing should only be carried out by personnel who have been trained in the use of the equipment and who are competent to interpret the results correctly.

Care should be taken to obtain a representative cross-section of the compartment by sampling at several depths and through as many deck openings as practicable. When tests are being carried out from deck level, ventilation should be stopped and a minimum period of about 10 minutes should be allowed to elapse before readings are taken.

Even when tests have shown a tank or compartment to be safe for entry, pockets of gas should always be suspected. Hence, when descending to the lower part of a tank or compartment, further atmosphere tests should be made. Regeneration of hydrocarbon gas should always be considered possible, even after loose scale has been removed. The use of personal detectors capable of continuously monitoring the oxygen content of the atmosphere, the presence of hydrocarbon vapour and, if appropriate, toxic vapour is strongly recommended. These instruments will detect any deterioration in the quality of the atmosphere and can provide an audible alarm to warn of the change in conditions.

While personnel remain in a tank or compartment, ventilation should be continuous and frequent atmosphere tests should be undertaken. In particular, tests should always be made before each daily commencement of work or after any interruption or break in the work. Sufficient samples should be drawn to ensure that the resulting readings are representative of the condition of the entire space.

11.3.2 Hydrocarbon Vapours

To be considered safe for entry, whether for inspection, cold work or hot work, a reading of not more than 1% LFL must be obtained on suitable monitoring equipment.

11.3.3 Benzene

Checks for benzene vapour should be made prior to entering any compartment in which a cargo that may have contained benzene has recently been carried (see Section 16.4). Entry should not be permitted without appropriate personal protective equipment if statutory or recommended Permissible Exposure Limits (PEL's) are likely to be exceeded. Tests for benzene vapours can only be undertaken using appropriate detector equipment, such as that utilising detector tubes. Detector equipment should be provided on board all vessels likely to carry cargoes in which benzene may be present.

11.3.4 Hydrogen Sulphide

Although a tank which has contained sour crude or sour products will contain hydrogen sulphide, general practice and experience indicates that, if the tank is thoroughly washed, the hydrogen sulphide should be eliminated (see also Section 16.5). However, the atmosphere should be checked for hydrogen sulphide content prior to entry and entry should be prohibited in the event of any hydrogen sulphide being detected. Hydrogen sulphide may also be encountered in pumprooms and appropriate precautions should therefore be taken (see Section 2.17).

11.3.5 Oxygen Deficiency

Before initial entry is allowed into any enclosed space which is not in daily use, the atmosphere should be tested with an oxygen analyser to check that the normal oxygen level in air of 21% by volume is present. This is of particular importance when considering entry into any space, tank or compartment that has previously been inerted.

11.4 CONDITIONS FOR ENTRY INTO ENCLOSED SPACES

11.4.1 General

An entry permit should be issued by a responsible officer prior to personnel entering an enclosed space. An example of an Enclosed Space Entry Permit is provided in Appendix I.

Suitable notices should be prominently displayed to inform personnel of the precautions to be taken when entering tanks or other enclosed spaces and of any restrictions placed upon the work permitted therein.

The entry permit should be rendered invalid if ventilation of the space stops or if any of the conditions noted in the check list change.

11.4.2 Entry Procedures

No one should enter any cargo tank, cofferdam, double bottom or other enclosed space unless an entry permit has been issued by a responsible officer who has ascertained immediately before entry that the atmosphere within the space is in all respects safe for entry. Before issuing an entry permit, the responsible officer should ensure that:

- The appropriate atmosphere checks have been carried out, namely oxygen content is 21% by volume, hydrocarbon vapour concentration is not more than 1% LFL and no toxic or other contaminants are present.

- Effective ventilation will be maintained continuously while the enclosed space is occupied.

- Lifelines and harnesses are ready for immediate use at the entrance to the space.

- Approved positive pressure breathing apparatus and resuscitation equipment are ready for use at the entrance to the space.

- Where possible, a separate means of access is available for use as an alternative means of escape in an emergency.

- A responsible member of the crew is in constant attendance outside the enclosed space in the immediate vicinity of the entrance and in direct contact with a responsible officer. The lines of communications for dealing with emergencies should be clearly established and understood by all concerned (see Section 11.7).

> **In the event of an emergency, under no circumstances should the attending crew member enter the tank before help has arrived and the situation has been evaluated to ensure the safety of those entering the tank to undertake rescue operations.**

Regular atmosphere checks should be carried out all the time personnel are within the space and a full range of tests should be undertaken prior to re-entry into the tank after any break.

The use of personal detectors (see Section 11.3.1) and carriage of emergency escape breathing apparatus are recommended.

Reference should be made to Section 2.17.4 for additional guidance on entry into pumprooms.

11.4.3 Evacuation from Enclosed Spaces

If any of the conditions stated on the entry permit or work permit change and become unsafe after personnel have entered the space, they should be ordered to leave the space immediately and not be permitted to re-enter until the situation has been re-evaluated and the safe conditions stated on the permit have been restored.

11.4.4 Entry into Enclosed Spaces with Atmospheres Known or Suspected to be Unsafe for Entry

It is stressed that entry into any space that has not been proved to be safe for entry should only be considered in an emergency situation when no practical alternative exists. In this highly hazardous situation, the personnel involved must be well trained in the use of breathing apparatus and be aware of the dangers of removing their face masks while in the hostile atmosphere.

When it is absolutely necessary to enter a compartment where it is suspected that the atmosphere is, or might become unsafe, a responsible officer must continuously supervise the operation and should ensure that:

- A permit has been issued by the master stating that there is no practicable alternative to the proposed method of entry and that such entry is essential for the safe operation of the ship.

- Ventilation is provided where possible.

- Personnel use positive pressure breathing apparatus and are connected to a lifeline.

- The number of persons entering the tank is kept to a minimum consistent with the work to be performed.

- Means of communication are provided and a system of signals is agreed and understood by the personnel involved.

- Spare sets of breathing apparatus, a resuscitator and rescue equipment are available outside the space and a standby party, with breathing apparatus donned, is in attendance in case of an emergency.

- All essential work that is to be undertaken is carried out in a manner that will avoid creating an ignition hazard.

11.5 RESPIRATORY PROTECTIVE EQUIPMENT

11.5.1 General

Breathing apparatus, of the positive pressure type, should always be used whenever it is necessary to make an emergency entry into a space which is known to contain toxic vapours or gas or to be deficient in oxygen, and/or is known to contain contaminants which cannot be effectively dealt with by air purifying equipment. Entry should only be permitted in exceptional circumstances when no other practicable, safe alternative exists.

11.5.2 Self Contained Breathing Apparatus

This consists of a portable supply of compressed air contained in a cylinder or cylinders attached to a carrying frame and harness worn by the user. Air is provided to the user through a face mask which can be adjusted to give an airtight fit. A pressure gauge indicates the pressure in the cylinder and an audible alarm sounds when the supply is running low. Only positive pressure type sets are recommended for use in enclosed spaces as these, as their name implies, maintain a positive pressure within the face mask at all times.

When using the equipment, the following should be noted:

- The pressure gauge must be checked before use.

- The operation of the audible low pressure alarm should be tested before use.

- The face mask must be checked and adjusted to ensure that it is airtight. In this regard, the presence of any facial hair may adversely effect the mask's seal and, should this be the case, another person should be selected to wear the apparatus.

- The pressure gauge should be monitored frequently during use to check on remaining air supply.

- Ample time should be allowed for getting out of the hazardous atmosphere. In any event, the user must leave immediately if the low pressure alarm sounds. It should be remembered that the duration of the air supply depends on the weight and fitness of the user and the extent of his exertion.

If the user suspects at any time that the equipment may not be operating satisfactorily or be concerned that the integrity of the face mask seal may be damaged, he should vacate the space immediately.

11.5.3 Air Line Breathing Apparatus

Air line breathing apparatus enables compressed air equipment to be used for longer periods than would be possible using self-contained equipment.

This equipment consists of a face mask which is supplied by air through a small diameter hose leading outside the space where it is connected to either compressed air cylinders or an air line served by a compressor. If the ships air supply is used, it is essential that it is properly filtered and adequately monitored for toxic or hazardous constituents. The hose is attached to the user by means of a belt or other arrangement which enables rapid disconnection in an emergency. Air supply to the face mask is regulated by a flow control valve or orifice.

If the air supply is from a compressor, the arrangement will include an emergency supply of air in cylinders for use in the event of the compressor failing. In such an emergency, the user should be signalled to vacate the space immediately .

A trained and competent person must be in control of the air line pressure and be alert to the need to change over to the alternative supply should normal working pressure not be maintained.

When using air line breathing apparatus:

- Check and ensure that the face mask is adjusted to be airtight.

- Check the working pressure before each use.

- Check the audible low pressure alarm before each use.

- To avoid damage, keep the air lines clear of sharp projections.

- Ensure that the air hose does not exceed 90 metres in length.

- Allow ample time to vacate the space when the low pressure alarm sounds. The duration of the emergency air carried by the user will depend on an individual's weight and fitness and each user should be aware of his particular limitations.

Should there be any doubt about the efficiency of the equipment, the user should vacate the space immediately.

The user should carry a completely separate supply of clean air for use in emergency evacuation from the space in the event of the air line failing.

11.5.4 Cartridge or Canister Face Masks

These units, which consist of a cartridge or canister attached to a face mask, are designed to purify the air of specific contaminants. It is important that they are only used for their designed purpose and within the limits prescribed by manufacturers.

> **Such units will not protect the user against concentrations of hydrocarbon or toxic vapours in excess of their design parameters, or against oxygen deficiency, and they should never be used in place of breathing apparatus.**

11.5.5 Hose Mask (Fresh Air Breathing Apparatus)

This equipment consists of a mask supplied by air from a large diameter hose connected to a rotary pump or bellows. It is cumbersome and provides no seal against the entry of gases.

> **Although this equipment may be found on some vessels, it is recommended that it is NOT used for enclosed space entry.**

11.5.6 Maintenance

All respiratory protective equipment should be examined and tested by a responsible officer at regular intervals. Defects should be made good promptly and a record kept of repairs. Air bottles must be recharged as soon as possible after use. Masks and helmets should be cleaned and disinfected after use. Any repair or maintenance must be carried out strictly in accordance with the manufacturer's instructions.

11.5.7 Stowage

Breathing apparatus should be stowed fully assembled in a place where it is readily accessible. Air bottles should be fully charged and the adjusting straps kept slack. Units should be sited so as to be available for emergencies in different parts of the ship or the jetty as appropriate.

11.5.8 Training

Practical demonstrations and training in the use of breathing apparatus should be carried out to give personnel experience in its use. Only trained personnel should use self-contained and air line breathing apparatus since incorrect or inefficient use can endanger the user's life.

11.6 WORK IN ENCLOSED SPACES

11.6.1 General Requirements

All conditions for entry, including the issue of an entry permit and, if appropriate, a work permit, must be observed.

Before work is undertaken, a check should be made to ensure that there is no loose scale, sludge or combustible material in the vicinity which, if disturbed or heated, could give off toxic or flammable gases. Effective ventilation should be maintained and, where practicable, directed towards the work area.

11.6.2 Opening up Equipment and Fittings

Whenever cargo pumps, pipelines, valves or heating coils are to be opened, they should first be thoroughly flushed with water. However, even after flushing, there will always be a possibility of some cargo remaining which could be a source of further flammable or toxic gas. Special care must therefore be taken whenever such equipment is opened up and additional gas tests should be made.

11.6.3 Use of Tools

Tools should not be carried into enclosed spaces but lowered in a canvas bag or bucket to avoid the possibility of their being dropped. Before any hammering or chipping is undertaken or any power tool is used, the responsible officer should be satisfied that there is no likelihood of hydrocarbon vapour being present in the vicinity. See Section 2.9.2 for general precautions relating to the use of hand tools.

11.6.4 Electric Lights and Electrical Equipment

Unless a compartment is approved safe for hot work (see Section 2.8), non-approved lights or non-intrinsically safe electrical equipment must not be taken into an enclosed space (see Section 2.4).

In port, any local regulations concerning the use of electric lights or electrical equipment should be observed.

11.6.5 Removal of Sludge, Scale and Sediment

When removing sludge, scale or sediment from an enclosed space, periodic gas tests should be undertaken and continuous ventilation should be maintained throughout the period the space is occupied.

There may be increases in gas concentrations in the immediate vicinity of the work and care should be taken to ensure that the atmosphere remains safe for personnel. It is strongly recommended that personal gas detectors are provided to some or all of the persons engaged in the work.

11.6.6 Cold Work

To be safe for cold work, the atmosphere within the enclosed space must satisfy all the requirements necessary for safe entry and a permit must be issued. In addition, it is advisable to remove any sludge, scale or sediment from the area in and around which the work is to take place.

When cold work is to be undertaken alongside a terminal, the terminal representative should be consulted as a work permit may need to be issued.

11.6.7 Hot Work

> **Hot work in an enclosed space should only be carried out when all applicable regulations and safety requirements have been met and a permit to work has been issued (see Section 2.8 for general precautions and approval for hot work; see Appendix F for hot work permits).**

11.6.8 Inflatable Work Boats

Only purpose-built inflatable work boats of an approved type are to be used for tank repair work and tank inspections. Before and during their use, the following precautions should be taken:

- If the tanks are connected by a common venting system, or an IG system, the tank in which the boat is to be used should be isolated to prevent a transfer of gas to or from other tanks. Procedures must be established that ensure the tank is re-connected to its venting system on completion of the work.

- The appropriate atmosphere checks should be carried out.

- An enclosed space entry permit should be issued.

- All deck apertures, such as tank washing plates, should be opened and effective ventilation maintained continuously while persons are in the tank.

- Adequate lighting of an approved type, such as air-driven lamps, should be available.

- The work boat should only be used when the water surface in the tank is calm.

- The work boat should only be used in tanks containing clean ballast water. The water level in the tank should be either stationary or falling; on no account must the level of the water be rising while the boat is in use.

- A responsible person should act as a look-out at the top of the tank and, if the boat is working at a point remote from the tank hatch, an additional look-out should be positioned down the access ladder at a point where a clear view of the boat is provided.

- Approved breathing apparatus and resuscitation equipment should be ready for use at the entrance to the tank.

- All personnel working in the compartment should wear a buoyancy aid.

11.6.9   Outside Contractors

The master or terminal operator should be satisfied that whenever outside contractors or work gangs are employed, arrangements are made to ensure their understanding of, and compliance with, all relevant safe working practices, and that they are effectively supervised and controlled by a responsible officer.

11.7   RESCUE FROM ENCLOSED SPACES

> **When an accident involving injury to personnel occurs in an enclosed space, the first action must be to raise the alarm. Although speed is often vital in the interests of saving life, rescue operations should not be attempted until the necessary assistance and equipment has been mustered. There are many examples of lives being lost through hasty, ill-prepared rescue attempts.**

Prior organisation is of great value in arranging quick and effective response. Lifelines, breathing apparatus, resuscitation equipment and other items of rescue equipment should always be kept ready for use and a trained emergency team should be available. A code of signals should be agreed in advance. (see Section 11.4.2).

> **Whenever it is suspected that an unsafe atmosphere has been a contributory factor to the accident, breathing apparatus and, where practicable, lifelines must be used by persons entering the space.**

The officer in charge of a rescue should remain outside the space, from where the most effective control can be exercised.

It is imperative that every member of the rescue team should know what is expected of him. Regular drills and exercises in rescue from enclosed spaces should be carried out.

11.8   RESUSCITATION

All terminal and tanker personnel should be instructed in resuscitation techniques for the treatment of persons who have been overcome by toxic gases or fumes, or whose breathing has stopped from other causes such as electric shock or drowning.

Most tankers and terminals are provided with special apparatus for use in resuscitation. This apparatus can be of a number of different types. It is important that personnel are aware of its presence and are trained in its proper use.

The apparatus should be stowed where it is easily accessible and not kept locked up. The instructions provided with it should be clearly displayed on board ship. The apparatus and the contents of cylinders should be checked periodically. Adequate spare bottles should be carried.

Chapter 12

Combination Carriers

This Chapter sets out safety measures to be taken on combination carriers in addition to those necessary for conventional tankers. For this purpose a combination carrier is a tanker designed to carry oil or solid cargoes in bulk, and is one of two main types, an Oil/Bulk/Ore ship or an Oil/Ore ship. Other types of combination carriers, which may for example carry liquefied gas and petroleum, or containers and general cargo, are not covered. Due account must be taken of any special local regulations.

12.1 GENERAL INSTRUCTIONS

Petroleum and dry bulk cargoes must not be carried simultaneously.

Attention should be paid to the gas contents of wing tanks when the vessel is discharging bulk ore. Similarly, it should be realised that damaged bulkheads may lead to flammable gas mixtures in ore holds.

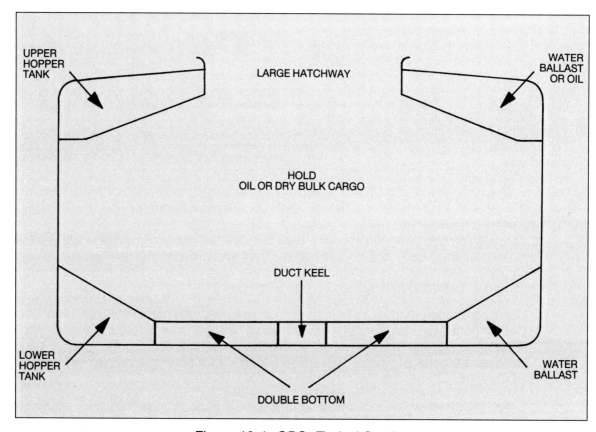

Figure 12-1. *OBO: Typical Section*

12.2 TYPES OF COMBINATION CARRIERS

12.2.1 Oil/Bulk/Ore (OBO)

The OBO ship is capable of carrying its full deadweight when trading as an ore carrier with cargoes of heavy ore concentrates. This type of ship is also designed to carry other types of dry bulk cargo such as grain and coal.

Holds are usually arranged to extend the full breadth of the ship, with upper and lower hopper tanks and double bottom tanks. In some cases holds may have wing tanks. Oil or dry bulk cargo is carried in the holds. Oil may in addition be carried in one or more sets of upper hopper tanks, and where there are wing tanks they may also be used. Normally wing tanks for the carriage of oily slops are fitted aft of the cargo holds. Permanent ballast may be carried in top and bottom hopper tanks and in double bottom tanks.

Conventional bulk carrier hatches, normally of the side rolling type, are fitted with a special sealing arrangement.

Cargo and ballast pipelines are typically installed in a duct keel or in two pipe tunnels located either side of the centre line and separated by a double bottom tank.

12.2.2 Oil/Ore (O/O)

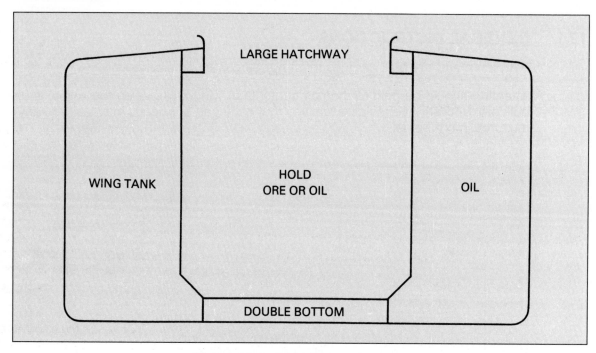

Figure 12-2. *O/O: Typical Section*

These ships are designed to carry their full deadweight when trading as tankers and also when carrying heavy ore concentrates. They are not usually designed to carry light bulk cargoes. Heavy ore concentrates are carried only in the centre holds. Oil cargo may be carried in both centre holds and cargo wing tanks.

Holds are constructed so as to extend approximately one half of the total breadth of the ship. Conventional wing tanks incorporate the main strengthening sections, allowing smooth sides in the centre holds. Holds are always constructed with double bottom spaces beneath them. Hatches are generally single piece side rolling with a sealing arrangement similar to that on OBO ships.

Cargo pipelines are usually installed in the wing tanks, whilst ballast pipelines are typically installed in the double bottom tanks. Where cargo pipelines pass through permanent ballast tanks, the possibility of pollution caused by pipeline failure should be borne in mind.

12.3 VOID SPACES, DUCT KEELS AND PIPE TUNNELS

Between cargo holds there may be a void space, through which various piping systems can pass and access be gained to tank valves and double bottom tanks.

A single duct keel may be fitted along the centre line. On some ships two duct keels are fitted, one on either side of the centre line.

Some duct keels and pipe tunnels may be fitted with wheeled trolleys on rails to permit easier access for personnel and equipment. These spaces may be fitted with fixed lighting, fixed washing systems and a fixed gas monitoring system.

Because of their restricted natural ventilation these spaces may be oxygen deficient. Furthermore, they are adjacent to cargo holds and ballast tanks, so both hydrocarbon vapour and inert gas may leak into them. The precautions for entry into enclosed spaces given in Chapter 11 should therefore be strictly applied. The rescue of an unconscious or injured person from these confined spaces may be extremely difficult.

12.4 SLACK HOLDS IN COMBINATION CARRIERS

12.4.1 General

Because of the broad beam and size of the holds, the very large free surface in slack holds (i.e. holds not filled to within the coaming) permits substantial movement of liquid, which can result in both loss of stability and 'sloshing'.

12.4.2 Loss of Stability

Particular care should be taken when loading or discharging liquid cargo from combination carriers and when handling ballast on such ships to ensure that the total free surface effect of cargo and ballast tanks is kept within safe limits, otherwise a sudden, and possibly violent, change of list could occur.

In compliance with government requirements all combination carriers are supplied with stability data and loading and unloading instructions. These instructions should be carefully studied and followed. Generally, these instructions will specify a maximum number of cargo holds or tanks which may be slack at any one time. Sometimes it may be necessary to adjust the quantity of cargo to be loaded in order to avoid slack holds. Where double bottom ballast tanks extend across the whole width of the vessel, the free surface effect of water in these tanks will be as great as that of full cargo holds and account must be taken of this fact.

Some combination carriers have a valve interlocking system which limits the number of tanks which may be loaded or discharged simultaneously. Such systems may fail or can be by-passed, and it is recommended that a conspicuous notice is displayed at the cargo control station warning of the danger of free surface effect and stating the maximum number of holds that can safely be slack at any one time.

Before arriving in port, a plan should be prepared for the anticipated loading or discharging sequence, bearing in mind the free surface effect and distribution of all cargo, fuel and ballast at all stages of the operation.

Terminal operators should appreciate that combination carriers may be subject to loading rate limitations and to specific discharge procedures. These arise from the danger of hatch seals leaking if placed under excessive pressure, as well as from the free surface effects.

If a loss of stability becomes evident during loading or discharge, all cargo, ballast and bunker operations must cease and a plan be prepared for restoring positive stability. If the vessel is at a terminal this plan should be agreed by the terminal representative and it may be necessary or prudent to disconnect the loading arms or hoses.

The specific action required to restore stability will be determined by the vessel's detailed stability information in relation to a particular condition.

In general the following principles will apply:

- The vertical centre of gravity must be lowered in the most effective way.

- Where slack double bottom ballast tanks exist these should be filled, starting with those on the low side, followed by those on the high side.

- If the pressing-up of slack double bottom tanks is insufficient to regain stability, it may be necessary to consider filling empty double bottom ballast tanks. It must be recognised that this will initially result in a further loss of stability caused by the additional free surface effect; this, however, will soon be corrected by the effect of the added mass below the vessel's original centre of gravity.

- No attempt should be made to correct a list by filling compartments on the high side as this is likely to result in a violent change of list to the opposite side.

- The restraint provided by moorings should be considered. To attempt to control a list by adjusting mooring rope tension could be dangerous and is therefore not recommended.

On completion of loading, the number of slack holds should be at a minimum and in any event not more than that specified in the stability information book.

12.4.3 'Sloshing'

'Sloshing' is the movement of liquid within a hold when the vessel is rolling or pitching.

It can give rise to:

- Structural damage caused by the slamming effect of the liquid against the ship's side or bulkheads.

- An electrostatically charged mist in the ullage space in holds partially filled with a mixture of oil and water, such as dirty ballast or retained tank washings. This can even occur with only a slight rolling motion.

In order to eliminate these problems, slack holds should be avoided wherever possible. This may be difficult when loaded with an oil cargo, but may be more readily achieved when the vessel is in ballast.

12.5 LONGITUDINAL STRESS

Consideration should be given to the distribution of the weights along the ship, taking account of the ship's longitudinal strength.

12.6 VENTING OF CARGO HOLDS

12.6.1 Venting Systems

The vent lines from the cargo holds may lead either to individual vent outlets, to a main gas line venting system which expels the hydrocarbon vapour through a riser at a safe height above the deck, or to an inert gas pipeline system.

12.6.2 Blockage of Vent Lines

Owing to the movement of liquid within the cargo hold in rough sea conditions, the possibility of liquid entering the vent line is greater than on a conventional tanker. Various trap systems may be incorporated, such as a U-bend or a special valve, but the possibility of a blockage should always be suspected after a rough voyage. A blockage may also occur if the vessel has been in very hot weather which has caused the cargo to expand above the gas line outlet.

Drains are normally fitted in each gas line and these should be routinely checked before commencing cargo operations in order to ensure that the cargo hold is able to 'breathe'.

These drains may become blocked, particularly during the carriage of high pour point cargoes, and gas lines should be blown through with inert gas to ensure they are clear.

12.6.3 Venting During Carriage of Dry Bulk Cargoes

During the carriage of dry bulk cargoes, the holds should be sealed from the main oil cargo pumping and gas venting systems and alternative venting systems utilised as required. Wing tanks should be maintained either in a gas free or an inert condition (see Section 12.10).

12.7 HATCH COVERS

12.7.1 Sealing

The hatches of combination carriers have a much more onerous duty to perform when these ships are carrying liquid cargo than when carrying dry bulk cargo as they are required to remain gas and liquid tight at all times, even when the ship is working in a seaway.

Regular attention should be paid to the closing devices, for example by adjusting them evenly and by lubrication of screw threads.

When closing hatch covers, the closing devices should be evenly and progressively pulled down in the correct sequence in accordance with the manufacturer's instructions.

In ships fitted with inert gas or fixed high-capacity gas freeing systems, a positive test of the efficiency of the sealing arrangements can be carried out by pressurising the holds and applying a soapy solution to the sealing arrangements. Any leakage is readily detectable and should be rectified by further adjustment of the closing devices in the affected area. (See Section 9.3.2(f) for advice on the use of a fixed gas freeing system.)

The cover joints should be examined for gas leakage when the compartment is loaded with liquid cargo and any gas or liquid leaks which cannot be stopped by adjusting the closing devices should be marked or noted so that the jointing material can be examined when the opportunity arises and the joint made good. Additional sealing by means of tape or compound may be necessary.

If the ship is fitted with an inert gas system, the gas tightness of the hatch covers will affect the frequency with which the inert gas pressure needs to be topped up.

Most combination carriers use synthetic rubber for the hatch seals, and this material should be examined whenever a suitable opportunity occurs. It is also advisable to have on board a reasonable stock of jointing material of the correct size so that the repairs can be carried out at sea.

12.7.2 Rubbing in a Seaway

The hatch covers on combination carriers generally work when a ship is in a seaway and it is thus possible for the steel hatch cover to rub on the steel coaming. Investigations have shown that this is unlikely to provide a source of ignition. However, the joints between the hatch cover and hatch coaming should be cleaned before closing the hatch, especially after a dry bulk cargo has been carried. After donning appropriate personnel protective equipment, a compressed air hose with a suitable nozzle might be used for this purpose.

12.7.3   Foreign Matter in Runways

It is important to keep hatch cover runways clear of foreign matter in order to ease the opening and closing of hatches. After donning appropriate personnel protective equipment and an initial clearing with a brush, runways can be cleaned using a compressed air hose or washdeck hose.

12.8   OPENINGS INTO CARGO HOLDS

Owing to the height of hatch coamings, which are partially filled on completion of loading a liquid cargo, all maindeck openings into cargo holds may have to withstand a positive pressure. It is essential therefore that all seals and gaskets on tank cleaning covers, access hatches, trimming hatches etc. provide an oil tight and gas tight seal. The seats should be cleaned to ensure a proper seal and all securing bolts should be hardened down prior to loading a bulk liquid cargo.

12.9   TANK WASHING

Any tank washing should be carried out in accordance with the guidelines given in Chapter 9.

Cargo holds should not be used as slop tanks during cleaning because of the risk of sloshing. Holds containing dirty ballast should not be discharged when the ship is rolling or pitching. Hatch covers should not be opened until the hold is gas free. All closing devices should be kept secured to prevent movement of the hatch covers.

When cargoes other than oil are intended to be carried it is essential that all holds and cargo tanks other than slop tanks are emptied of oil and oil residues and cleaned and ventilated to such a degree that the tanks are completely gas free. They should then be inspected internally to confirm this condition. The pumproom, cargo pumps, pipelines, duct keel and other void spaces should be checked to ensure that they are free of oil and hydrocarbon gas.

Most dry bulk ports require a gas free certificate to be issued in respect of a combination carrier presenting to load or discharge dry bulk cargo. Such certificates normally relate to holds and other spaces but will not confirm that pumps and pipelines are free from oil and/or hydrocarbon gas.

12.10   CARRIAGE OF SLOPS WHEN TRADING AS A DRY BULK CARRIER

In addition to compliance with the requirements set out in Section 12.9, every effort should be made to ensure that before a combination carrier is to be operated as a dry bulk carrier, any oil contained in the slop tanks is discharged ashore. After discharging the slops, the empty tanks should be cleaned and either gas freed or inerted prior to loading any dry bulk cargo.

If, however, slops cannot be discharged and have to remain on board the following precautions should be taken:

• All slops must be collected in the slop tank specially designated for this purpose.

• Blanking plates or other approved means of closure must be fitted in all pipelines, including common vent lines, leading to or from the slop tank to ensure that the contents and atmosphere of the slop tank are isolated from other compartments.

• The slop tank should be purged with inert gas and a positive pressure maintained within the tank at all times.

- Carbon dioxide must never be used in liquid form to provide inert gas to the ullage space of the dirty slop tank because of the risk of generating an electrostatic charge.

- Unless the tank is fully inerted, the slops should be handled in such a way as to avoid a free fall of slops into the receiving tank, as this may cause a build up of an electrostatic charge.

Unless the vessel reverts to carrying oil, oil slops should not be contained on board for more than one voyage. If, however, it is impossible to remove the slops because of the lack of shore reception facilities for oily residues, the slop tank should be treated as indicated above and a report forwarded to the owner and the appropriate administration.

12.11 LEAKAGE INTO BALLAST TANKS ON COMBINATION CARRIERS

On combination carriers, a serious problem occurs if there is leakage of oil from the cargo holds into the permanent ballast tanks.

The known weak structural points are as follows:

- On vessels with vertically corrugated transverse bulkheads, cracks may occur in the welded seams between these bulkheads and the upper hopper tanks. On vessels where the upper hopper tanks and the lower hopper tanks are connected by a trunkway or a pipe, the contamination would affect the lower hopper tank in addition to the area around the actual fracture. On vessels where the upper hopper tank is connected to the lower hopper tank by means of a pipe, it may be advisable to install a valve in the drop line to confine oil contamination to the upper hopper tank.

- In double hulled vessels, leaks may be found in the upper welded seams of the longitudinal bulkhead between ballast tank and cargo tank abutting the sloped deckhead of the cargo tank.

12.12 INERT GAS SYSTEMS

Inert gas systems will generally be fitted on combination carriers for use when trading as oil tankers. They should be operated as described in Chapter 10.

An additional problem on combination carriers is that owing to the size of the hatch cover there is a greater chance of petroleum gas or inert gas leaks than on conventional tankers, particularly in view of the tendency of covers to work in a seaway. Adequate checks should be made to locate leaks and reduce the loss of inert gas (see Section 12.7.1).

12.13 TESTING OF CARGO TANKS AND ENCLOSED SPACES ON DRY BULK VOYAGES

Before loading a dry bulk cargo, all spaces which have previously contained oil should be cleaned, gas freed and inspected internally. Once all tank cleaning has been completed, daily checks for petroleum gas should be made in all empty cargo holds, empty cargo tanks and empty double bottom and ballast tanks, as well as in pumprooms, pipeducts, cofferdams, stool tanks and similar void spaces. If no petroleum gas has been detected after 14 days, the frequency of the readings may be reduced to every two days, unless the ship passes through areas with higher sea or air temperatures, in which case the daily checks should continue.

If the next voyage is to continue in dry bulk cargo the readings on that voyage need be taken only every three days.

If petroleum gas is detected during any dry cargo voyage, the space should be ventilated with air. If the petroleum gas cannot be controlled by ventilation, the space should be inerted and remain so until it can be cleaned again.

12.14 CARGO CHANGE-OVER CHECK LISTS

The following check lists are of a general nature and each ship should develop its own comprehensive check lists using these as a guide.

12.14.1 Oil to Dry Bulk Cargo

- Wash cargo holds and tanks including access trunks.

- Flush all main suctions into cargo holds and tanks and strip dry.

- Gas free all cargo holds and tanks.

- Hose off, blow through, disconnect and stow heating coils as required. Plug securing sockets as necessary.

- Complete hand hosing and digging of holds and sumps to the requirements of the next cargo.

- Drain cargo holds and suction wells.

- Blank off main suctions to holds as necessary. Ensure stripping discharge line to after hold is securely blanked.

- Ensure sounding pipes to bilge wells are open and clear of obstructions.

- Fit main and stripping suction recess doors as necessary. Also fit heating coil connecting pipe recess doors.

- Wash cargo pipeline system thoroughly, including pumps, deck lines, bottom lines and pumproom.

- Ensure gauging system, where fitted, is stowed or blanked as necessary to manufacturer's recommendations.

- Drain, vent and prove gas free all gas lines and risers.

- Blank off gas line to holds as necessary.

- Set venting system to the requirements of the next cargo.

- Check hatch cover sealing arrangements and closing devices.

- Check ballast tanks, void spaces, cofferdams and pumprooms for flammable gas. Ventilate as necessary and prove gas free.

- If slops are retained, ensure designated pipeline segregations are fitted, slop tanks are fully inerted and the relevant venting system adopted as necessary.

12.14.2 Dry Bulk Cargo to Oil

- Sweep holds clean and lift cargo remains out of hold for disposal.

- Wash cargo remains off bulkheads with a high pressure water jet, stripping slowly to remove water, leaving solid residues.

- Remove solid residues from the tank top and sumps, and prove that the stripping suction is clear.

- Remove suction doors and attach securely to stowage positions.

- Close off sounding pipes to sumps as required.

- Remove blanks from main cargo suctions and stripping discharges to after hold.

- Lower, secure in place, connect and prove tight heating coils as necessary.

- Remove requisite blanks from gauging system and render fully operational.

- Wash all stripping lines thoroughly to remove solid residues.

- Open, clean and check all strainers in cargo systems.

- Check and clean hatch cover sealing arrangements, trackways etc.

- Close hatches and check sealing and bolting down arrangements.

- Remove blanks from gas lines as necessary.

- Set venting system for next cargo.

- Prove all valves and non-return valves in cargo system operational.

- Inert holds prior to loading where applicable. During inerting prove tightness of hatch covers, tank cleaning covers, access hatches and all openings into cargo spaces.

12.15 DISCHARGE OF DRY BULK CARGO

During the discharge of dry bulk cargo it may be necessary to ballast one or more holds to reduce the air draught of the ship. This is unlikely to introduce hazards if the pipeline system has been well washed. However if a pump or pipeline has not been adequately washed, the ballasting operation may discharge residual oil into the hold. Atmospheric tests in the hold (in accordance with Section 2.8.4), should therefore be made before any hot work is carried out in, adjacent to, or above a ballasted hold.

Chapter 13

Packaged Cargoes

This Chapter provides guidance about the carriage on tankers of small quantities of packaged petroleum and other flammable liquids and gases. It also refers to certain anti-knock compounds (tetraethyl lead and tetramethyl lead) which may be carried on petroleum tankers, but does not attempt to give guidance on the many hazardous chemical cargoes which may be shipped from time to time. Guidance on the properties of such cargoes may be obtained from the ICS Tanker Safety Guide (Chemicals) or from the shipper. Recommendations on handling and stowage, necessary for compliance with the SOLAS Convention and any national requirements, are given in the International Maritime Dangerous Goods (IMDG) Code.

13.1   DANGEROUS GOODS

Dangerous goods are classified in Chapter VII of the International Convention for the Safety of Life at Sea (SOLAS 1974).

The master should only permit aboard the ship packaged dangerous goods which have been properly identified by the shipper of the goods and declared as being properly packaged, marked and labelled so that they comply with the appropriate provisions of the International Maritime Dangerous Goods (IMDG) Code, taking into consideration as appropriate the IMO Recommendations on the Safe Transport, Handling and Storage of Dangerous Substances in Port Areas.

Before accepting the cargo, the master should check that he has received adequate advice on any special properties of the cargo, on procedures for entering an enclosed compartment containing the cargo, and for dealing with any leak, spill, inhalation, skin contact or fire.

> **Attention is drawn to the advice for dealing with spillage or fire contained in the IMO guide 'Emergency Procedures for Ships Carrying Dangerous Goods — Group Emergency Schedules'.**

The master should ensure that the dangerous goods loaded in the ship are properly stowed and segregated as recommended in the IMDG Code, taking into consideration as appropriate the IMO Recommendations on the Safe Transport, Handling and Storage of Dangerous Substances in Port Areas.

13.2 PETROLEUM AND OTHER FLAMMABLE LIQUIDS

13.2.1 General

The following procedures should be observed in addition to the general safety precautions for handling bulk petroleum.

13.2.2 Loading and Discharging

Packaged petroleum and other flammable liquids should not be handled during the loading of volatile petroleum in bulk except by permission of the responsible officer and the terminal representative.

13.2.3 Precautions During Handling

The handling of packaged petroleum and other flammable liquids should be supervised by a responsible officer.

The following precautions should be taken:

- Stevedores must comply with smoking restrictions and other safety regulations.

- When permanent hatch protection is not fitted, temporary protection should be provided to avoid the risk of sparks being caused by hoists striking the hatch coamings, hatch sides or hold ladders.

- All hoists should be of a size suitable for passing through hatches with ample clearance.

- Fibre rope slings, cargo nets, or drum hooks on wire rope or chain slings should be used for handling loose drums.

- Goods should preferably be palleted and secured. Pallets should be lifted with pallet lifting gear with safety nets. If goods are not presented on pallets, cargo trays or fibre rope slings may be used. Cargo nets are liable to cause damage.

- Loose gas cylinders should be handled with cargo nets of a sufficiently small mesh.

- Each package should be inspected for leakage or damage before being stowed and any found defective to an extent likely to impair its safety should be rejected.

- Packages should be placed on dunnage on the deck or in the hold.

- Packages should not be dragged across the deck or hold and should not be allowed to slide or roll free.

- Cans and drums should be stowed with caps and end plugs uppermost.

- Where required to secure the cargo, each tier should be separated by dunnage. The height to which cargo can be safely stowed should be related to the nature, size and strength of the packages. Advice should be obtained from the terminal.

- Sufficient suitable dunnage should be used to prevent possible damage during the voyage.

- Cargo should be secured to prevent any movement during the voyage.

- During darkness, adequate approved lighting should be provided overside and in the hold.

- Empty receptacles, unless gas free, should be treated in all respects as filled receptacles.

- No materials liable to spontaneous combustion should be used as dunnage or stowed in the same compartment as the packages. Attention is drawn to the combustible nature of certain protective packings such as straw, wood shavings, bitumenized paper, felts and polyurethane.

- On completion of loading or discharge and prior to closing hatches, the hold should be inspected to check that everything is in order.

13.2.4 Entry Into Holds

Before entry into any hold which contains, or which has contained, packaged petroleum and/ or other flammable liquids, all the precautions for entry into enclosed spaces should be taken (see Chapter 11). Holds should be ventilated during all cargo handling operations. If handling operations are interrupted and hatches closed, the atmosphere should again be tested before resuming work.

13.2.5 Portable Electrical Equipment

The use of portable electrical equipment (other than approved air driven lamps) should be prohibited in holds or spaces containing packaged petroleum or other flammable liquids, or on deck or in spaces over or adjacent to such holds or spaces, unless the ship complies with the conditions for the use of such equipment on tankers (see Section 2.4).

13.2.6 Smothering Type Fire Extinguishing Systems

When packaged petroleum or other flammable liquids are being handled, the control valves of any smothering system in the holds should be closed and precautions taken to prevent unauthorised or accidental opening of these valves. On completion of loading or discharge operations and when hatches have been secured, any fixed smothering system that has been closed should be returned to operational readiness.

13.2.7 Fire-Fighting Precautions

In addition to the precautions outlined in Section 4.4.1, at least two fire extinguishers of the dry chemical type and fire hoses equipped with spray nozzles should be ready for use while cargo handling is taking place.

13.2.8 Centrecastle and Forecastle Spaces

Packaged petroleum or other flammable liquids should not be carried in the centrecastle and forecastle spaces or any other space unless such spaces have been specifically designed and classified for this purpose.

13.2.9 Deck Cargo

When drums or other receptacles are carried on deck they should be given some protection against the sea and weather, and normally stowed only one tier high.

All packages should be stowed well clear of all deck fittings (including tank and valve controls, fire hydrants, steam pipes, deck lines, tank washing openings, doorways and ladders), adequately dunnaged and properly secured to the vessel's structure.

13.2.10 Barges

Barge personnel should comply with the requirements of Chapter 4 as appropriate, particularly with regard to smoking, naked lights and cooking appliances, and, if alongside a tanker, with any instructions given in Section 6.11.3. Barges containing packaged petroleum or other flammable liquids should be allowed to remain alongside a tanker during the hours of darkness only if adequate safe illumination is provided and there are means of ensuring compliance with smoking restrictions and other safety requirements.

13.3 LIQUEFIED GASES

In addition to the general precautions for handling packaged petroleum and other flammable liquids given in Section 13.2, the following safeguards should be observed when handling packaged liquefied gas cargoes:

- Pressurised receptacles should be suitably protected against physical damage from other cargo, stores or equipment.

- Pressurised receptacles should not be overstowed with other heavy cargo.

- Pressurised receptacles should be stowed in such a position that the safety relief device is in communication with the vapour space within the receptacle.

- Valves should be suitably protected against any form of physical damage.

- Cylinders stowed underdeck should be in compartments or holds capable of being ventilated and away from all sources of heat, accommodation and working areas.

- Oxygen cylinders should be stowed separately from flammable gas cylinders.

Temperatures should be kept down and hold temperatures not permitted to rise above 50°C. Hold temperatures should be constantly checked, and if they approach this level the following measures should be taken:

- The cargo hold should be ventilated.

- The liquefied gas containers should be sprayed with water if loading or discharge operations are carried out in direct tropical sunlight.

- An awning should be rigged over the hold.

- The deck should be dampened down.

13.4 TETRAETHYL LEAD (TEL) AND TETRAMETHYL LEAD (TML)

Extreme care is necessary when handling anti-knock compounds because of the toxic hazards arising from skin contact or vapour inhalation. It is essential that before handling packaged cargoes of TEL and TML advice is given to the master about the nature and properties of the substances and that the recommendations contained in handbooks issued by the manufacturing companies are strictly followed.

Chapter 14

Emergency Procedures

This Chapter deals with the preparation of plans both by the terminal and by the tanker to meet an emergency that may in any way concern the cargo or cargo handling, as well as the immediate action to be taken in such an emergency. Particular attention is paid to the procedures to be followed and the action to be taken in the event of a fire, because this is potentially the most extreme type of emergency likely to be encountered, but much of the guidance is applicable in other circumstances, and it should be read with this in mind. This Chapter does not deal with rescue from enclosed spaces which is covered in Chapter 11. Additional information on fire fighting is contained in Chapter 22. Many of the following measures may be equally applicable to the control and combat of pollution.

14.1 GENERAL

All tankers and terminals should have procedures ready for immediate implementation in the event of an emergency. The procedures must anticipate and cover all types of emergency which might be encountered in the particular activities of the tanker or terminal. Although the main aim of the procedures will be to respond to a fire, all other possible emergencies such as hose or pipeline bursts, cargo overflow, pumproom flooding, men overcome by gas within tanks, breakouts of vessels, weather or blackouts, must be covered. Similarly, while the deployment of fire-fighting equipment will be prominent in any emergency procedures, equipment such as breathing apparatus, resuscitation apparatus and stretchers must also be covered, together with details of means of escape or exit.

The procedures should be familiar to the personnel involved, who should be adequately trained and clearly understand the action they would be required to take when responding to the emergency. This can best be achieved by regularly exercising the plan. Exercises will also serve to highlight the need for any revisions to be made to the plan, associated emergency procedures and further training requirements.

Care should be taken when formulating an emergency plan to ensure that procedures to alert people or to arrange equipment do not depend too heavily on one man doing a number of tasks simultaneously.

14.2 TERMINAL EMERGENCY PLAN

14.2.1 Preparation

A terminal emergency plan which covers all aspects of the action to be taken in the event of an emergency should be developed by all terminals. This plan should be drawn up in consultation with the port authority, fire brigade, police etc. and be compatible with any port emergency plan. The plan should include:

- The specific initial action to be taken by those at the location of the emergency to report, contain and overcome the incident.

- Procedures to be followed in mobilising the resources of the terminal as required by the incident.

- Alerting responsibility and procedures.

- Reporting location for personnel involved.

- Emergency organisation giving specific duties of each person.

- Communication systems.

- Control centres.

- An inventory, including location details, of emergency equipment.

Each terminal should have an emergency team whose duties involve planning, implementing and revising emergency procedures as well as executing them. An emergency plan, when formulated, must be properly documented in an emergency procedures manual which should be available to all personnel whose work is connected with the terminal. The main points of the initial response to an emergency, such as reporting and action to contain and control it, together with the location of all emergency equipment, should be conspicuously displayed on notices at all strategic locations within the terminal.

Ships alongside the terminal berths must be advised of the terminal's emergency plan, particularly:

- Alarm signals.

- Emergency escape routes.

- How to summon assistance in the event of an emergency on board.

14.2.2 Control

It is essential that the terminal emergency plan makes absolutely clear the person, or persons in order of priority, with overall responsibility for dealing with the emergency. The responsibility, under that person, for the actions of those parts of the terminal organisation which may be called upon to participate in the effort to contain and control the incident must also be clearly laid down. Failure to define lines of responsibility can easily lead to confusion and to the loss of valuable time.

It is particularly important that the role of any civil fire-fighting brigade commander is clearly stated. In some countries it is mandatory that he takes overall charge of all fire-fighting activities and the terminal's plan must reflect the true relationship between civil and terminal fire-fighting controllers before and after the arrival of the civil fire brigade on the scene.

At major terminals, an office should be designated as a control centre, ready for use in the event of emergencies. This control centre should be located at a convenient central point not adjacent to likely hazards, possibly in the main terminal office.

During an emergency the control centre should be manned by a leading representative from the terminal, port authority, fire brigade, tug company, police or other appropriate civil authority. When possible, it may also be desirable that a responsible officer from the casualty vessel be in attendance at the control centre to give advice. A public relations officer should be designated to relay information to the public.

It is essential that the persons who are to man the control centre are aware of its location and of their duty to proceed there without delay immediately they are alerted. All other alerted personnel should also report to the main control centre unless another location is specified in the emergency plan.

A secondary unit, the forward control, may be needed, particularly in the case of major fires, to take charge of operations at the site of the incident, under the overall command of the control centre. The forward control should be manned by an emergency team trained in emergency techniques and completely familiar with their duties.

To fulfil its purposes the control centre must have good means of communication (see Sections 14.2.3, 14.2.4 and 14.2.5). It should also be equipped with;

- The terminal emergency plan.

- A prepared list of human and material resources and their location.

- Tape recorder (radio and telephone calls should be recorded).

- Technical information on the installations, etc.

14.2.3 Communications

The control centre should be capable of directing, co-ordinating and controlling, either directly or through the forward control, all fire-fighting and other emergency activities, including advice to shipping. For these purposes it must have a communications system linking it with:

Within the terminal:

- Fire service (shore and afloat).

- Personnel.

- Medical service.

Outside the terminal:

- Fire service.

- Medical service.

- Harbour authorities.

- Tugs and launches.

- Pilots.

- Police.

- Other appropriate civil authorities.

It may not in practice be possible for small terminals to implement all the recommendations regarding communications which follow, but they should endeavour to deploy a communications system adequate for their requirements, including a fire alarm.

Reliable communications are essential in dealing successfully with emergency situations. Because of their importance, consideration should be given to setting up a secondary system to take over if the main system is put out of action.

14.2.4 Communications System

The purpose of the system should be to handle:

- The sounding of the terminal fire alarm.

- The summoning of assistance.

- The co-ordination and control of all fire-fighting and emergency activities, including movement of vessels.

The communications system must have the flexibility to cover operations:

- On a tanker.

- On a jetty.

- On adjacent water.

- Elsewhere in the terminal.

Most of the equipment should therefore be portable or mobile, particularly that for use by the forward control. Moreover, it should be of a type approved for any location in which it is likely to be used. The most satisfactory system to meet all these requirements is a UHF/VHF transceiver system. Tugs, water-borne fire-fighting equipment and designated rescue launches, if available, should be permanently fitted with UHF/VHF transceiver equipment capable of operation on the channel designated for emergency use. This channel or channels should be made known to relevant personnel involved in the emergency.

As fire-fighting tugs may be used for either the movement of ships or fire-fighting, they should have at least two separate UHF/VHF channels. When fire-fighting, tugs must be in direct communication with and under the control of the senior fire-fighting officer in charge.

For communication links from the control centre, the following are typical methods:

Internal fire service	Special fire alarm and normal communication system.
Forward control	UHF/VHF transceiver; normal communication system in reserve.
Personnel and internal medical services	Normal communication system.
Fire-fighting craft and rescue launches	UHF/VHF transceiver; via harbour or port authorities as reserve.
Ships at berths	Normal UHF/VHF transceiver link used in cargo handling operations. There may be occasions when it would be helpful to station a terminal man with a portable radio on a tanker at a berth.
Civil authorities including fire services, police and medical services	Direct telephone link with failure alarm, UHF/VHF transceiver or public telephone system.
Harbour authorities, pilots, tugs and other harbour craft	UHF/VHF transceiver and public telephone system.

In order to avoid the public telephone system being swamped by incoming telephone calls, an unlisted outgoing only public telephone should be installed in the control room.

14.2.5 Communications Discipline

All personnel should understand and appreciate the necessity for strictly observing rules laid down for using communication links in an emergency. They should receive frequent instruction on such requirements, which should include the following:

- All sections to be allocated a call sign which should always be used to identify the section concerned.

- Calls, announcements and conversations to be as brief as possible consistent with intelligibility.

- Calls, announcements and conversations to be interrupted only when the demands of another section are vital to the outcome of the emergency operation.

- Calls from the control centre to take priority over all other calls.

- Only persons authorised to do so under the terminal emergency plan to use the communications system.

A log of the incident, communications and primary events should be kept at the control centre.

14.2.6 Fire-Fighting Equipment Plan

A fire-fighting equipment plan showing clearly the location and particulars of all fire-fighting equipment on or immediately adjacent to the berth should be permanently displayed on the berth.

14.2.7 Access to Equipment

Fixed and portable fire-fighting equipment, resuscitation equipment etc. should be kept free of obstructions at all times.

14.2.8 Vehicle Movement and Control

Jetty approaches and jetty heads should be kept free of obstructions to the movement of vehicles at all times. Packaged cargo or stores for a ship should therefore not be stacked on the jetty in the path of what will be the direct access in the event of an emergency. Vehicles permitted onto a jetty or a jetty approach should not be immobilised and ignition keys should not be removed unless in a designated car park not forming part of an emergency turning or passing area. Escape routes should be clearly identified. Where possible a one-way traffic system should be considered.

During an emergency, traffic into a terminal or on to berths must be strictly limited to vehicles required to deal with the emergency or to render assistance. When available, and if it is practicable, local police should be requested to exercise control well outside the terminal so that the roads which converge on the terminal are kept free for essential traffic movement.

14.2.9 Use of Municipal and Port Services

A terminal emergency plan should make the best possible use of the services which can be relied upon to be available. In such circumstances, success in dealing with an emergency could depend upon the degree of co-operation achieved and upon prior combined training carried out with these services. Frequent opportunities should be taken to have combined exercises simulating terminal emergencies.

If a terminal is located in an area where a concentration of industry exists, it may be practicable to sponsor a mutual assistance plan.

14.2.10 Harbour Authorities, Police and Fire Services

All emergencies should be reported to the harbour authority.

Any emergency that requires, or might require, assistance beyond the resources of the terminal should immediately be reported to the local fire services or the local police.

14.2.11 Pilots

If, in an emergency, the partial or total evacuation of jetties is decided upon, the local pilotage organisations may be called upon at short notice to provide a number of pilots to advise on the handling of ships not involved.

14.2.12 Tugs

If tugs are used to berth or unberth tankers at a terminal, all or some of them may be fitted with fire-fighting equipment specially designed to fight fires on tankers at the terminal berths or on the terminal itself, and they may also be equipped to pump fire-fighting water into the terminal's fire main system.

Where the fire-fighting capability of tugs is part of a terminal's planned response to fires on tankers or on the terminal itself, they must be made available as soon as they are required if their contribution is to be effective. Arrangements must be made with the pilots so that, should these tugs be assisting a ship berthing or unberthing at the terminal or in some other part of the harbour when a fire emergency occurs, they can be released in the shortest possible time to assist in fire-fighting. When these tugs are idle between routine tasks, they must be moored with easily slipped moorings, within easy reach and, where possible, within sight of the terminal, and must keep a continuous radio and visual watch on the terminal. Where the attendance of these fire-fighting tugs at a fire cannot be assured within a reasonable time scale, their contribution to the fire-fighting plans of the terminal should be downgraded accordingly.

The decision to use tugs to assist in fighting a fire on a tanker or on the terminal, or to use them to sail other vessels in danger of becoming involved, should be made by the person in overall charge of the fire-fighting and in conjunction with the harbour authority. Fire-fighting tugs should be equipped with UHF/VHF radio with separate channels for towing and fire-fighting and, when fire-fighting, they must be in direct contact with and under the control of the person in overall charge of the fire-fighting. Tugs should not fight fires independently of the person in charge of fire-fighting as this could impede his fire-fighting strategy.

Tugs with fire-fighting equipment should be inspected regularly to ensure that their equipment and foam compound stocks are in good condition. Tests of the fire pump and monitors should be carried out weekly. The foam filling points on the tugs must be kept clear so as to be immediately ready for use.

A decision should be made as part of the terminal emergency plan as to whether trained fire fighters should board the tug or whether the crew will be used for fire-fighting duties. The decision should be supported with appropriate training for the chosen fire fighters (see Section 14.2.17).

14.2.13 Rescue Launches

A launch or launches, if available, should be detailed in an emergency to provide for:

- The recovery of personnel who may be in the water.

- The evacuation of personnel trapped on a tanker or on a berth.

Launches detailed for these duties should have the following equipment:

- A communication link capable of being integrated into the control centre communication system.

- Fixed or portable searchlights for operations during darkness or periods of reduced visibility.

- Blankets, as personnel recovered from the water are likely to be suffering from cold and shock.

- Portable boarding ladders to facilitate entry into the launch; personnel in the water may have little or no reserve energy and may be unable to help themselves.

- Self contained breathing apparatus.

- Resuscitation equipment.

The crews of the launches should receive instruction in rescuing survivors from the water, bearing in mind that these may be seriously injured or suffering from extensive burns. They should also receive instruction in artificial respiration. Launch crews should be made aware that survival time in water could be very short and the prompt rescue of personnel is therefore important.

14.2.14 Medical Facilities

Terminal and outside medical facilities should be alerted at once depending upon the nature of the emergency. As soon as possible they should be told:

- The nature and location of the emergency.

- The likelihood or number of casualties.

- Whether medical staff are required at the location of the emergency.

As soon as details of casualties are known, they should be passed to the appropriate medical authorities, together with their names if available.

14.2.15 Harbour Authorities and Vessel Traffic Control Centres

The local harbour authority and vessel traffic control centre, if there is one, should be informed of any emergency involving the terminal, or ships berthed or moored at the terminal, with details of:

- The nature and extent of the emergency.

- The nature of the ship or ships involved, with locations and cargo details.

- The nature of assistance required.

This information will be required to enable the harbour authority and vessel traffic control centre to decide whether to restrict navigation within the port area or to close the port.

14.2.16 Emergency Removal of a Tanker From a Berth

If a fire on a tanker or on a berth cannot be controlled it may be necessary to consider whether or not the tanker should be removed from the berth. Planning for such an eventuality may require consultation between a port authority representative or harbour master, the responsible terminal official, the master of the tanker and the senior local authority fire officer. The plan should stress the need to avoid precipitate action which might increase, rather than lessen, the danger to the personnel, the tanker, the terminal, other ships berthed nearby and other adjacent installations.

If it is necessary to remove from a berth a tanker which may be on fire, the circumstances may be such that the ship's crew is unable to assist. The terminal emergency plan should therefore make provision for manpower for closing valves, disconnecting hoses or arms, unmooring the tanker and for operating fire-fighting equipment without assistance from the tanker's personnel. (see Section 3.7).

The plan should cover:

- Designation of the person, or persons in order of priority, with the authority to decide whether or not to remove a tanker which is on fire from its berth.

- Action to be taken with respect to ships at other berths.

- Designation of safe locations to which a tanker on fire can be moved under controlled conditions, if it is decided to move the ship.

The decision whether to remove a tanker under controlled conditions or to retain it at the berth should, in the first instance, be based on the preservation of life, but can also involve consideration of:

- The capability of fire-fighting equipment at the terminal and readily available from nearby sources.

- The availability of tugs to assist in removing the tanker from the berth.

- The ability of the tanker to move under its own power.

- The availability of safe locations to which a tanker on fire can proceed or be towed and possibly beached.

- The availability of adequate fire-fighting equipment and personnel to fight a fire if a tanker is towed to a safe, and probably remote, location.

- The proximity of other ships at the terminal.

- The shipping and other facilities in the area and the possibility of closure of the port for a period.

- The availability of equipment for controlling any pollution.

- The relative investment and earning capacity of the tanker and of the terminal facilities that could become inoperative or be destroyed by the fire.

14.2.17 Training and Drills

The degree of training given to terminal personnel in fire prevention and fire-fighting may depend upon whether there is a permanent fire-fighting unit attached to the terminal or to a plant nearby, or whether arrangements have been made for speedy assistance from an outside source.

Selected terminal personnel should receive instruction in the use of the fire-fighting and emergency equipment available at the terminal. All personnel working at terminals should receive instruction in fire prevention and in basic fire-fighting techniques. Periodic refresher training should be provided, supplemented by fire drills.

Crews of tugs which can be used for fire-fighting should receive instruction and training in fighting oil fires in co-operation with land-based fire-fighting services. In order to utilise fully the tugs' fire-fighting equipment and capability during an emergency, it may be necessary to supplement the crew with trained shore personnel. Opportunities should be provided at frequent intervals for combined practices involving the tugs and shore fire-fighting services.

Opportunities may arise whereby a combined fire practice or conference can be arranged between shore personnel and crew members of a tanker at a berth without imposing an operational delay on either the terminal or the tanker. This would help to make the tanker personnel familiar with the fire-fighting equipment ashore. Shore personnel would also have the opportunity of becoming familiar with the types and locations of fire-fighting equipment on board and of being instructed in any design features on tankers which may require special attention in case of fire.

14.3 TANKER EMERGENCY PLAN

14.3.1 Preparation

Planning and preparation are essential if personnel are to deal successfully with emergencies on board tankers. The master and other officers should consider what they would do in the event of various types of emergency, such as fire in cargo tanks, fire in the engine room, fire in the accommodation, the collapse of a person in a tank, the ship breaking adrift from her berth, the emergency release of a tanker from her berth etc.

They will not be able to foresee in detail what might occur in all such emergencies but good advance planning will result in quicker and better decisions and a well organised reaction to the situation. (see Section 3.7)

The following information should be readily available:

- Type of cargo, amount and disposition.

- Whereabouts of other hazardous substances.

- General arrangement plan.

- Stability information.

- Fire-fighting equipment plans.

14.3.2 Emergency Organisation

An emergency organisation should be set up which will come into operation in the event of an emergency. The purpose of this organisation will be in each situation to:

- Raise the alarm.

- Locate and assess the incident and possible dangers.

- Organise manpower and equipment.

The following suggestions are for guidance in planning an emergency organisation, which should cover the following four elements:

Command Centre
There should be one group in control of the response to the emergency with the master or the senior officer on board in charge. The command centre should have means of internal and external communication.

Emergency Party
This group should be under the command of a senior officer and should assess the emergency and report to the command centre on the situation, advising what action should be taken and what assistance should be provided, either from on board or, if the ship is in port, from ashore.

Back up Emergency Party
The back up emergency party under the command of an officer should stand by to assist the emergency party as instructed by the command centre and to provide back up services, e.g. equipment, stores, medical services including cardio-pulmonary resuscitation etc.

Engineering Group
This group should be under the command of the chief engineer or the senior engineering officer on board and should provide emergency assistance as instructed by the command centre. The prime responsibility for dealing with any emergency in the main machinery spaces will probably rest with this group. It may be called on to provide additional manpower elsewhere.

The plan should ensure that all arrangements apply equally well in port and at sea.

14.3.3 Preliminary Action

The person who discovers the emergency must raise the alarm and pass on information about the situation to the officer on duty who, in turn, must alert the emergency organisation. While this is being done, those on the scene should attempt immediate measures to control the emergency until the emergency organisation takes effect.

Each group in the emergency organisation should have a designated assembly point, as should those persons not directly involved as members of any group. Personnel not directly involved should stand by to act as required.

14.3.4 Ship's Fire Alarm Signal

At a terminal the sounding of the ship's fire alarm system should be supplemented by a series of long blasts on the ship's whistle, each blast being not less than 10 seconds in duration, or by some other locally required signal.

14.3.5 Fire-Fighting Equipment Plans

Fire-fighting equipment plans must be permanently displayed in prominent positions showing clearly, for each deck, the location and particulars of all fire-fighting equipment, dampers, controls, etc. These plans should also be displayed, or be readily available, at the access points to the ship when it is in port.

14.3.6 Inspection and Maintenance

Fire-fighting equipment should always be ready for immediate use and should be checked frequently. The dates and details of such checks should be recorded and indicated on the appliance as appropriate. The inspection of all fire-fighting and other emergency equipment should be carried out by a responsible officer, and any necessary maintenance work completed without delay. As soon as possible after an incident there should be a thorough check of all the equipment used. All breathing apparatus used should be checked and the bottles recharged. Foam systems should be flushed through etc.

14.3.7 Training and Drills

Ship's personnel should be familiar with the theory of fire-fighting outlined in Chapter 22 and should receive instruction in the use of fire-fighting and emergency equipment. Practices and drills should be arranged at intervals to ensure that personnel retain their familiarity with the equipment.

If an opportunity arises for a combined fire practice or conference with shore personnel at a terminal (see Section 14.2.17) the master should make an officer available to show the shore personnel the location of portable and fixed fire-fighting equipment on board and also to instruct them on any design features of the ship which may require special attention in case of fire.

14.4 FIRE ON A TANKER AT SEA OR AT ANCHOR

Ship's personnel who discover an outbreak of fire must immediately raise the alarm, indicating the location of the fire. The ship's fire alarm must be operated as soon as possible.

Personnel in the vicinity of the fire should apply the nearest suitable extinguishing agent to attempt to limit the spread of the fire, to extinguish it, and thereafter to prevent re-ignition. If they are unsuccessful, their actions should very quickly be superseded by the operation of the tanker's emergency plan.

Any cargo, ballast, tank cleaning or bunkering operations should be stopped immediately and all valves closed. Any craft alongside should be removed.

After all personnel have been evacuated from the vicinity, all doors, openings and tank apertures should be closed as quickly as possible and mechanical ventilation should be stopped. Decks, bulkheads and other structures in the vicinity of the fire, and adjacent tanks which contain petroleum liquids or are not gas free, should be cooled with water.

The tanker should be manoeuvred so as to resist the spread of the fire and allow it to be attacked from windward.

14.5 FIRE ON A TANKER AT A TERMINAL

14.5.1 Action by Ship's Personnel

If a fire breaks out on a tanker while at a terminal, the tanker must raise the alarm by sounding the recognised alarm signal consisting of a series of long blasts on the ship's whistle, each blast being not less than 10 seconds in duration, unless the terminal has notified the ship of some other locally recognised alarm signal. All cargo, bunkering, or ballasting operations must be stopped and the main engines and steering gear brought to a stand by condition.

Once the alarm has been raised, responsibility for fighting the fire on board the ship will rest with the master or other responsible officer assisted by the ship's crew. The same emergency organisation should be used as when the ship is at sea (see Section 14.3.2) with an additional group under the command of an officer or senior rating to make preparations, where possible, for disconnecting metal arms or hoses from the manifold.

On mobilisation of the terminal and, where applicable, the civil fire-fighting forces and equipment, the master or other responsible officer, in conjunction with the professional fire fighters, must make a united effort to bring the fire under control.

14.5.2 Action by Terminal Personnel

On hearing a tanker sounding its fire alarm, the person in charge of a berth must immediately advise the control room. The control room personnel will sound the terminal fire alarm, inform the port authority and commence shutting down any loading, discharging, bunkering or deballasting operations which may be taking place.

The terminal's fire emergency plan will be activated and this may involve shutting down cargo, bunkering, and ballast handling operations on ships on adjacent or neighbouring berths. All other ships at the terminal should be informed of the emergency and, where considered necessary, make preparations to disconnect metal arms or hoses and bring their engines and steering gear to a state of readiness.

Where there are fire-fighting tugs, the terminal control room will summon them to assist in fighting the fire until a decision is made by the person in overall control whether or not to use them to assist in the evacuation of unaffected ships (see Section 14.2.16 for the emergency removal of a tanker on fire from a berth).

The terminal control room will be responsible for summoning any outside assistance such as the civil fire brigade, rescue launches, medical aid and ambulances, police, harbour authority and pilots.

14.6 FIRE OR EXPLOSION ON A BERTH

14.6.1 Action by Vessels

Should a fire or explosion occur on a berth, the ship or ships at the berth must immediately report the incident to the terminal control room by the quickest possible method (VHF/UHF/ telephone contact, sounding ship's siren etc.); shut down all cargo, bunkering, deballasting and tank cleaning operations; and drain all arms or hoses ready for disconnecting. The ships' fire mains should be pressurised and water fog applied in strategic places. The ships' engines, steering gear and unmooring equipment must be brought to a state of immediate readiness. A pilot ladder should be put over on the offshore side.

14.6.2 Action by Vessels at Other Berths

On hearing the terminal alarm being sounded or on being otherwise advised of a fire at the terminal, a ship whose berth is not involved in the fire should shut down all cargo, bunkering and ballasting operations; bring her fire-fighting capability to a state of readiness; and make engines, steering gear and mooring equipment ready for immediate use.

14.7 JETTISON OF CARGO

The jettison of cargo is an extreme measure justified only as a means of saving life at sea or for the safety of the vessel. A decision to jettison cargo should therefore not be taken until all the alternative options have been considered in the light of available information on stability and reserve buoyancy.

If it is necessary to jettison cargo the following precautions should be taken:

- Engine room personnel should be alerted. Depending on the circumstances prevailing at the time, consideration should be given to changing over engine room intakes from high to low level.

- Discharge should take place through the sea valve and where possible on the side opposite to the engine room intakes.

- All non-essential inlets should be closed.

- If discharge must be from the deck level, flexible hoses should be rigged to extend below the water surface.

- All safety precautions relating to normal operations which involve the presence of flammable gas in the vicinity of the deck must be observed.

- A radio warning should be broadcast.

Part II

Technical Information

Chapter 15

Basic Properties of Petroleum

This Chapter describes the physical and chemical properties which have the greatest bearing on the hazards arising from handling petroleum liquids. These properties are vapour pressure, the flammability of the gases evolved from the liquids and the density of these gases.

15.1 VAPOUR PRESSURE

15.1.1 True Vapour Pressure

All crude oils and the usual petroleum products are essentially mixtures of a wide range of hydrocarbon compounds (i.e. chemical compounds of hydrogen and carbon). The boiling points of these compounds range from – 162°C (methane) to well in excess of +400°C, and the volatility of any particular mixture of compounds depends primarily on the quantities of the more volatile constituents (i.e. those with a lower boiling point).

The volatility (i.e. the tendency of a crude oil or petroleum product to produce gas) is characterised by the vapour pressure. When a petroleum mixture is transferred to a gas free tank or container it commences to vaporise, that is, it liberates gas into the space above it. There is also a tendency for this gas to re-dissolve in the liquid, and an equilibrium is ultimately reached with a certain amount of gas evenly distributed throughout the space. The pressure exerted by this gas is called the equilibrium vapour pressure of the liquid, usually referred to simply as the vapour pressure.

The vapour pressure of a pure compound depends only upon its temperature. The vapour pressure of a mixture depends on its temperature, constituents and the volume of the gas space in which vaporisation occurs; that is, it depends upon the ratio of gas to liquid by volume.

The True Vapour Pressure (TVP) or bubble point vapour pressure is the equilibrium vapour pressure of a mixture when the gas/liquid ratio is effectively zero. It is the highest vapour pressure which is possible at any specified temperature.

As the temperature of a petroleum mixture increases its TVP also increases. If the TVP exceeds atmospheric pressure the liquid commences to boil.

The TVP of a petroleum mixture provides a good indication of its ability to give rise to gas. Unfortunately it is a property which is extremely difficult to measure, although it can be calculated from a detailed knowledge of the composition of the liquid. For crude oils it can also be estimated from the stabilisation conditions, making allowance for any subsequent changes of temperature or composition. In the case of products, reliable correlations exist for deriving TVP from the more readily measured Reid Vapour Pressure and temperature.

15.1.2 Reid Vapour Pressure

The Reid Vapour Pressure (RVP) test is a simple and generally used method for measuring the volatility of petroleum liquids. It is conducted in a standard apparatus and in a closely defined way. A sample of the liquid is introduced into the test container at atmospheric pressure so that the volume of the liquid is one fifth of the total internal volume of the container. The container is sealed and immersed in a water bath where it is heated to 37.8°C. After the container has been shaken to bring about equilibrium conditions rapidly, the rise in pressure due to vaporisation is read on an attached pressure gauge. This pressure gauge reading gives a close approximation, in bars, to the vapour pressure of the liquid at 37.8°C.

RVP is useful for comparing the volatilities of a wide range of petroleum liquids in a general way. It is, however, of little value in itself as a means of estimating the likely gas evolution in specific situations, mainly because the measurement is made at the standard temperature of 37.8°C and at a fixed gas/liquid ratio. For this purpose TVP is much more useful; as already mentioned, in some cases correlations exist between TVP, RVP and temperature.

15.2 FLAMMABILITY

15.2.1 General

In the process of burning, hydrocarbon gases react with the oxygen in the air to produce carbon dioxide and water. The reaction gives enough heat to form a flame which travels through the mixture of hydrocarbon gas and air. When the gas above a liquid hydrocarbon is ignited the heat produced is usually enough to evaporate sufficient fresh gas to maintain the flame, and the liquid is said to burn; in fact it is the gas which is burning and is being continuously replenished from the liquid.

15.2.2 Flammable Limits

A mixture of hydrocarbon gas and air cannot be ignited and burn unless its composition lies within a range of gas in air concentrations known as the 'flammable range'. The lower limit of this range, known as the lower flammable limit (LFL), is that hydrocarbon concentration below which there is insufficient hydrocarbon gas to support and propagate combustion. The upper limit of the range, known as the upper flammable limit (UFL), is that hydrocarbon concentration above which there is insufficient air to support and propagate combustion.

The flammable limits vary somewhat for different pure hydrocarbon gases and for the gas mixtures derived from different petroleum liquids. Very roughly the gas mixtures from crude oils, motor or aviation gasolines and natural gasoline type products can be represented respectively by the pure hydrocarbon gases propane, butane and pentane. Table 15-1 gives the flammable limits for these three gases. It also shows the amount of dilution with air needed to bring a mixture of 50% by volume of each of these gases in air down to its LFL; this type of information is very relevant to the ease with which vapours disperse to a non-flammable concentration in the atmosphere.

Gas	Flammable limits % vol. hydrocarbon in air		Number of dilutions by air to reduce 50% by volume mixture to LFL
	Upper	Lower	
Propane	9.5	2.2	23
Butane	8.5	1.9	26
Pentane	7.8	1.5	33

Table 15-1 *Flammable Limits, Propane, Butane, Pentane*

In practice the lower and upper flammable limits of oil cargoes carried in tankers can, for general purposes, be taken as 1% and 10% by volume respectively.

15.2.3 Effect of Inert Gas on Flammability

When an inert gas, typically flue gas, is added to a hydrocarbon gas/air mixture the result is to increase the lower flammable limit hydrocarbon concentration and to decrease the upper flammable limit concentration. These effects are illustrated in Fig. 15-1, which should be regarded only as a guide to the principles involved.

Every point on the diagram represents a hydrocarbon gas/air/inert gas mixture, specified in terms of its hydrocarbon and oxygen contents. Hydrocarbon gas/air mixtures without inert gas lie on the line AB, the slope of which reflects the reduction in oxygen content as the hydrocarbon contents increases. Points to the left of AB represent mixtures with their oxygen content further reduced by the addition of inert gas.

The lower and upper flammability limit mixtures for hydrocarbon gas in air are represented by the points C and D. As the inert gas content increases, the flammable limit mixtures change as indicated by the lines CE and DE, which finally converge at the point E. Only those mixtures represented by points in the shaded area within the loop CED are capable of burning.

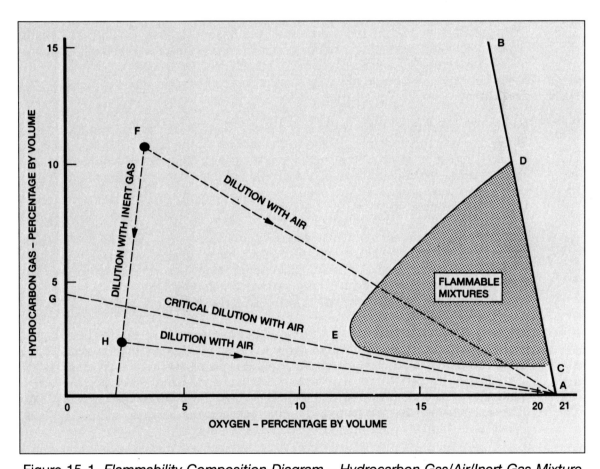

Figure 15-1. *Flammability Composition Diagram – Hydrocarbon Gas/Air/Inert Gas Mixture*

This diagram is illustrative only and should not be used for deciding upon acceptable gas compositions in practical cases.

On such a diagram, changes of composition due to the addition of either air or inert gas are represented by movements along straight lines directed either towards the point A (pure air), or towards a point on the oxygen content axis corresponding to the composition of the added inert gas. Such lines are shown for the gas mixture represented by the point F.

It is evident from Fig. 15-1 that as inert gas is added to hydrocarbon gas/air mixtures the flammable range progressively decreases until the oxygen content reaches a level, generally taken to be about 11% by volume, when no mixture can burn. The figure of 8% by volume of oxygen specified in this guide for a safely inerted gas mixture allows a margin beyond this value.

When an inerted mixture, such as that represented by the point F, is diluted by air its composition moves along the line FA and therefore enters the shaded area of flammable mixtures. This means that all inerted mixtures in the region above the line GA go through a flammable condition as they are mixed with air, for example during a gas freeing operation. Those below the line GA, such as that represented by point H, do not become flammable on dilution. Note that it is possible to move from a mixture such as F to one such as H by dilution with additional inert gas (i.e. purging to remove hydrocarbon gas).

15.2.4 Tests for Flammability

Since hydrocarbon gas/air mixtures are flammable within a comparatively narrow range of concentrations of hydrocarbon gas in air, and concentration in air is dependent upon vapour pressure, it should in principle be possible to evolve a test for flammability by measuring vapour pressure. In practice, the very wide range of petroleum products and the range of temperatures over which they are handled has prevented the development of one simple test for this purpose.

Instead the oil industry makes use of two standard methods. One is the Reid Vapour Pressure test (see Section 15.1.2) and the other is the flashpoint test, which measures flammability directly. However, with some residual fuel oils it has been shown that the flashpoint test will not always provide a direct indication of flammability (see Chapter 24).

15.2.5 Flashpoint

In this test a sample of the liquid is gradually heated in a special pot and a small flame is repeatedly and momentarily applied to the surface of the liquid. The flashpoint is the lowest liquid temperature at which the small flame initiates a flash of flame across the surface of the liquid, thereby indicating the presence of a flammable gas/air mixture above the liquid. For all oils, except some residual fuel oils, this gas/air mixture corresponds closely to the lower flammable limit mixture.

There are many different forms of flashpoint apparatus but they fall into two classes. In one the surface of the liquid is permanently open to the atmosphere as the liquid is heated and the result of such a test is known as an 'open cup flashpoint'. In the other class, the space above the liquid is kept closed except for brief moments when the initiating flame is introduced through a small port. The result of this class of test is termed a 'closed cup flashpoint'.

Because of the greater loss of gas to atmosphere in the open cup test the open cup flashpoint of a petroleum liquid is always a little higher (by about 6°C) than its closed cup flashpoint. The restricted loss of gas in the closed cup apparatus also leads to a much more repeatable result than can be obtained in open cup testing. For this reason, the closed cup method is now more generally favoured and is used in this guide in the classification of petroleum. Open cup test figures, however, may still be found in the legislation of various national administrations, in classification society rules and other such documents.

15.2.6 Flammability Classification of Petroleum

There are many schemes for dividing the complete range of petroleum liquids into different flammability classes based on flashpoint and vapour pressure and there is a considerable variation in these schemes between countries. Usually the basic principle is to consider whether or not a flammable equilibrium gas/air mixture can be formed in the space above the liquid when the liquid is at ambient temperature.

Generally in this guide it has been sufficient to group petroleum liquids into two categories entitled non-volatile and volatile, defined in terms of flashpoint as follows:

Non-volatile

Flashpoint of 60°C or above as determined by the closed cup method of testing. These liquids produce, when at any normal ambient temperature, equilibrium gas concentrations below the lower flammable limit. They include distillate fuel oils, heavy gas oils and diesel oils. Their RVPs are below 0.007 bar and are not usually measured.

Volatile

Flashpoint below 60°C as determined by the closed cup method of testing. Some petroleum liquids in this category are capable of producing an equilibrium gas/air mixture within the flammable range when in some part of the normal ambient temperature range, while most of the rest give equilibrium gas/air mixtures above the upper flammable limit at all normal ambient temperatures. Examples of the former are jet fuels and kerosenes and of the latter gasolines and most crude oils. In practice, gasolines and crude oils are frequently handled before equilibrium conditions have been attained and gas/air mixtures in the flammable range may then be present.

The choice of 60°C as the flashpoint criterion for the division between non-volatile and volatile liquids, is to some extent arbitrary. Since less stringent precautions are appropriate for non-volatile liquids it is essential that under no circumstances is a liquid capable of giving a flammable gas/air mixture ever inadvertently included in the non-volatile category. The dividing line must therefore be chosen to make allowance for such factors as the misjudging of the temperature, inaccuracy in the flashpoint measurement and the possibility of minor contamination by more volatile materials. The closed cup flashpoint figure of 60°C makes ample allowances for these factors and is also compatible with the definitions adopted internationally by the International Maritime Organization (IMO) and by a number of regulatory bodies throughout the world. (See Chapter 24 for information on the relationship between the flashpoint and flammability of residual fuel oils.)

15.3   DENSITY OF HYDROCARBON GASES

The densities of the gas mixtures evolved from the normal petroleum liquids, when undiluted with air, are all greater than the density of air. Layering effects are therefore encountered in cargo handling operations and can give rise to hazardous situations.

The following table gives gas densities relative to air for the three pure hydrocarbon gases, propane, butane and pentane, which represent roughly the gas mixtures that are produced respectively by crude oils, by motor or aviation gasolines and by natural gasolines. These figures are not significantly changed if inert gas is substituted for air.

Gas	Density relative to air		
	Pure hydrocarbon	50% by volume hydrocarbon/50% by volume air	Lower flammable limit mixture
Propane	1.55	1.25	1.0
Butane	2.0	1.5	1.0
Pentane	2.5	1.8	1.0

Table 15-2 *Propane, Butane, Pentane: Densities Relative to Air*

It will be seen that the density of the undiluted gas from a product such as motor gasoline is likely to be about twice that of air, and that from a typical crude oil about 1.5 times. These high densities, and the layering effects that result from them, are only significant while the gas remains concentrated. As it is diluted with air the density of the gas/air mixture from all three types of cargo approaches that of air, and at the lower flammable limit is indistinguishable from it.

Chapter 16

Toxicity of Petroleum and Associated Substances

The toxicity hazards of petroleum and its products are described in this Chapter, together with those of inert gas. Although not strictly a matter of toxicity, the effects of oxygen deficiency are also described.

16.1 GENERAL

The toxic hazards to which personnel are exposed in tanker operations arise almost entirely from exposure to gases of various kinds.

A number of indicators are used to measure the concentrations of toxic vapours and many substances have been assigned Permissible Exposure Limits (PELs) and/or Threshold Limit Values (TLVs).

The term Threshold Limit Value has been in use within the industry for a number of years and is often expressed as a Time Weighted Average (TWA). The use of the term Permissible Exposure Limit is becoming more commonplace and refers to the maximum exposure to a toxic substance that is allowed by an appropriate regulatory body. The PEL is usually expressed as a Time Weighted Average, normally averaged over an eight hour period, or as a Short Term Exposure Limit (STEL), normally expressed as a maximum airborne concentration averaged over a 15 minute period. The values are expressed as parts per million (ppm) by volume of gas in air.

16.2 LIQUID PETROLEUM

16.2.1 Ingestion

The risk of swallowing significant quantities of liquid petroleum during normal tanker and terminal operations is very slight. Petroleum has low oral toxicity to man, but when swallowed it causes acute discomfort and nausea. There is then a possibility that liquid petroleum may be drawn into the lungs during vomiting and this can have serious consequences, especially with higher volatility products such as gasolines and kerosenes.

16.2.2 Skin Contact

Many petroleum products, especially the more volatile ones, cause skin irritation and remove essential oils from the skin, leading to dermatitis. They are also irritating to the eyes. Certain heavier oils can cause serious skin disorders on repeated and prolonged contact.

Direct contact with petroleum should always be avoided by wearing the appropriate protective equipment, especially impervious gloves and goggles.

16.3 PETROLEUM GASES

The main effect of petroleum gas on personnel is to produce narcosis. The symptoms include headache and eye irritation, with diminished responsibility and dizziness similar to drunkenness. At high concentrations these lead to paralysis, insensibility and death.

The toxicity of petroleum gases can vary widely depending on the major hydrocarbon constituents of the gases. Toxicity can be greatly influenced by the presence of some minor components such as aromatic hydrocarbons (e.g. benzene) and hydrogen sulphide. A TLV of 300 ppm, corresponding to about 2% LFL, is established for gasoline vapours. Such a figure may be used as a general guide for petroleum gases but must not be taken as applicable to gas mixtures containing benzene or hydrogen sulphide.

The human body can tolerate concentrations somewhat greater than the TLV for short periods. The following are typical effects at higher concentrations:

Concentration	% LEL	Effects
0.1% vol. (1,000 ppm)	10%	Irritation of the eyes within one hour.
0.2% vol. (2,000 ppm)	20%	Irritation of the eyes, nose and throat, dizziness and unsteadiness within half an hour.
0.7% vol. (7,000 ppm)	70%	Symptoms as of drunkenness within 15 minutes.
1.0% vol. (10,000 ppm)	100%	Rapid onset of 'drunkenness' which may lead to unconsciousness and death if exposure continues.
2.0% vol. (20,000 ppm)	200%	Paralysis and death occur very rapidly.

Table 16-1: *Typical Effects of Exposure to Petroleum Gases*

The smell of petroleum gas mixtures is very variable, and in some cases the gases may dull the sense of smell. The impairment of smell is especially serious if the mixture contains hydrogen sulphide. The absence of smell should therefore never be taken to indicate the absence of gas.

The TLV concentration is considerably below the lower flammable limit and combustible gas indicators cannot be expected to measure concentrations of this order accurately.

16.4 BENZENE AND OTHER AROMATIC HYDROCARBONS

16.4.1 Aromatic Hydrocarbons

The aromatic hydrocarbons include benzene, toluene and xylene. These substances are components in varying amounts, in many typical petroleum cargoes such as, gasolines, gasoline blending components, reformates, naphthas, special boiling point solvents, turpentine substitute, white spirits and crude oil.

The health hazards of aromatic hydrocarbons are not fully established but it is recommended that personnel engaged in cargo operations involving products containing them follow the precautions and procedures described in Section 7.2.4 and 7.6.3 in order to minimise exposure due to cargo handling operations.

The Threshold Limit Value (TLV) or Permissible Exposure Limit (PEL), of an aromatic hydrocarbon vapour is generally less than that of other hydrocarbons.

16.4.2 Benzene

Repeated over exposure to high levels of benzene vapour may have chronic effects which can lead to disorders of the blood and bone marrow. Personnel engaged in operations involving the products containing benzene should therefore follow the precautions described in Section 7.2.4 in order to minimise exposure during cargo handling operations.

Benzene primarily presents an inhalation hazard. It has poor warning qualities, as its odour threshold is well above the Permissible Exposure Limit.

Exposure to concentrations in excess of 1,000 ppm can lead to unconsciousness and even death. Benzene can also be absorbed through the skin and is toxic if ingested.

- **Procedures**

Cargoes containing benzene should be handled using the closed operation procedures described in 7.6.3 as this will significantly reduce exposure to benzene vapour.

Operators should adopt procedures to verify the effectiveness of the closed loading system in reducing the concentrations of benzene vapours around the working deck.

This will involve surveys to determine the potential exposure of personnel to benzene vapour during all operations such as loading, discharging, sampling, hose handling, tank cleaning and gas freeing and gauging of cargoes containing benzene. These surveys will also need to be carried out to ascertain vapour concentrations when tank cleaning, venting or ballasting tanks whose previous cargo contained benzene.

Spot checks on vapour concentrations using detector tubes and pumps can be carried out by ship's personnel to ascertain if vapour levels are being exceeded and if personal protective equipment may need to be worn.

- **Personal Protective Equipment (PPE)**

Operators should establish procedures for the use of respiratory protective equipment where personnel are at risk of being exposed to benzene vapours in excess of Permissible Exposure Limits (PEL).

Personnel should be required to wear respiratory protective equipment under the following circumstances–

- When PEL's specified by national or international authorities are exceeded.

- When monitoring cannot be carried out.

- When closed operations cannot be conducted for any reason.

The need to use respiratory protective equipment may extend to those personnel not directly involved in cargo operations.

- **Tank Entry**

Prior to entry into a tank which has recently carried petroleum products containing benzene, the tank should initially be ventilated to a reading of not more than 1% LFL on a combustible gas indicator and then checked using the appropriate instruments to ensure that the concentration of benzene vapours do not exceed Permissible Exposure Limits.

16.5 HYDROGEN SULPHIDE

Many crude oils come out of the well with high levels of hydrogen sulphide (H_2S), but this level is usually reduced by a stabilisation process before the crude oil is delivered to the vessel. However, the amount of stabilisation may be temporarily reduced at times. Thus a tanker may receive a cargo with a hydrogen sulphide content higher than usual. In addition, some crude oils are never stabilised and always contain a high hydrogen sulphide level. Hydrogen sulphide can also be encountered in other cargoes such as naphtha, fuel oil, bitumens and gas oils.

The Permissible Exposure Limit (PEL) of hydrogen sulphide expressed as a Time Weighted Average (TWA) is 10 ppm. The effects of the gas at concentrations in air in excess of the TWA are:

Concentration	Effects
50-100 ppm	Eye and respiratory tract irritation after exposure of one hour.
200-300 ppm	Marked eye and respiratory tract irritation after exposure of one hour.
500-700 ppm	Dizziness, headache, nausea etc. within 15 minutes, loss of consciousness and possible death after 30-60 minutes exposure.
700-900 ppm	Rapid unconsciousness, death occurring a few minutes later.
1,000-2,000 ppm	Instantaneous collapse and cessation of breathing.
Note: Persons over exposed to H_2S vapour should be removed to clean air as soon as possible. The adverse effects of H_2S can be reversed and the probability of saving the person's life improved if prompt action is taken.	

Table 16-2: *Typical Effects of Exposure to Hydrogen Sulphide (H_2S)*

It is important to distinguish between concentrations of hydrogen sulphide in the atmosphere expressed in ppm by volume and concentrations in liquid expressed in ppm by weight. For example a crude oil containing 70 ppm (by weight) hydrogen sulphide has been shown to produce a concentration of 7,000 ppm (by volume) in the gas stream leaving an ullage port above the cargo tank. Thus, it is not possible to predict the likely vapour concentration from known liquid concentrations.

The following procedures should be followed when handling all cargoes containing hazardous concentrations of hydrogen sulphide:

- **Closed Operations**

    - Cargoes containing hydrogen sulphide should be handled using the closed operation procedures described in 7.6.3.

- **Vapour Monitoring**

    - Exposure of personnel to hydrogen sulphide should be monitored by using suitable instrumentation for detecting and measuring the concentration of the gas.

      Personnel, likely to be exposed to hydrogen sulphide, should be provided with personal monitoring instruments which will quickly identify if they are being exposed to high levels of hydrogen sulphide vapour.

    - Spot checks on vapour concentrations can be carried out by ship's personnel to verify that vapour levels are not being exceeded, particularly during such operations as gauging and sampling for custody transfer, connection and disconnection of pipe lines and mopping up spills. These spot checks are carried out using detector tubes, pumps or electronic instruments.

- **Personal Protective Equipment (PPE)**

    - Procedures should be defined for the use of respiratory protective equipment, when concentrations of vapour are detected by the vapour monitoring equipment. This should be implemented on a phased basis depending on the equipment available on the ship and the concentration of vapour detected.

    - Consideration should be given to providing Emergency Escape Breathing Apparatus to personnel working in hazardous areas. These are very portable and can be donned quickly if gas is detected.

- These precautions should also be observed during ballasting, tank cleaning and gas freeing operations associated with the carriage of cargoes with a hydrogen sulphide content.

Personnel should be required to wear respiratory protective equipment under the following circumstances

- When Permissible Exposure Limits specified by national or international authorities are exceeded.

- When monitoring cannot be carried out.

- When closed operations cannot be conducted for any reason and hydrogen sulphide concentrations could exceed Permissible Exposure Limits.

Prior to entry into a tank which has previously carried petroleum products containing hydrogen sulphide, the tank should initially be ventilated to a reading of not more than 1%LFL on a combustible gas indicator and then checked using the appropriate instruments to ensure that there are no detectable traces of hydrogen sulphide.

16.6 GASOLINES CONTAINING TETRAETHYL LEAD (TEL) OR TETRAMETHYL LEAD (TML)

The amounts of tetraethyl lead (TEL) or tetramethyl lead (TML) normally added to gasolines are insufficient to render the gases from these products significantly more toxic than those from unleaded gasolines. The effects of the gases from leaded gasolines are therefore similar to those described for petroleum gases in Section 16.3.

16.7 INERT GAS

16.7.1 Inert Gas – General

Inert gas is principally used to control cargo tank atmospheres and so prevent the formation of flammable mixtures. The primary requirement for an inert gas is low oxygen content. Its composition can, however, be variable and the table below provides an indication of typical inert gas components expressed as a percentage by volume:

Component	IG from main boiler flue gas
Nitrogen (N_2)	83%
Carbon dioxide (CO_2)	13%
Carbon monoxide (CO)	present
Oxygen (O_2)	4%
Sulphur dioxide (SO_2)	50 ppm
Oxides of Nitrogen (NO_x)	present
Water vapour (H_2O)	present
Ash and soot (C)	present
Dewpoint	high if not dried
Density	1.044

Table 16-3: *Inert Gas Composition*

16.7.2 Toxic Constituents

The main hazard associated with inert gas is its low oxygen content. However, inert gas produced by combustion either in a steam raising boiler or in a separate inert gas generator contains trace amounts of various toxic gases which may increase the hazard to personnel exposed to it.

The precautions necessary to protect personnel against toxic hazards are contained in Section 10.6.11. These precautions do not include requirements for direct measurement of the concentration of the trace constituents of flue gas, because gas freeing the atmosphere of a cargo tank from a hydrocarbon gas concentration of about 2% by volume to 1% LFL, and until a steady 21% by volume oxygen reading is obtained, is sufficient to dilute these constituents to below their TLVs.

16.7.3 Nitrogen Oxides

Fresh flue gases typically contain about 200 ppm by volume of mixed nitrogen oxides. The majority is nitric oxide (NO) which is not removed by water scrubbing. Nitric oxide reacts slowly with oxygen forming nitrogen dioxide (NO_2). As the gas stands in tanks the total concentration of nitrogen oxide falls over a period of 1-2 days to a level of 10-20 ppm as the more soluble nitrogen dioxide goes into solution in free water, or by condensation, to give nitrous and nitric acids. Further decrease below this level is very slow.

Nitric oxide is a colourless gas with little smell at its TLV of 25 ppm. Nitrogen dioxide is even more toxic with a TLV of 3 ppm.

16.7.4 Sulphur Dioxide

Flue gas produced by the combustion of high sulphur content fuel oils typically contains about 2,000 ppm of sulphur dioxide (SO_2). Inert gas system water scrubbers remove this gas with an efficiency which depends upon the design and operation of the scrubber, giving inert gas with sulphur dioxide content usually between 2 and 50 ppm.

Sulphur dioxide produces irritation of the eyes, nose and throat and may also cause breathing difficulties in sensitive people. It has a distinctive smell at its TLV of 2 ppm.

16.7.5 Carbon Monoxide

Carbon monoxide (CO) is normally present in flue gas at a level of only a few parts per million, but abnormal combustion conditions and slow running can give rise to levels in excess of 200 ppm. Carbon monoxide is an odourless gas with a TLV of 50 ppm. It is insidious in its attack, which is to restrict oxygen uptake by the blood, causing a chemically induced form of asphyxiation.

16.8 OXYGEN DEFICIENCY

The oxygen content of the atmosphere in enclosed spaces may be low for several reasons. The most obvious one is if the space is in an inert condition, and the oxygen has been displaced by the inert gas. Also, oxygen can be removed by chemical reactions such as rusting or the hardening of paints or coatings.

As the amount of available oxygen decreases below the normal 21% by volume breathing tends to become faster and deeper. Symptoms indicating that an atmosphere is deficient in oxygen may give inadequate notice of danger. Most persons would fail to recognise the danger until they were too weak to be able to escape without help. This is especially so when escape involves the exertion of climbing.

While individuals vary in susceptibility, all will suffer impairment if the oxygen level falls to 16% by volume.

Exposure to an atmosphere containing less than 10% oxygen content by volume inevitably causes unconsciousness. The rapidity of onset of unconsciousness increases as the availability of oxygen diminishes, and death will result unless the victim is removed to the open air and resuscitated.

An atmosphere containing less than 5% oxygen by volume causes immediate unconsciousness with no warning other than a gasp for air. If resuscitation is delayed for more than a few minutes, irreversible damage is done to the brain even if life is subsequently restored.

Entry into oxygen deficient spaces must never be permitted without breathing apparatus until such spaces have been thoroughly ventilated and test readings indicate an oxygen level of 21% by volume throughout (see Section 11.4).

Chapter 17

Hydrocarbon Gas Evolution and Dispersion

The gases evolved and vented during cargo handling and associated operations are discussed in this Chapter. The dispersion of these gases in the atmosphere is illustrated by reference to the results of wind tunnel experiments. This Chapter also describes the problems which may be encountered with high vapour pressure cargoes and the special precautions that may be taken.

17.1   INTRODUCTION

During many cargo handling and associated operations, petroleum gas is expelled from cargo tank vents in sufficient quantity to give rise to flammable gas mixtures in the atmosphere outside the tanks. In this guide, a major objective is to avoid such a flammable gas mixture being exposed to a source of ignition. In many cases this is achieved either by eliminating the source of ignition or by ensuring that there are barriers, such as closed doors and ports, between the gas and unavoidable potential sources of ignition.

However, it is impossible to cover every possibility of human error and every combination of circumstances. An additional safeguard is introduced if operations can be arranged so that petroleum gas issuing from vents is dispersed sufficiently well to avoid flammable gas mixtures reaching those areas where sources of ignition may exist.

There can be a flammability problem from gas concentrations external to cargo tanks in the case of high vapour pressure volatile cargoes, the main types of which are:

- Crude oil.

- Motor and aviation gasolines.

- Natural gasolines.

- Light distillate feedstocks (LDFs) and naphthas.

The gases from these petroleum liquids are denser than air, and this has an important bearing on how they behave both inside and outside the tanks (see Section 15.3).

The gas which is vented is formed within the tanks, and the way in which it is formed affects both the concentration when vented and the length of time during which a high concentration is vented. Situations which lead to gas evolution include loading, standing of cargo in full or part filled tanks (including slop tanks), evaporation of tank residues after discharge and crude oil washing.

The initial tank atmosphere, whether air or inert gas, has no bearing on gas evolution or venting.

17.2 GAS EVOLUTION AND VENTING

17.2.1 Evolution During Loading

As a high vapour pressure petroleum cargo enters an empty gas free tank there is a rapid evolution of gas. Because of its high density, the gas forms a layer at the bottom of the tank which rises with the oil surface as the tank is filled. Once it has been formed the depth of the layer increases only slowly over the period of time normally required to fill a tank, although ultimately an equilibrium gas mixture is established throughout the ullage space.

The amount and concentration of gas forming this layer at the beginning of loading depend upon many factors, including:

- The true vapour pressure (TVP) of the cargo.

- The amount of splashing as the oil enters the tank.

- The time required to load the tank.

- The occurrence of a partial vacuum in the loading line.

The hydrocarbon gas concentration in the layer varies with distance above the liquid surface. Very close to the surface it has a value close to that corresponding to the TVP of the adjoining liquid. For example, if the TVP is 0.75 bar the hydrocarbon has concentration just above the surface is about 75% by volume. Well above the surface the hydrocarbon gas concentration is very small, assuming that the tank was originally gas free. In order to consider further the influence of gas layer depth, it is necessary to define this depth in some way.

When considering dispersion of gases outside cargo tanks, only high gas concentrations in the vented gas are relevant. For this purpose therefore, the gas layer depth will be taken as the distance from the liquid surface to the level above it where the gas concentration is 50% by volume. It should be remembered that hydrocarbon gas will be detectable at heights above the liquid surface several times the layer depth defined in this way.

Most high vapour pressure cargoes give rise to a gas layer with a depth in these terms of less than 1 metre. Its precise depth depends upon the factors listed above, and most of the advice with respect to vented gas given in this guide is intended for such cargoes. However, gas layers greater than 1 metre in depth may be encountered if the cargo TVP is great enough. Cargoes giving rise to these deeper gas layers may require special precautions (see Section 17.6).

17.2.2 Venting During the Loading of Cargo

Once the dense hydrocarbon gas layer has formed above the surface of the liquid its depth, as defined in Section 17.2.1, increases only very slowly. As the liquid rises in the tank the hydrocarbon gas layer rises with it. Above this layer the atmosphere originally present in the tank persists almost unchanged and it is this gas which in the early stages of loading enters the venting system. In an initially gas free tank, therefore, the gas vented at first is mainly air (or inert gas) with a hydrocarbon concentration below the LFL. As loading proceeds, the hydrocarbon content of the vented gas rises.

Concentrations in the range 30%-50% by volume are quite usual in the vented gas towards the end of loading, although the very high concentration immediately above the liquid surface remains in the final ullage space on completion of loading.

Subsequently evaporation continues until an equilibrium hydrocarbon gas concentration is established throughout the ullage space. This may be very high indeed, depending upon the cargo composition and temperature; values as high as 90%-95% by volume have been observed with crude oils. However, this gas is only vented by breathing of the tank, and thus only intermittently. When the oil is discharged, this very dense gas mixture travels to the bottom of the tank with the descending liquid surface and may contribute to the gas vented during the next operation in the tank.

If the tank is not initially gas free the hydrocarbon gas concentration in the vented gas during loading depends upon the previous history of the tank. For example:

- In an unwashed crude oil tank loaded soon after discharge of a previous cargo, there is a layer of highly concentrated gas at the bottom of the tank, with hardly any hydrocarbon gas above it. This gas is expelled immediately ahead of the layer which is formed as fresh cargo enters the tank.

- In an unwashed crude oil tank after a long ballast voyage, there is a homogenous hydrocarbon gas concentration of up to 10% by volume throughout the tank. When the tank is next loaded this is the gas that is expelled until the concentrated gas layer immediately above the liquid surface begins to exert its influence. Thereafter this concentrated layer dominates the composition of the vented gas which is thereafter similar to that in an initially gas free tank.

- In a crude oil tank that has been washed or sprayed with crude oil but not subsequently purged with inert gas or gas freed, a uniform gas concentration exists throughout the tank. Depending on the crude oil used and its temperature, this concentration is usually well above the flammable range and may be as high as 40% by volume. This mixture is displaced from the tank throughout the subsequent loading until the possibly even richer gas adjacent to the liquid surface approaches the top of the tank.

- Shortly after the discharge of a motor or aviation gasoline cargo, there is a layer at the bottom of the tank where concentrations of 30%-40% by volume of hydrocarbons have been measured. If loaded at this stage the gas enters the venting system immediately ahead of the concentrated layer formed by the next cargo.

- In motor or aviation gasoline tanks that have been battened down after discharge and not gas freed, uniform hydrocarbon gas concentrations as high as 40% by volume have been measured throughout the tanks. This concentration is expelled to the vent system throughout the next loading until the concentrated layer above the liquid surface approaches the top of the tank.

Note that in all loading operations, whether the tank is initially gas free or not, very high gas concentrations enter the venting system towards completion of loading.

17.2.3 Ballasting

The atmosphere in cargo tanks before ballasting will be similar to that before the loading of oil cargo, given a similar tank history. The gas concentration expected to enter the venting system during ballasting will therefore be comparable to that in the examples given (see Section 17.2.2.)

For ships using crude oil washing, vapour emissions to the atmosphere during filling of departure ballast must be avoided in some ports by containing the vapour in empty cargo tanks, by simultaneous ballasting and cargo discharge, or by other approved means.

17.2.4 Inert Gas Purging

If inert gas purging is being carried out by the displacement method (see Section 10.4) any dense concentrated hydrocarbon layer at the bottom of the tank is expelled in the early stages, followed by the remainder of the tank atmosphere as it is pressed downwards by the inert gas. If there is a uniformly high concentration throughout the tank, for example after crude oil washing, the hydrocarbon concentration of the vented gas remains high throughout the purging process until the inert gas reaches the bottom of the tank.

If inert gas purging is being carried out by the dilution method (see Section 10.4), the gas concentration at the outlet is highest at the beginning of the operation and falls continuously as it proceeds.

17.2.5 Gas Freeing

In a gas freeing operation air is delivered into the tank, where it mixes with the existing tank atmosphere and also tends to mix together any layers that may be present. The resultant mixture is expelled to the outside atmosphere. Because the process is one of continuous dilution with the air, the highest hydrocarbon concentration is vented at the beginning of gas freeing and decreases thereafter. For example, on a non-inerted ship, gas freeing of a motor gasoline tank that has been battened down can give initial concentrations as high as 40% by volume, but in most circumstances the concentration in the vented gas is much lower, even at the start of the operations.

On inerted ships, where purging to remove hydrocarbon vapour before gas freeing is a requirement, even the initial concentration will be low, 2% by volume or less.

17.3 GAS DISPERSION

Whether the hydrocarbon gas at the outlet is mixed with air or with inert gas will have no bearing on the dispersion of the gas after it has left the outlet.

As the hydrocarbon gas displaced during loading, ballasting, gas freeing or inert gas purging issues from the vent or vents on the tanker, it immediately starts to mix with the atmosphere. The hydrocarbon concentration is progressively reduced until, at some distance from the vent, it passes below the lower flammable limit. At any point below the LFL it ceases to be of concern as a flammability hazard because it cannot be ignited. Thus there exists in the vicinity of any vent a flammable zone within which the gas concentration is above the LFL.

There is a potential danger of fire and explosion if this flammable zone reaches any location where there may be sources of ignition, such as:

- Superstructures and deckhouses which the gas can enter through doors, ports or ventilation intakes.

- The cargo deck which, although it is usually regarded as free of sources of ignition, is a work area and thoroughfare.

- An adjacent jetty which, although it is usually regarded as free of sources of ignition, is a work area and thoroughfare.

17.4 VARIABLES AFFECTING DISPERSION

17.4.1 The Dispersion Process

A mixture of hydrocarbon gas and air (or inert gas) issuing vertically from an outlet rises under its own momentum as a plume above the outlet. If there is no wind the plume remains vertical but otherwise it is bent over in the downwind direction. The rise of the plume due to its momentum is opposed by a tendency to sink because its density is greater than that of the surrounding air.

The flow velocity of the issuing gas is at its maximum as it passes through the outlet, and decreases as air is drawn into the plume. This air decreases the hydrocarbon gas concentration and hence the gas density in the plume. The progressive decreases in velocity, hydrocarbon concentration and density, together with the wind speed and other meteorological factors, determine the final shape of the plume and hence of the flammable zone.

17.4.2 Wind Speed

For many years it has been recognised that the dispersion of hydrocarbon gas/air mixtures is inhibited by low wind speeds. This recognition is based upon experience on tankers and little experimental work has been done to obtain quantitative information on the effect of wind speed. Much depends upon the quantity of gas being vented and how it is vented, but experience at terminals seems to suggest that at wind speeds above about 5 metres/sec dispersion is sufficient to avoid any flammability risk.

17.4.3 Rate of Flow of Gas

As the rate of flow of a hydrocarbon gas/air mixture of fixed composition is increased through a given opening several effects come into play. In the first place, the rate of emission of the hydrocarbon constituent increases in proportion to the total gas flow rate and therefore the distance the plume travels before it is diluted to the LFL should be greater. On the other hand, the higher the velocity, the more efficient is the mixing of the initially hydrocarbon rich gas with the air and this tends to counterbalance the first effect.

In addition, at low rates of total gas flow the initial momentum of the plume may not be enough to counteract the tendency of the plume to sink because of its initially high density.

The results of the interaction of these different processes at low wind speed are illustrated (Fig. 17-1). The gas mixture used in obtaining these diagrams was 50% by volume propane and 50% by volume air and is typical of that to be expected when topping off a crude oil cargo. At the lowest flow rate (Fig. 17-1(a)) the density effect predominates and the gas sinks back towards the deck. At the highest flow rate (Fig. 17-1(c)) mixing is far more efficient and there is no tendency for the plume to sink.

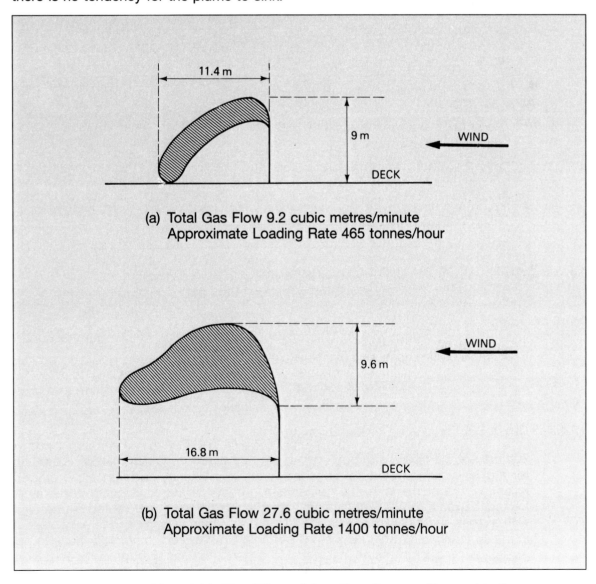

(a) Total Gas Flow 9.2 cubic metres/minute
Approximate Loading Rate 465 tonnes/hour

(b) Total Gas Flow 27.6 cubic metres/minute
Approximate Loading Rate 1400 tonnes/hour

Figure 17-1 (a) and (b). *The Effect of Gas Flow Rate on Flammable Zone*

The flammable zones generated by the same operations with motor or aviation gasolines would be similar but with a more pronounced density effect, and this effect would be even more pronounced with a natural gasoline type cargo. Also, the greater dilution required to reach the LFL with motor or aviation gasolines (see Section 15.2.2) would tend to make the flammable zones larger than with crude oils, and this effect would be even more pronounced with the natural gasolines. Thus the dispersion problem becomes progressively more pronounced as one goes from crude oils, through motor or aviation gasolines, to natural gasoline type cargoes.

17.4.4 Concentration of Hydrocarbon Gas

With a constant total rate of flow of gas, changes in hydrocarbon concentration have two effects. The rate of emission of hydrocarbon gas increases in proportion to the concentration so that, other things being equal, the extent of the flammable zone increases. Also, the initial density of the gas mixture as it issues from the opening becomes greater so that there is a greater tendency for the plume to sink.

At low concentrations therefore, a flammable zone similar in outline to that in Fig. 17-1(c) is to be expected but it is likely to be small because of the relatively small amount of hydrocarbon gas. As the concentration increases, the flammable zone tends to assume such shapes as Fig. 17-1(b) and 17-1(a) as the increasing density exerts its influence. In addition the overall size of the zone becomes greater due to the greater rate of emission of hydrocarbon gas.

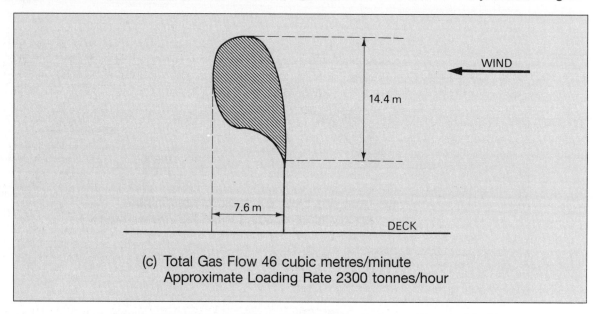

(c) Total Gas Flow 46 cubic metres/minute
Approximate Loading Rate 2300 tonnes/hour

Figure 17-1 (c). *The Effect of Gas Flow Rate on Flammable Zone*

Illustrations based upon wind tunnel data of:
Gas mixture: 50% by volume propane in air
Diameter of opening: 254 millimetres
Wind speed: 1.1 metres/second

17.4.5 Cross Sectional Area of the Opening

The area of the opening through which the hydrocarbon gas/air mixture issues determines, for a given volumetric rate of flow, the linear flow velocity and hence the efficiency of the mixing of the plume with the atmosphere. Effects of this kind occur, for example, in gas freeing. If fixed turbo-blower fans are used the mixture is usually vented through a stand pipe with a cross-sectional area small enough to give a high velocity and to encourage dispersion in the atmosphere. When using small portable blowers, which normally have to be operated against a low back pressure, it is usual to exhaust the gas through an open tank hatch. The efflux velocity is then very low with the outlet close to the deck, circumstances which encourage the gas to remain close to the deck.

17.4.6   The Design of the Vent Outlet

The outlets from the venting systems on tankers take many forms. Some are simple openings so that the mixture flows out unimpeded in a vertical direction. In other designs louvres or cowls may be installed which have the effect of diverting the direction of flow either sideways or downwards. As an example of the effect of such devices, Fig. 17-2 shows the result of installing a simple flat plate baffle just above a vent outlet. In this example the vent outlet is well above the deck. If it were lower, extensive areas of the deck would be covered with a flammable gas mixture.

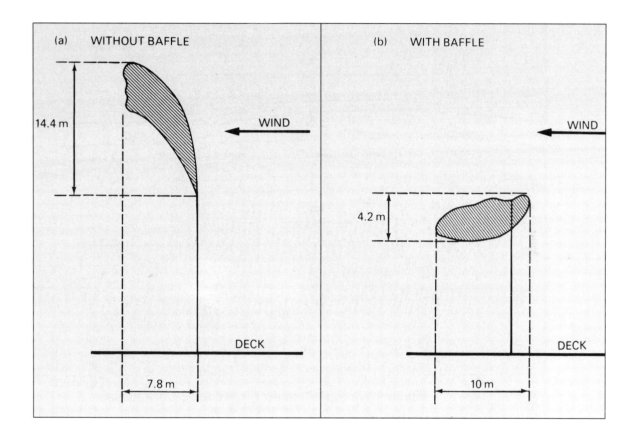

Figure 17-2 (a) and (b). *The Effect of Baffling a Vent Outlet on Flammable Zone*

Illustrations based upon wind tunnel data

Gas mixture:	50% by volume propane in air
Diameter of opening:	254 millimetres
Wind speed:	1.1 metres/second
Total gas flow:	60 cubic metres/minute
Approximate loading rate:	3000 tonnes/hour

17.4.7   Position of the Vent Outlet

If vent outlets are situated near structures such as deckhouses, the shape of the flammable zone is influenced by turbulence produced in the air as it passes over them. A diagram illustrating the kind of eddies formed is given in Fig. 17-3. It shows how, on the upwind side, there are downward eddies below a level indicated by the line X-X and how, above and in the lee of the structure, there is a tendency for turbulent air to form eddies close to the structure. These movements can adversely affect the efficient dispersion of hydrocarbon gas.

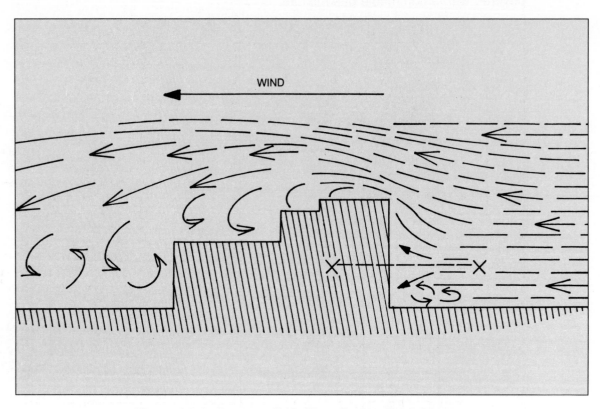

Figure 17-3. *Pattern of Air Flow Over a Deck House*

If the rate of flow of gas is low there are marked effects in the lee of structures; examples are given in Fig. 17-4(a) and (b) which show a clear tendency for the gas to be pulled back towards and against the downwind end of the structure. Figure 17-4(c) shows the behaviour of gas from a similar vent upwind of the structure. The flammable zone in this case is little affected by the presence of the structure; both the eddies and the density of the issuing gas contribute to the downwind, downward migration of the gas.

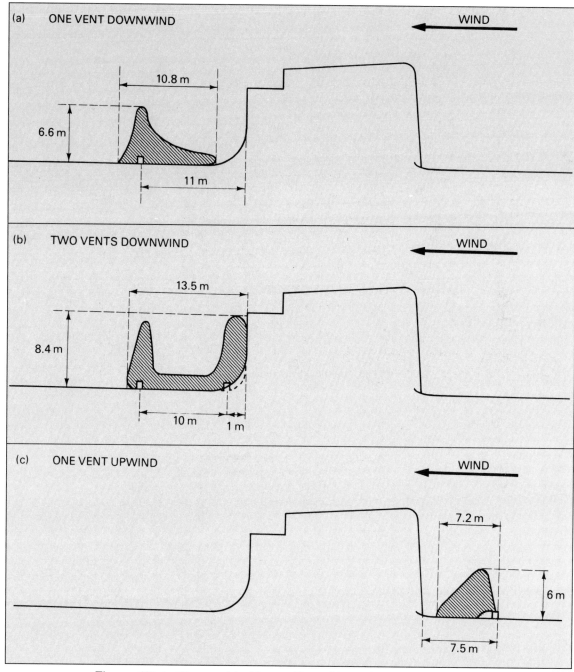

Figure 17-4. *Flammable Zones From Vents Near a Deck House*

Illustrations based upon wind tunnel data:

Gas mixture:	50% by volume propane in air
Diameter of openings:	152 millimetres
Wind speed:	1.1 metres/second
Total gas flow per opening:	6.7 cubic metres/minute
Approximate loading rate: per opening	330 tonnes/hour

If the exit velocity from a vent near a structure is high, it can overcome the influence of eddies. For example, Fig. 17-5(a) shows the flammable zone from a vent situated only about 1.5 metres upwind of a deckhouse; the plume is almost vertical and only just touches the deckhouse. However, a somewhat lower rate of loading would have resulted in serious impingement of the zone upon the deckhouse. Fig. 17-5(b) illustrates the effect of an additional vent which doubles the amount of gas released. Partly as the result of eddies and partly due to the denser combined plume the flammable zone is in close contact with the top of the deckhouse.

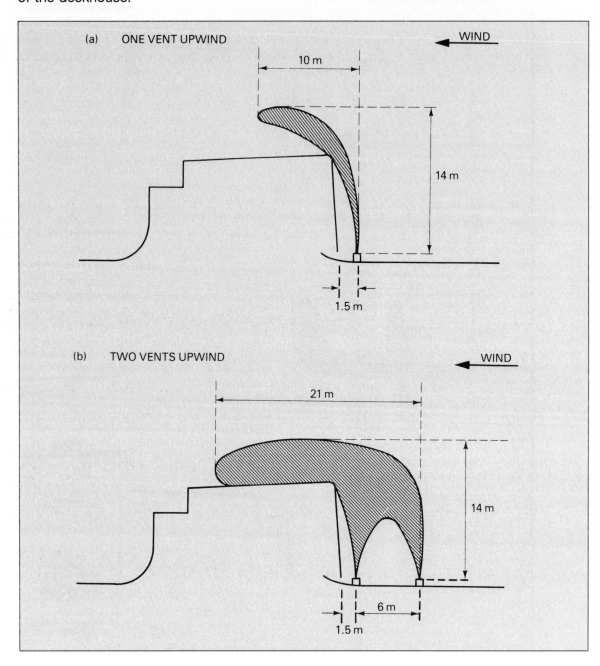

Figure 17-5. *Flammable Zones From Vents Near a Deck House*

Illustrations based upon wind tunnel data:

Gas mixture:	50% by volume propane in air
Diameter of openings:	152 millimetres
Wind speed:	1.1 metre/second
Total gas flow per opening:	20 cubic metres/minute
Approximate loading rate per opening:	1000 tonnes/hour

17.5　MINIMISING HAZARDS FROM VENTED GAS

The objective of venting arrangements and their operational control is to minimise the possibilities of flammable gas concentrations entering enclosed spaces containing sources of ignition or reaching deck areas where, notwithstanding all other precautions, there might be a source of ignition. Previous sections illustrate the means of promoting rapid dispersion of gas and minimising its tendency to sink to the deck. Although this section is concerned with flammability, the same principles apply to dispersion of gas down to concentrations safe to personnel.

The following conditions are desirable in any operation where flammable mixtures are displaced to the atmosphere or mixtures are displaced which could become flammable on dilution with air, such as on inerted ships:

- An unimpeded vertical discharge at a high efflux velocity.

- Positioning the outlet sufficiently high above the deck.

- Placing the outlet an adequate distance from the superstructure and other enclosed spaces.

When using a vent outlet of fixed diameter, usually designed for 125% of the maximum cargo loading rate, the efflux velocity will drop at lower loading rates. Vent outlets with automatically variable areas have been designed and produced to maintain a high efflux velocity under all loading conditions. The permitted height of the outlet above deck is dependent on whether venting is by free-flow or through a high velocity vent valve.

The fitted venting arrangements should always be used during loading and ballasting operations but, unless tanks have closed gauging arrangements, there will be periods when sighting ports have to be opened, particularly during topping-off operations. The emission then is generally at a lower rate and close to the deck so that to minimise risk ullage ports should be opened for as short a time as possible.

When gas freeing by fixed mechanical blower, or purging with inert gas either by displacement or dilution through designated outlets, sufficiently high efflux velocities should be reached to ensure rapid gas dispersion in any conditions.

When gas freeing by portable blowers, it may be necessary to open a tank hatch lid to act as a gas outlet, resulting in a low gas outlet velocity and calling for vigilance to ensure that gas does not accumulate on deck. If an inerted tank is being gas freed through the hatch lid there may be localised areas where the atmosphere is deficient in oxygen. If practicable it is preferable to gas free through a small diameter opening, such as a tank cleaning opening, with a temporary stand-pipe rigged.

In all operations where gas is being vented great vigilance should be exercised, especially under adverse conditions (e.g. if there is little or no wind). Under such conditions, it may be prudent to stop operations until conditions improve.

17.6　LOADING OF VERY HIGH VAPOUR PRESSURE CARGOES

17.6.1　Gas Evolution

This Chapter has so far dealt with gas evolution and dispersion from high vapour pressure cargoes which give rise to concentrated hydrocarbon gas layers of a depth of 1 metre or less when loaded (see Section 17.2.1). Cargoes yielding layers of greater depth are sometimes encountered. The main examples are crude oils, which may have their vapour pressures increased by the addition of extra gas (such as butane); and some natural gasolines, by-products of LNG/LPG production, which are sometimes known as pentanes plus.

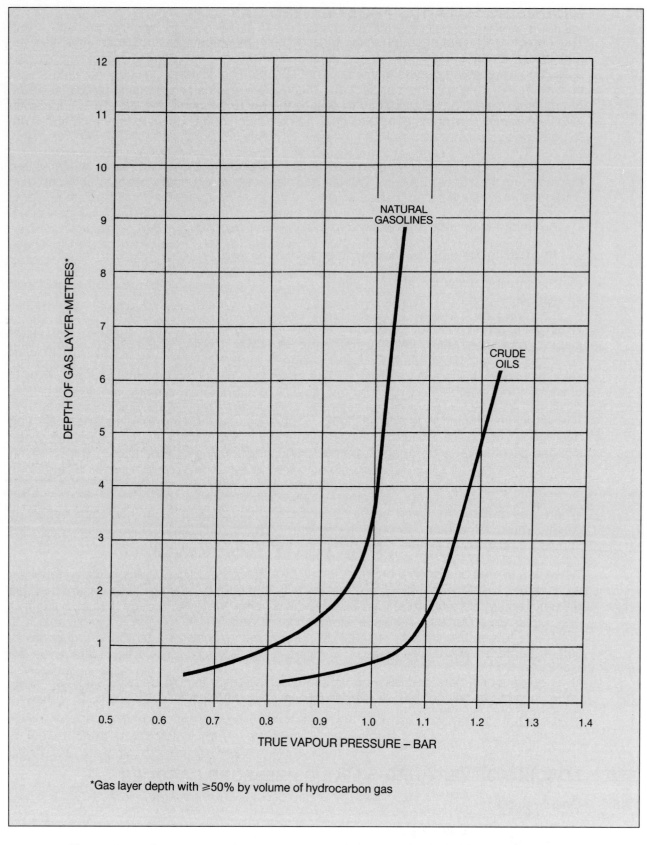

Figure 17-6. *Relationship Between Depth of Gas Layer and True Vapour Pressure*

Examples of the variation of gas layer depth (to the 50% by volume concentration level) related to true vapour pressure (TVP) are shown in Figure 17-6 for typical natural gasolines and crude oils. There are some cargoes with intermediate properties, for example flash stabilised condensates, some distillation overhead products and crude oils with abnormally low methane and ethane contents.

The natural gasoline curve in Figure 17-6 is for a series of blends of different TVPs and the crude oil curve is for a series produced by adding increasing amounts of butane to a crude oil. Below a gas layer depth of about 1 metre, the dependence of depth on TVP is not very marked for either type of cargo. At greater TVPs it becomes progressively steeper, indicating that in this range a small increase in TVP could cause a very large increase in gas evolution.

Boiling commences when the TVP exceeds 1 bar. In the case of the natural gasoline blends this coincides quite closely with the steep increase in gas layer thickness. However with the crude oil/butane blends the steep increase does not occur until a TVP significantly above 1 bar is reached. Crude oils may be stabilised so that their TVPs are near, or somewhat above, 1 bar as they enter the ship. In practice therefore some boiling may occur even without butanisation, but the gas evolution is not necessarily excessive.

In boiling, gas bubbles form below the surface of the liquid, but only down to a depth at which the total pressure (atmospheric plus hydrostatic) is equal to the TVP. The consequent loss of gas in this region may lead to a local fall in TVP; moreover the latent heat required to evaporate the gas results in cooling which also reduces the TVP. The reduction in TVP in the liquid near the surface from both these causes tends to delay boiling, despite the fact that the TVP of the bulk of the liquid is above 1 bar.

That is why crude oils can be handled with their TVPs somewhat above 1 bar. It does not apply to the same extent to the natural gasoline type of product because the gaseous constituents in a crude oil are only a small proportion of the total, whereas a natural gasoline usually consists almost entirely of potentially gaseous compounds. This means that the availability of gas, where boiling is taking place, is far greater with the natural gasolines than with crude oils. Natural gasolines suffer hardly any decrease of TVP due to gas depletion when they begin to boil, and boiling is much more likely to continue in their case than in the case of crude oils.

17.6.2 Special Precautions with Very High Vapour Pressure Cargoes

When unusually deep gas layers are encountered, very high concentrations of gas, approaching 100% by volume, may be vented for prolonged periods during loading. Excessive amounts of gas may then be present on or around the tanker, which may call for special precautions to be taken.

Curves of the kind given in Figure 17-6 suggest that the TVP at the loading temperature of the cargo should be used as the criterion for determining when special precautions are necessary. The Reid vapour pressure of a cargo gives very little guidance unless the temperature of the cargo when loaded is also specified. However, it has proved to be difficult to select TVP criteria because they depend ultimately on subjective judgements of acceptable gas conditions on ships. As a general guide, the available information suggests that consideration should be given to the need for special precautions when the TVP is expected to exceed the following values:

- For natural gasoline type cargoes, for example pentanes plus, 0.75 bar.

- For crude oils, with or without added gas, 1.0 bar.

- For some intermediate cargoes, for example flash stabilised condensates, some distillation overhead products and crude oils with abnormally low methane and ethane contents, TVP limits between these two values might be appropriate.

Precautions that might then be applied are given in Section 7.6.13.

Chapter 18

Gas Indicators

This Chapter describes the principles, uses and limitations of portable instruments for measuring concentrations of hydrocarbon gas in inerted and non-inerted atmospheres, of other toxic gases and of oxygen. Certain fixed installations are also described. For all instruments reference should also be made to the manufacturer's instructions.

18.1   MEASUREMENT OF HYDROCARBON CONCENTRATION

The Catalytic Filament Combustible Gas (CFCG) Indicator is used for measuring hydrocarbon gas in air at concentrations below the lower flammable limit (LFL). The scale is graduated in % LFL. A CFCG Indicator must not be used for measuring hydrocarbon gas in inert atmospheres.

Two types of instrument are available commercially for measuring hydrocarbon gas concentrations in excess of the LFL or in oxygen deficient (inerted) atmospheres - the Non-Catalytic Heated Filament Gas Indicator and the Refractive Index Meter. The scale is graduated in % volume hydrocarbon gas.

18.2   CATALYTIC FILAMENT COMBUSTIBLE GAS INDICATOR (CFCG)

18.2.1   Operating Principle

The sensing element of a CFCG indicator is usually a catalytic metal filament heated by an electric current. In some instruments the filament is replaced by a ceramic pellet with a catalyst (a pellister) but the mode of action is the same. When a mixture of hydrocarbon gas with air is drawn over the filament the gas oxidises on the hot filament and makes it hotter. This increases its resistance and the change of resistance provides a measure of the concentration of hydrocarbon gas in the mixture.

A simplified diagram of the electrical circuit of a CFCG indicator is shown in Figure 18-1. It is a Wheatstone bridge with the sensor filament forming one arm of the bridge.

The indicator is made ready for use by balancing the bridge with the filament at the correct operating temperature in contact with fresh air, so that the meter reading is zero. The increased resistance of the sensor filament brought about by combustion of the sample mixture throws the bridge out of balance and causes the meter to deflect by an amount proportional to the combustible gas concentration. The deflection is shown on a scale calibrated to read 0%-100% LFL. Some instruments incorporate additional circuitry to give a second, expanded, range 0%-10% LFL. To maintain consistent readings the voltage across the bridge must be kept constant and a control is provided for this purpose.

Another arm of the bridge consists of a second filament (compensator filament) identical with the sensor filament and the two are mounted close to each other in the instrument. The second filament, however, remains permanently in contact with pure air and the arrangement provides automatic compensation for the effect of ambient temperature changes on the

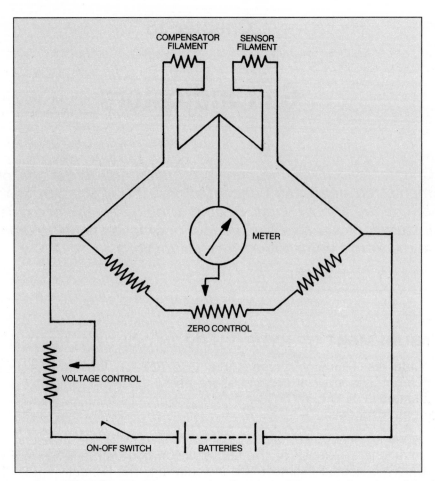

Figure 18-1. *Simplified Circuit Diagram of a Catalytic Filament Combustible Gas Indicator*

instrument reading. The resistances in the other two arms of the bridge are made from an alloy, the electrical resistance of which is practically independent of temperature.

In taking a measurement the manufacturer's detailed instructions should be followed. After the instrument has been initially set at zero with fresh air in contact with the sensor filament, a sample is drawn into the meter by means of a rubber aspirator bulb or a pump. The reading is taken when the pointer has ceased to rise on the scale.

The out-of-balance voltage across the meter is proportional to hydrocarbon concentration up to 2-3 times the LFL although a reading cannot go beyond 100% LFL. If the concentration is more than about twice the LFL there is insufficient oxygen in the mixture to burn the hydrocarbon gas completely. The response of the instrument to such a concentration is that the needle initially deflects to the maximum on the scale and then falls back to a reading near zero. Continuous observation of the needle is necessary to avoid overlooking this kind of response. Prolonged operation with such a gas mixture causes the deposition of carbonaceous matter on the sensor filament and may alter the response of the instrument. In such cases the response of the instrument should be checked.

For the same reason the instrument does not give a reliable reading with atmospheres deficient in oxygen, such as those in inerted tanks. The meter must not be used for measuring hydrocarbon concentrations in inerted tanks.

Non-hydrocarbon gases, such as hydrogen sulphide or carbon monoxide, or gases from lead compounds, which may be present in a tank atmosphere can affect the meter response, but only if they are present in very high concentrations.

The instrument is normally fitted with a filter to remove solid particles and liquid. It will not indicate the presence of combustible mists (such as lubricating oils) or dusts.

18.2.2 Instrument Check Procedures

The instrument is set up to read correctly in the factory using a hydrocarbon gas/air mixture, the composition of which should be indicated on the label fixed to the instrument.

The response should be checked at the beginning of every day during which it is intended to use the instrument. Such a check should also be made after replacing a filament. Test kits for use in the field are available for this purpose providing a mixture of hydrocarbon gas in air (such as 50% LFL butane in air). At intervals, the instrument should be checked more thoroughly in a laboratory equipped with suitable gas blending facilities.

During operation it is important to check the instrument and sample lines occasionally for leakage, since the ingress of air would dilute the sample, giving false readings.

Leak testing may be achieved by pinching the sample line and squeezing the aspirator bulb; the bulb should not expand as long as the sampling line is pinched.

18.2.3 Precision of Measurement

The response of the instrument depends upon the composition of the hydrocarbon gas and in practice this composition is not known. The calibration of the instrument is such that the response is usually on the safe side for the gases encountered in tanker operations.

Factors that can affect the measurements are large changes in ambient temperature and excessive pressure of the tank atmosphere being tested, leading to high flow rates which in turn affect the filament temperature. To avoid the effect of gas flow rate, it is recommended practice to take a reading when there is no flow, i.e. between two squeezes of the rubber aspirator bulb.

The use of dilution tubes which enable catalytic filament indicators to measure concentrations in over rich hydrocarbon gas/air mixtures is not recommended.

18.2.4 Operational Features

Only instruments fitted with flashback arresters in the inlet and outlet of the detector filament chamber should be used. The arresters are essential to prevent the possibility of flame propagation from the combustible chamber; a check should therefore always be made that they are fitted properly in their place.

Some authorities require, as a condition of their approval, that PVC covers be fitted around meters with aluminium cases to avoid the risk of incendive sparking if the case impacts on rusty steel.

When hydrocarbons are being measured no filters should be used other than the cotton filter inserted in the gas inlet of the detector to remove solid particles or liquid from the gas sample, although a water absorbent material or water trap may be necessary in the sampling line if the gas is very wet (see Section 18.10).

18.3 NON-CATALYTIC HEATED FILAMENT GAS INDICATOR

18.3.1 Operating Principle

The sensing element of this instrument is a non-catalytic hot filament. The composition of the surrounding gas determines the rate of loss of heat from the filament, and hence its temperature and resistance.

The sensor filament forms one arm of a Wheatstone bridge. The initial zeroing operations balance the bridge and establish the correct voltage across the filament, thus ensuring the correct operating temperature. During zeroing the sensor filament is purged with air or inert gas free from hydrocarbons. As in the CFCG indicator, there is a second identical filament in another arm of the bridge which is kept permanently in contact with air and acts as a compensator filament.

The presence of hydrocarbon changes the resistance of the sensor filament and this is shown by a deflection on the bridge meter. The rate of heat loss from the filament is a non-linear function of hydrocarbon concentration and the meter scale reflects this non-linearity. The meter gives a direct reading of % volume hydrocarbons.

The non-catalytic filament is not affected by gas concentrations in excess of its working scale. The instrument reading goes off the scale and remains in this position as long as the filament is exposed to the rich gas mixture.

In taking a measurement, the manufacturer's detailed instructions should be followed. After the instrument has been initially set at zero with fresh air in contact with the sensor filament, a sample is drawn into the meter by means of a rubber aspirator bulb. The bulb should be operated until the meter pointer comes to rest on the scale (usually within 15-20 squeezes) then aspirating should be stopped and the final reading taken. It is important that the reading should be taken with no flow through the instrument and with the gas at normal atmospheric pressure.

18.3.2 Instrument Check Procedures

The checking of a non-catalytic heated filament instrument requires the provision of gas mixtures of a known total hydrocarbon concentration.

The carrier gas may be air, nitrogen or carbon dioxide or a mixture of these. Since this type of instrument may be required to measure accurately either low concentrations (1%-3% by volume) or high concentrations (greater than 10% by volume) it is desirable to have either two test mixtures, say 2% and 15% by volume, or one mixture between these two numbers, say 8% by volume. Gas mixtures may be obtained in small aerosol-type dispensers or small pressurized gas cylinders, or may be prepared in a special test kit.

18.3.3 Precision of Measurement

Correct response from these instruments is achieved only when measuring gas concentrations in mixtures for which the instrument has been calibrated and which remain gaseous at the temperature of the instrument.

Relatively small deviations from normal atmospheric pressure in the instrument produce significant differences in the indicated gas concentration. If a space which is under elevated pressure is sampled, it may be necessary to detach the sampling line from the instrument and allow the sample pressure to equilibrate with the atmosphere pressure.

18.4 REFRACTIVE INDEX METER

18.4.1 Operating Principle

This is an optical device depending on the difference between the refractive indices of the gas sample and air.

In this type of instrument a beam of light is divided into two, and these are then recombined at the eyepiece. The recombined beams exhibit an interference pattern which appears to the observer as a number of dark lines in the eyepiece.

One light path is through chambers filled with air. The other path is via chambers through which the sample gas is pumped. Initially the latter chambers are filled with air and the instrument is adjusted so that one of the dark lines coincides with the zero line on the instrument scale. If a gas mixture is then pumped into the sample chambers the dark lines are displaced across the scale by an amount proportional to the change of refractive index.

The displacement is measured by noting the new position on the scale of the line which was used initially to zero the instrument. The scale may be calibrated in concentration units or it may be an arbitrary scale whose readings are converted to the required units by a table or graph. The response of the instrument is linear and a one point test with a standard mixture at a known concentration is sufficient for checking purposes.

The instrument is normally calibrated for a particular hydrocarbon gas mixture. As long as the use of the instrument is restricted to the calibration gas mixture it provides accurate measurements of gas concentrations.

The measurement of the concentration of hydrocarbon gas in an inerted atmosphere is affected by the carbon dioxide present when flue gas is used for inerting. In this case the use of sodalime as an absorbent for carbon dioxide is recommended, provided the reading is corrected appropriately.

The refractive index meter is not affected by gas concentrations in excess of its scale range. The instrument reading goes off the scale and remains in this position as long as the gas chambers are filled with the gas mixture.

18.4.2　Instrument Check Procedures

A mixture of known hydrocarbon, e.g. butane in nitrogen at a known concentration, should be used to check the instrument. If the hydrocarbon test gas differs from the original calibration gas the indicated reading should be multiplied by the appropriate correction factor before judging the accuracy and stability of the instrument.

18.5　FIXED FLAMMABLE GAS DETECTION INSTALLATIONS

Fixed installations have been employed to a limited extent in a few petroleum tankers to monitor the flammability of the atmosphere in spaces such as pipe tunnels in double bottoms and pumprooms. Three general arrangements have been developed for fixed monitoring installations thus:

- A multiplicity of sensing devices is distributed throughout the spaces to be monitored. Signals are taken sequentially from them by a central control.

- A gas measurement system is installed in the central control room. Samples of the atmospheres to be checked are drawn sequentially, usually by vacuum pump, through sample lines to the central gas measurement system. It is important to ensure that there is no leakage of air into the system which would dilute the samples and cause misleading readings.

- Infra-red sensors are located in the space being monitored and the electronics necessary for processing the signals are located in a safe location, usually the central control room.

18.6　MEASUREMENT OF LOW CONCENTRATIONS OF TOXIC GASES

Probably the most convenient and suitable equipment to use for measuring very low concentrations of toxic gases on board tankers is chemical indicator tubes.

These consist of a sealed glass tube containing a proprietary filling which is designed to react with a specific gas and to give a visible indication of the concentration of that gas. To use the device the seals at each end of the glass tube are broken, the tube is inserted in a bellows-type fixed volume displacement hand pump, and a prescribed volume of gas mixture is drawn through the tube at a rate fixed by the rate of expansion of the bellows. A colour change occurs along the tube and the length of discolouration, which is a measure of the gas concentration, is read off a scale integral with the tube. In some versions of these instruments a hand operated injection syringe is used instead of a bellows pump.

It is important that all the components used for any measurement should be from the same manufacturer. It is not permissible to use a tube from one manufacturer with a hand pump from another manufacturer. It is also important that the manufacturer's operating instructions should be carefully observed.

Since the measurement depends on passing a fixed volume of gas through the glass tube, if an extension hose is used it should be placed between the glass tube and the hand pump.

The tubes are designed and intended to measure concentrations of gas in the air. Thus measurements made in a ventilated tank, in preparation for tank entry, should be reliable.

Under some circumstances errors can occur if several gases are present at the same time, as one gas can interfere with the measurement of another. The manufacturer should be consulted for guidance.

For each type of tube the manufacturers must guarantee the standards of accuracy laid down in national standards. Tanker operators should consult the regulatory authority appropriate for the ship's flag.

18.7   MEASUREMENT OF OXYGEN CONCENTRATIONS

Oxygen analysers are normally used to determine whether an atmosphere, for example inside a cargo tank, may be considered fully inerted or safe for entry. The fixed types of analysers are used for monitoring the oxygen content of the boiler uptakes and the inert gas main.

The following are the most common types of oxygen analysers in use:

- Paramagnetic sensors.

- Electrolytic sensors.

- Selective chemical absorption liquids.

All analysers regardless of type should be used strictly in accordance with the manufacturer's instructions. If so used, and subject to the limitations listed below, the analysers may be regarded as reliable.

18.8   USE OF OXYGEN ANALYSERS

18.8.1 Paramagnetic Sensors

Oxygen is strongly paramagnetic whereas most other common gases are not. This property therefore enables oxygen to be determined in a wide variety of gas mixtures.

One commonly used oxygen analyser of the paramagnetic type has a sample cell in which a lightweight body is suspended in a magnetic field. When sample gas is drawn through the cell the suspended body experiences a torque proportional to the magnetic susceptibility of the gas. An equal and opposing torque is produced by an electric current passing through a coil wound round the suspended body. The equalizing current is a measure of the magnetic force and is thus a measure of the magnetic susceptibility of the sample, i.e. related to its oxygen content.

Before use the analyser should be calibrated, using nitrogen or carbon dioxide to purge the sample cell for a zero check and with air at 21% oxygen for span.

The analyser readings are directly proportional to the pressure in the measuring cell. The unit is calibrated to a specific atmospheric pressure and the small error due to atmospheric pressure variations can be corrected if required. Reading errors can be more significant during pressure variations using some gas sampling arrangements, but can be avoided by reducing the sampling pressure to atmospheric during readings. Continuous samples should be supplied to the instrument by positive pressure. They should not be drawn through the analyser by negative pressure as the measuring pressure then becomes uncertain.

The filter should be cleared or replaced when an increase in sample pressure is required to maintain a reasonable gas flow through the analyser. The same effect is produced if the filter becomes wet due to insufficient gas drying. The need for filter cleaning or replacement should be checked regularly.

18.8.2 Electrolytic Sensors

Analysers of this type determine the oxygen content of a gas mixture by measuring the output of an electrolytic cell. In one common analyser, oxygen diffuses through a membrane into the cell causing current to flow between two special electrodes separated by a liquid or gel electrolyte. The current flow is related to the oxygen concentration in the sample, and the scale is arranged to give a direct indication of oxygen content. The cell may be housed in a separate sensor head connected by cable to the read-out unit.

The analyser readings are directly proportional to the pressure in the measuring cell but only small errors are caused by normal variations in atmospheric pressure,

Certain gases may affect the sensor and give rise to false readings. Sulphur dioxide and oxides of nitrogen interfere if they are present in concentrations of more than 0.25% by volume. Mercaptans and hydrogen sulphide can poison the sensor if their levels are greater than 1% by volume. This poisoning does not occur immediately but over a period of time; a poisoned sensor drifts and cannot be calibrated in air. In such cases reference should be made to the manufacturer's instructions.

18.8.3 Selective Chemical Absorption Liquids

In this type of analyser, a known volume of sample gas in brought into contact with a liquid which absorbs oxygen, causing a volume change in the liquid. The relationship of this volume change to the original volume is a measure of the oxygen content of the sample.

The use of this type of analyser for checking the condition of the ullage space in a loaded compartment is not recommended, because of the effect of high concentrations of hydrocarbon gases on the reagents.

18.8.4 Maintenance, Calibration and Test Procedures

As these analysers are of vital importance, they should be carefully maintained and tested strictly in accordance with the manufacturer's instructions.

It is essential that each time an instrument is to be used, a check is made of batteries (if fitted), zero setting and calibration. During use frequent checks should be made to ensure accurate readings are obtained at all times. Calibration is simple on all analysers, using atmospheric air as standard. Zero calibration can be checked with nitrogen or carbon dioxide.

18.8.5 Personal Oxygen Monitors

Personal oxygen monitors which are capable of continuously measuring the oxygen content of the atmosphere are available. These monitors employ an electrolytic sensor. They should automatically provide an audible and visual alarm when the atmosphere becomes deficient in oxygen so as to give the wearer adequate warning of unsafe conditions. The monitors should be tested at regular intervals (see also Sections 10.7.3 and 16.8).

18.9   GAS SAMPLE LINES AND SAMPLING PROCEDURES

18.9.1   Gas Sample Lines

The material and condition of sample lines can affect the accuracy of gas measurements.

Metal tubes are unsuited to most cargo tank gas measurements and flexible lines must be used.

The gases from crude oils and many petroleum products are composed essentially of paraffinic hydrocarbons and there are a number of suitable materials available for flexible sample tubing. The problem of material selection is more difficult for those gases containing substantial proportions of aromatic hydrocarbons, in particular xylene. It is recommended that in such cases suppliers of sample tubing should be asked to provide test data showing the suitability of their product for the purposes for which it will be employed.

Sample tubing must be resistant to water.

Sample tubing which is cracked or blocked, or which has become contaminated with cargo residues, greatly affects instrument readings. Users should check the condition of the tubing regularly and replace defective tubing.

18.9.2   Sampling Procedures

Every tank has 'dead spots' where the rate of change of gas concentration during ventilation or purging is less than the average in the bulk of the tank. The location of these dead spots depends on the positions of the inlet and outlet through which ventilating air or inert gas is admitted and expelled and also on the disposition of the structural members in the tank. Generally, but not invariably, the dead spots are to be found within the tank bottom structure. The sample line must be long enough to permit sampling in the bottom structure.

The differences in gas concentration between the bulk volume of the tank and the dead spots vary depending on the operating procedures in use. For example, the powerful water jets produced by fixed washing machines are excellent mixing devices which tend to eliminate major differences in gas concentration between one location in the tank and another. Similarly, the introduction of ventilating air or inert gas as powerful jets directed downwards from the deckhead produces good mixing and minimises variations in concentration.

Because of the hazards associated with these dead spots, it is important to refer to Chapter 11, and to Section 11.3.1 in particular, before entering any tank or other enclosed space.

18.10   FILTERS IN SAMPLE LINES

Cotton filters are normally used in hydrocarbon gas meters of either the catalytic or non-catalytic filament types, and additional filters are not normally needed. In extremely wet conditions, e.g. tank washing, excessive water can be removed from the gas sample using materials that retain water but do not affect the hydrocarbons. Suitable materials are granular anhydrous calcium chloride or sulphate. If required, soda asbestos selectively retains hydrogen sulphide without affecting the hydrocarbons. However, it also retains carbon dioxide and sulphur dioxide and must not be used in tanks inerted with scrubbed flue gas.

The use of water retaining filters is essential with oxygen meters, particularly the paramagnetic type, because the presence of water vapour in the sample can damage the measuring cell. Only manufacturers recommended filters should be used.

Chapter 19

Electrical Equipment and Installations

In this Chapter a description is given of the different approaches to the classification of dangerous areas on board tankers and hazardous areas in terminals with regard to electrical installations and equipment. General guidance is given on the safety precautions to be observed during maintenance and repair of electrical equipment. The standards for, and the installation of, electrical equipment do not come within the scope of this safety guide.

19.1 DANGEROUS AND HAZARDOUS AREAS

19.1.1 Dangerous Areas in a Tanker

In a tanker, certain areas are defined by international convention, Administrations and classification societies as being dangerous for the installation or use of fixed electrical equipment, either at all times or only during loading, ballasting, tank cleaning or gas freeing operations. These areas are described in the International Electrotechnical Commission Publication 92-5 which refers to the types of electrical equipment which can be installed in them.

19.1.2 Hazardous Areas at a Terminal

At a terminal, account is taken of the probability of a flammable gas mixture being present by grading hazardous areas into three zones:

- *Zone 0*
  An area in which a flammable gas mixture is continuously present or is present for long periods.

- *Zone 1*
  An area in which there is likely to be a flammable gas mixture under normal operating conditions.

- *Zone 2*
  An area in which the presence of a flammable gas mixture is unlikely, but if such a mixture is present it is likely to persist for only a short period.

19.1.3 Application of Hazardous Area Classifications to a Tanker at a Berth

When a tanker is at a berth, it is possible that an area in the tanker which is regarded as safe may fall within one of the hazardous zones of the terminal. If such a situation should arise, and if the area in question contains unapproved electrical equipment then such equipment may have to be isolated whilst the tanker is at the berth.

19.2 ELECTRICAL EQUIPMENT AND INSTALLATIONS

19.2.1 Electrical Equipment and Installations on Board Ship

Electrical equipment and installations in tankers will be in accordance with classification society or national requirements, or the recommendations of the International Electrotechnical Commission. Additional recommendations in respect of the use of temporary electrical installations and portable electrical equipment are given in Sections 2.4, 4.10 and 11.6.4.

19.2.2 Electrical Equipment and Installations at Terminals

At terminals, the types of electrical equipment and methods of installation will normally be governed by national requirements and, where applicable, by the recommendations of the International Electrotechnical Commission.

19.3 INSPECTION AND MAINTENANCE OF ELECTRICAL EQUIPMENT

19.3.1 General

All apparatus, systems and installations, including cables, conduits and the like, should be maintained in good condition. To ensure this they should be regularly inspected.

Correct functional operation does not necessarily imply compliance with the required standards of safety.

19.3.2 Inspections and Checks

All equipment, systems and installations should be inspected when first installed. Following any repair, adjustment or modification, those parts of the installation which have been disturbed should be checked.

If at a terminal there is at any time a change in the area classification or in the characteristics of the flammable material handled, a check should be made to ensure that all equipment is of the correct group and temperature class and continues to comply with the requirements for the revised area classification.

19.3.3 Insulation Testing

Insulation testing should be carried out only when no flammable gas mixture is present.

19.3.4 Alterations to Equipment, Systems and Installations

No modification, addition or removal should be made to any approved equipment, system or installation at a terminal without the permission of the appropriate authority, unless it can be verified that such a change does not invalidate the approval.

No modification should be made to the safety features of equipment which relies on the techniques of segregation, pressurising, purging or other methods of ensuring safety, without the permission of the engineer responsible.

When equipment in a terminal hazardous zone is permanently withdrawn from service, the associated wiring should be removed from the hazardous zone or should be correctly terminated in an enclosure appropriate to the area classification.

When equipment in a terminal hazardous zone is temporarily removed from service, the exposed conductors should be correctly terminated as above, or adequately insulated, or solidly bonded together and earthed. The cable cores of intrinsically safe circuits should either be insulated from each other or bonded together and insulated from earth.

19.3.5 Periodic Mechanical Inspections

During inspections of electrical equipment or installations particular attention should be paid to the following:

- Cracks in metal, cracked or broken glasses, or failure of cement around cemented glasses in flameproof or explosion proof enclosures.

- Covers of flameproof enclosures to ensure that they are tight, that no bolts are missing, and that no gaskets are present between mating metal surfaces.

- Each connection to ensure that it is properly connected.

- Possible slackness of joints in conduit runs and fittings.

- Clamping of armouring of cable.

- Stesses on cables which might cause fracture.

19.4 ELECTRICAL REPAIRS, MAINTENANCE AND TEST WORK AT TERMINALS

19.4.1 General

As a general safety precaution the use of mechanical lock off devices and safety tags is strongly recommended.

19.4.2 Cold Work

Work should not be carried out on any apparatus or wiring, nor should any flame-proof or explosion-proof enclosure be opened, nor the special safety characteristics provided in connection with standard apparatus be impaired, until all voltage has been cut off from the apparatus or wiring concerned. The voltage should not be restored until work has been completed and the above safety measures have been fully reinstated. Any such work, including changing of lamps, should be done only by an authorised person.

19.4.3 Hot Work

For the purpose of repairs, alterations or carrying out tests, it is permissible to use soldering apparatus or other means involving a flame, fire, or heat, or to use industrial type apparatus, in any terminal hazardous area, provided that the area has first been made safe and certified gas free by an authorised person and is then maintained in that condition as long as the work is in progress. When such hot work is considered necessary on a berth at which a tanker is moored or on a tanker berthed at a terminal, the joint agreement of the terminal and tanker should first be obtained and a hot work permit issued.

It is also permissible to restore voltage to apparatus for testing during a period of repair or alteration subject to the same conditions.

Before undertaking any hot work, refer to Section 2.8

Chapter 20

Static Electricity

This Chapter deals with the generation of static electricity during the loading and discharging of cargo and during tank cleaning. In addition the Chapter deals with ship to shore and ship to ship electric currents.

20.1 PRINCIPLES OF ELECTROSTATIC HAZARDS

20.1.1 General

Static electricity presents fire and explosion hazards during the handling of petroleum, and tanker operations. Certain operations can give rise to accumulations of electric charge which may be released suddenly in electrostatic discharges with sufficient energy to ignite flammable hydrocarbon gas/air mixtures; there is, of course, no risk of ignition unless a flammable mixture is present. There are three basic stages leading up to a potential static hazard: charge separation, charge accumulation and electrostatic discharge. All three of these stages are necessary for an electrostatic ignition.

20.1.2 Charge Separation

Whenever two dissimilar materials come into contact charge separation occurs at the interface. The interface may be between two solids, between a solid and a liquid or between two immiscible liquids. At the interface a charge of one sign (say positive) moves from material A to material B so that materials A and B become respectively negatively and positively charged. Whilst the materials stay in contact and immobile relative to one another, the charges are extremely close together. The voltage difference between the charges of opposite sign is then very small, and no hazard exists.

The charges can be widely separated by many processes, such as:

- The flow of liquids (e.g. petroleum or mixtures of petroleum and water) through pipes or fine filters.

- The settling of a solid or an immiscible liquid through a liquid (e.g. rust or water through petroleum).

- The ejection of particles or droplets from a nozzle (e.g. steaming operations).

- The splashing or agitation of a liquid against a solid surface (e.g. water washing operations or the initial stages of filling a tank with oil).

- The vigorous rubbing together and subsequent separation of certain synthetic polymers (e.g. the sliding of a polypropylene rope through PVC gloved hands).

When the charges are separated, a large voltage difference develops between them. Also a voltage distribution is set up throughout the neighbouring space and this is known as an electrostatic field. As examples, the charge on a charged petroleum liquid in a tank produces an electrostatic field throughout the tank both in the liquid and in the ullage space, and the charge on a water mist by tank washing produces a field throughout the tank.

If an uncharged conductor is present in an electrostatic field it has approximately the same voltage as the region it occupies. Furthermore the field causes a movement of charge within the conductor; a charge of one sign is attracted by the field to one end of the conductor and an equal charge of opposite sign is left at the opposite end. Charges separated in this way are known as induced charges and as long as they are kept separate by the presence of the field they are capable of contributing to an electrostatic charge.

20.1.3 Charge Accumulation

Charges which have been separated attempt to recombine and to neutralize each other. This process is known as charge relaxation. If one, or both, of the separated materials carrying charge is a very poor electrical conductor, recombination is impeded and the material retains or accumulates the charge upon it. The period of time for which the charge is retained is characterised by the relaxation time of the material, which is related to its conductivity; the lower the conductivity the greater is the relaxation time.

If a material has a comparatively high conductivity, the recombination of charges is very rapid and can counteract the separation process, and consequently little or no static electricity accumulates on the material. Such a highly conducting material can only retain or accumulate charge if it is insulated by means of a poor conductor, and the rate of loss of charge is then dependent upon the relaxation time of this lesser conducting material.

The important factors governing relaxation are therefore the electrical conductivities of the separated materials and of any additional materials which may be interposed between them after their separation.

20.1.4 Electrostatic Discharges

Electrostatic breakdown between any two points, giving rise to a discharge, is dependent upon the strength of the electrostatic field in the space between the points. This field strength, or voltage gradient, is given approximately by dividing the difference in voltage between the points by their distance apart. A field strength of about 3,000 kilovolts per metre is sufficient to cause breakdown of air or petroleum gases.

The field strength near protrusions is greater than the overall field strength in the vicinity and discharges therefore generally occur at protrusions. A discharge may occur between a protrusion and the space in its vicinity without reaching another object. These single electrode discharges are rarely, if ever, incendive in the context of normal tanker operations.

The alternative is a discharge between two electrodes adjacent to each other. Examples are:

- Between sampling apparatus lowered into a tank and the surface of a charged petroleum liquid.

- Between an unearthed object floating on the surface of a charged liquid and the adjacent tank structure.

- Between unearthed equipment suspended in a tank and the adjacent tank structure.

Two-electrode discharges may be incendive if various requirements are met. These include:

- A discharge gap short enough to allow the discharge to take place with the voltage difference present, but not so short that any resulting flame is quenched.

- Sufficient electrical energy to supply the minimum amount of energy to initiate combustion.

- The nearly instantaneous release of this energy into the discharge gap.

Whether the last requirement can be fulfilled depends to a large extent on the conductivity of the electrodes. In order to consider this further it is necessary to classify solids and liquids into three main groups.

The first group is the conductors. In the case of solids these are the metals, and in the case of liquids the whole range of aqueous solutions including sea water. The human body, consisting of about 60% water, is effectively a liquid conductor. The important property of conductors is that not only are they incapable of holding a charge unless insulated, but also that if they are insulated and an opportunity for an electrical discharge occurs all the charge available is almost instantaneously released into the discharge.

Discharges between two conductors very frequently occur as sparks, and are much more energetic and potentially dangerous than those occurring between objects, one of which is not a conductor. In the latter case, discharges often take a more diffuse and much less dangerous form, known as corona or brush discharge, rather than a spark.

The second group is the non-conductors, which have such low conductivites that once they have received a charge they retain it for a very long period. Alternatively they can prevent the loss of charge from conductors by acting as insulators. Charged non-conductors are of primary concern because they can transfer charge to, or induce charge on, neighbouring insulated conductors which may then give rise to sparks. Very highly charged non-conductors may themselves contribute directly to incendive sparks.

Liquids are considered to be non-conductors when they have conductivities less than 50picoSiemens/metre (pS/m) giving relaxation times greater than 0.35 seconds; they are often known as static accumulators. In the case of petroleum, clean oils (distillates) frequently fall into this category. An antistatic additive is a substance which is deliberately added to a petroleum distillate to raise its conductivity above 50 pS/m.

The solid non-conductors are highly insulating materials such as polypropylene, PVC, nylon and many types of rubber. They become more conductive as their surfaces are contaminated with dirt or moisture.

The third group is a range of liquids and solids with conductivities intermediate between those of the first two groups. The liquids have conductivities exceeding 50 pS/m and are often known as static non-accumulators. Examples are black oils (containing residual materials) and crude oils, which typically have conductivities in the range of 10,000-100,000 pS/m. Some chemicals, for example alcohols, are also static non-accumulators.

The solids in this intermediate category include such materials as wood, cork, sisal and naturally occurring organic substances generally. They owe their conductivity to their ready absorption of water and they become more conductive as their surfaces are contaminated by moisture and dirt. In some cases thorough cleaning and drying may lower their conductivities sufficiently to bring them into the non-conductive range.

If materials in the intermediate conductivity group are not insulated from earth, their conductivities are normally sufficiently high to prevent accumulation of an electrostatic charge. However, their conductivities are normally low enough to inhibit production of energetic sparks.

The incendivity of a discharge from a material of intermediate conductivity depends upon so many factors in addition to conductivity that generalisations beyond the foregoing are impossible, and it is necessary to rely upon practical experience to indicate when it is acceptable to use them.

Under normal conditions gases are highly insulating; this has important implications with respect to mists and particulate suspensions in air and other gases. Charged mists are formed during the ejection of wet steam from a nozzle, while using tank washing machines and during crude oil washing. Although the liquid, for example water, may have a very high conductivity, the relaxation of the charge on the droplets is hindered by the insulating properties of the surrounding gas. Fine particles present in inert flue gas or created during discharge of pressurised liquid carbon dioxide are frequently charged. The gradual charge relaxation which does occur is the result of the settling of the particles or droplets and, if the field strength is high, of corona discharge at protrusions which supplies a neutralising charge of the opposite polarity.

In summary, electrostatic discharges can occur as a result of accumulations of charge on:

- Liquid or solid non-conductors, for example a static accumulator oil (such as kerosene) pumped into a tank, or a polypropylene rope.

- Electrically isolated liquid or solid conductors, for example mists, sprays or particulate suspensions in air, or a metal rod hanging on the end of a synthetic fibre rope.

For materials with intermediate conductivities the risk of electrostatic discharge is small, particularly if current practices are adhered to, and the chance of their being incendive is even smaller.

20.2   GENERAL PRECAUTIONS AGAINST ELECTROSTATIC HAZARDS

The most important countermeasure that must be taken to prevent an electrostatic hazard is to bond all metal objects together. Bonding eliminates the risk of discharges between metal objects, which can be very energetic and dangerous. To avoid discharges from conductors to earth, it is normal practice to include bonding to earth (earthing or grounding). On ships, bonding to earth is effectively accomplished by connecting metallic objects to the metal structure of the ship, which is naturally earthed through the sea.

Some examples of objects which might be electrically insulated in hazardous situations and which must therefore be bonded are:

- Ship/shore hose couplings and flanges if more than one length of non-conducting hose or pipe is used in a string.

- Portable tank cleaning machines.

- Conducting manual ullaging and sampling equipment.

- The float of a permanently fitted ullage device if it lacks an earthing path through the metal tape.

The most certain method of bonding and earthing is by means of a metallic connection between the conductors. This method should be used whenever possible, although for electrostatic purposes an adequate bond can in principle be made using a material of intermediate conductivity.

Certain objects may be insulated during tanker operations, for example:

- A metal object such as a can floating in a static accumulating liquid.

- A loose metal object while it is falling in a tank during washing operations.

Every effort should be made to ensure that such objects are removed from the tank, since there is evidently no possibility of deliberately bonding them. This necessitates careful inspection of tanks, particularly after shipyard repairs.

20.3 ELECTROSTATIC HAZARDS WHEN HANDLING STATIC ACCUMULATOR OILS

20.3.1 Pumping Oil into Tanks

Petroleum distillates often have electrical conductivities less than 50 picoSiemens/metre and thus fall into the category of accumulators.

Since their conductivities are not normally known, all distillates must be treated as static accumulators unless they contain an antistatic additive (see Section 20.3.4). During and for some time after entry into the tank a static accumulator oil may carry sufficient charge to constitute a hazard.

The charge may arise through one or more of several different processes:

- Flow of the oil through the pipeline system into the tank. Charge generation is enhanced if water droplets are suspended in the oil as it flows through the pipes.

- Flow through a micropore filter of the kind used for aircraft jet fuels. These filters have the ability to charge fuels to a very high level, probably because all the fuel is brought into intimate contact with the filter surface, where charge separation occurs.

- Turbulence and splashing in the early stages of pumping the oil into an empty tank.

- The settling of water droplets, rust or other particles entering the tank with the oil or stirred up by it in the tank.

The generally accepted method for controlling electrostatic generation in the initial stages of loading is to restrict the flow rate of the static accumulator oil into the tank until all splashing and surface turbulence in the tank has ceased.

At the commencement of loading an empty tank the linear velocity in the branch line to each individual cargo tank should not exceed 1 metre/second. The reasons for such a low rate are twofold:

- It is at the beginning of filling a tank that there is the greatest likelihood of water being mixed with the oil entering the tank. Mixtures of oil and water constitute a most potent source of static electricity.

- A low loading rate minimises the extent of turbulence and splashing as oil enters the tank; this helps reduce the generation of static electricity and also reduces the dispersal of any water present, so that it more quickly settles out to the bottom of the tank where it can lie relatively undisturbed when the loading rate is subsequently increased.

During subsequent loading, the limitations on flow rate imposed by the design of pipeline systems, coupled with precautions in the introduction of dipping, ullaging and sampling equipment (see Section 20.5) and the avoidance of electrically isolated conductors, have proved sufficient to maintain operational safety. If, however, markedly different pipeline or pumping systems were to be introduced, enabling higher flow rates or velocities to be achieved, then flow rate limitations might have to be imposed throughout loading.

The limitation on the initial loading rate for static accumulator oils applies whenever a flammable gas mixture may be present. These situations are fully described in Section 7.4 and are summarised in Table 7-1.

It is not uncommon during loading to encounter water from operations such as water washing, ballasting or line flushing and care should be taken to prevent excess water and unnecessary mixing. For example, cargo tanks and water flushed lines should be drained before loading and water should not be permitted to accumulate in tanks. Lines should not be displaced with water back into a tank containing a static accumulator oil.

Coarse filters are sometimes used in tanker operations. These generate an insignificant amount of charge provided that they are kept clean. However, if micropore filtration is used on the jetty, sufficient time must be allowed for the charge to relax before the liquid reaches the tank. It is desirable for the liquid to spend a minimum of 30 seconds in the piping downstream of the filter.

20.3.2   Fixed Equipment in Cargo Tanks

Equipment permanently mounted from the top of a tank, such as fixed washing machines or high level alarms, may act as isolated probes. A metal probe remote from any other tank structure but near a highly charged liquid surface will have a high voltage gradient at the probe tip. During the loading of static accumulator oils, this high voltage gradient may cause electrostatic discharges to the approaching liquid surface.

An isolated probe configuration can be avoided by installing the device adjacent to a wall or other tank structure to reduce the voltage gradient at the probe tip. Alternatively, a support can be added running from the lower end to the tank structure so that the rising liquid meets an edge rather than the isolated tip of a probe. Another solution possible in some cases is to construct the probe-like device entirely of a non-conductive material. These measures are not necessary if the vessel is limited to crude, black oil service or the tanks are inerted.

20.3.3   Air Release in the Bottom of Tanks

If air or inert gas is blown into the bottom of a tank containing a static accumulator oil a strong electrostatic field can be generated, especially in the presence of water or particulate matter. Accordingly precautions should be taken to minimise the amount of air or inert gas entering tanks containing static accumulator oils.

20.3.4   Antistatic Additives

If the oil contains an effective antistatic additive, it is no longer a static accumulator. Although strictly this means that the precautions applicable to an accumulator can be relaxed, it is still advisable to adhere to them in practice.

20.4   OTHER SOURCES OF ELECTROSTATIC HAZARDS

20.4.1   Free Fall in Tanks

Loading or ballasting overall delivers charged liquid to a tank in such a manner that it can break up into small droplets and splash into the tank. This may produce a charged mist as well as increasing the petroleum gas concentration in the tank. Restrictions upon loading or ballasting overall are given in Section 7.6.15.

20.4.2   Water Mists

The spraying of water into tanks, for instance during water washing, gives rise to electrostatically charged mist. This mist is uniformly spread throughout the tank being washed. The electrostatic levels vary widely from tank to tank, both in magnitude and in sign.

When washing is started in a dirty tank the charge in the mist is initially negative, reaches a maximum negative value, then goes back through zero and finally rises towards a positive equilibrium value. It has been found that, among the many variables affecting the level and polarity of charging, the characteristics of the wash water and the degree of cleanliness of the tank have the most significant influence. The electrostatic charging characteristics of the water are altered by recirculation or by the addition of tank cleaning chemicals, either of which may cause very high electrostatic potentials in the mist. Potentials are higher in large tanks than in small ones. The size and number of washing machines in a tank affect the rate of change of charge but they have little effect on the final equilibrium value.

The charged mist droplets created in the tank during washing give rise to an electrostatic field which is characterised by a distribution of potential (voltage) throughout the tank space. The walls and structure are at earth (zero) potential; the space potential increases with distance from these surfaces and is highest at points furthest from them. The field strength, or voltage gradient, in the space is greatest near the tank walls and structure, more especially where there are protrusions into the tank. If the field strength is high enough, electric breakdown occurs into the space, giving rise to a corona. Because protrusions cause concentrations of field strength, a corona occurs preferentially from such points. A corona injects a charge of the opposite sign into the mist and is believed to be one of the main processes limiting the amount of charge in the mist to an equilibrium value. The corona discharges produced during tank washing are not strong enough to ignite the hydrocarbon gas/air mixtures that may be present.

Under certain circumstances, discharges with sufficient energy to ignite hydrocarbon gas/air mixtures can occur from unearthed conducting objects already within, or introduced into, a tank filled with charged mist. Examples of such unearthed conductors are a metal sounding rod suspended on a non-conducting rope or a piece of metal falling through the tank space. Primarily by induction, an unearthed conductor within a tank can acquire a high potential when it comes near an earthed object or structure, particularly if the latter is in the form of a protrusion. The unearthed conductor may then discharge to earth giving rise to a spark capable of igniting a flammable hydrocarbon gas/air mixture.

The processes by which unearthed conductors give rise to ignitions in a mist are fairly complex, and a number of conditions must be satisfied simultaneously before an ignition can occur. These conditions include the size of the object, its trajectory, the electrostatic level in the tank and the geometrical configuration where the discharge takes place.

As well as solid unearthed conducting objects, an isolated slug of water produced by the washing process may similarly act as a spark promoter and cause an ignition. Experiments have shown that high capacity, single nozzle fixed washing machines can produce water slugs which, owing to their size, trajectory and duration before breaking up, may satisfy the criteria for producing incendive discharges. On the other hand, there is no evidence of such water slugs being produced by portable types of washing machine.

Following extensive experimental investigations and using the results of long-term experience, the tanker industry has drawn up the tank washing guidelines set out in Chapter 9. These guidelines are aimed at preventing excessive charge generation in mists and at controlling the introduction of unearthed conducting objects when there is charged mist in the tank.

Charged mists very similar to those produced during tank washing occur from time to time in partly ballasted holds of OBOs. Due to the design of these ships there may be violent mist-generating impacts of the ballast against the sides of the hold when the ship rolls in even a moderate sea. The impacts also give rise to free flying slugs of water in the tank, so that if the atmosphere of the tank is flammable all the elements for an ignition are present. The most effective counter-measure is to have tanks either empty or fully pressed up so that the violent wave motion in the tank cannot take place.

20.4.3   Steam

Steaming can produce mist clouds which may be electrostatically charged. The effects and possible hazards from such clouds are similar to those described for the mists created by water washing, but the introduction of steam can cause very much higher levels of charging than those produced by water washing. The time required to reach maximum charge levels is also very much less. Furthermore, although a tank may be almost free of hydrocarbon gas at the start of steaming, the heat and disturbance will often release gases and pockets of flammability may build up. For these reasons, steam should not be injected into cargo tanks where there is any risk of the presence of a flammable atmosphere.

20.4.4 Inert Gas

Small particulate matter carried in inert gas can be electrostatically charged. The charge separation originates in the combustion process and the charged particles are capable of being carried through the scrubber, fan and distribution pipes into the cargo tanks. The electrostatic charge carried by the inert gas is usually small but levels of charge have been observed well above those encountered with the water mists formed during washing. Because the tanks are normally in an inert condition, the possibility of an electrostatic ignition has to be considered only if it is necessary to inert a tank which already contains a flammable atmosphere or if a tank already inerted is likely to become flammable because the oxygen content rises as a result of ingress of air. Precautions are then required during dipping, ullaging and sampling (see Section 20.5.5).

20.4.5 Discharge of Carbon Dioxide

During the discharge of pressurised liquid carbon dioxide, the rapid cooling which takes place can result in the formation of particles of solid carbon dioxide which become charged on impact and contact with the nozzle and can thereby lead to incendive sparks. Carbon dioxide should therefore not be injected into cargo tanks or pump rooms which may contain unignited flammable gas mixtures.

20.4.6 Clothing and Footwear

A person who is highly insulated from earth by his footwear or the surface on which he is standing can become electrostatically charged. This charge can arise from physical separation of insulating materials caused, for instance, by walking on a very dry insulating surface (separation between the soles of the shoes and the surface) or by removing a garment.

Experience over a very long period indicates that electrostatic discharges caused by clothing and footwear do not present a significant hazard in the oil industry. This is especially true in a marine environment where surfaces rapidly become contaminated by deposits of salt and moisture which reduce electrical resistances, particularly at high humidities.

20.4.7 Synthetic Materials

An increasing number of items manufactured from synthetic materials are being offered for use on board ships. It is important that those responsible for their provision to tankers should be satisfied that, if they are to be used in flammable atmospheres, they will not introduce electrostatic hazards.

20.5 DIPPING, ULLAGING AND SAMPLING

20.5.1 General

There is a possibility of discharges whenever equipment is lowered into cargo tanks within which there may be electrostatic charges either in the liquid contents or on water or oil mists or on inert gas particulates. If there is any possibility of the presence of a flammable hydrocarbon gas/air mixture, precautions must be taken to avoid incendive discharges throughout the system.

20.5.2 Equipment

If any form of dipping, ullaging or sampling equipment is used in a possibly flammable atmosphere where an electrostatic hazard exists or can be created, it is essential at all times to avoid the presence of an unearthed conductor. Metallic components of any equipment to be lowered into a tank should be securely bonded together and earthed to the ship before introduction and should remain earthed until after removal.

Equipment should be designed to facilitate earthing. For example, the frame holding the wheel on which a metal measuring tape is wound should be provided with a threaded stud to which a sturdy bonding cable is bolted. The stud should have electrical continuity through the frame to the metal measuring tape. The other end of the bonding cable should terminate in a spring loaded clamp suitable for attachment to the rim of an ullage opening during use of the tape.

The suitability of equipment made wholly or partly of non-metallic components depends upon the conductivities of the materials employed and their manner of use. For example, in the case of non-conductors it is known that a significant electrostatic charge can be generated when a polypropylene rope runs rapidly through a PVC-gloved hand. For this reason only natural fibre ropes should be used for dipping, ullaging and sampling. Non-conducting materials may be acceptable in other circumstances — for example, a sample bottle holder made of a synthetic plastic — but those responsible for the provision of such equipment to ships must be satisfied that they are safe to use. It is essential in all cases that non-conducting components do not lead to the insulation of any metal components from earth.

A material of intermediate conductivity, such as wood or natural fibre, generally has sufficient conductivity intrinsically, or as a result of water absorption, to avoid the accumulation of electrostatic charge. There should be a leakage path to earth from such materials so that they are not totally insulated but this need not have the very low resistance normally provided for the bonding and earthing of metals. In practice, on ships such a path usually occurs naturally either by direct contact with the ship or by indirect contact through the operator of the equipment.

20.5.3 Static Accumulator Oils

It is wise to assume that the surface of a non-conducting liquid (static accumulator) may be at a high potential during and immediately after loading. It has already been said that metallic dipping, ullaging and sampling equipment should be bonded and earthed. There is therefore a possibility of a discharge between the equipment and the liquid surface as the two approach each other. Since such discharges can be incendive, no dipping, ullaging or sampling with metallic equipment should take place while a static accumulator is being loaded when there is any possibility of the presence of a flammable gas mixture. Moreover there should be a delay of 30 minutes after the completion of loading of each tank before commencing these operations; this is to allow the settlement of water or particulate matter in the liquid and the dissipation of any electrical potential.

The situations where these restrictions on the use of metallic equipment should be applied are fully described in Section 7.4 and are summarised in Table 7-1.

Discharges between the surface of a static accumulator oil and non-metallic objects have not in practice been found to be incendive. Dipping, ullaging or sampling with such equipment is therefore permissible at any time provided that the equipment complies with the conditions described in Section 20.5.2.

The potential within a metal sounding pipe is always low due to the small volume and to shielding from the rest of the tank. Dipping, ullaging and sampling within a metal sounding pipe are therefore permissible at any time, even with metallic equipment.

20.5.4 Non-Static Accumulator Oils

The possibility exists of a flammable atmosphere being present above a non-static accumulator oil in a non-inerted or non-gas free environment and therefore the precautions summarised in Chapter 7, Table 7-1, should be followed (see also Chapter 24).

20.5.5 Water Mists Due to Washing

When tank washing operations are performed, it is essential that there should be no unearthed metallic conductor in the tank, and that none should be introduced while the charged mist persists (i.e. during washing and for 5 hours after the completion of the operation). Earthed and bonded metallic equipment can be used at any time because any discharges to the water mist take the form of non-incendive corona. The equipment can contain or consist entirely of non-metallic components; both intermediate conductors and non-conductors are acceptable although the use of polypropylene ropes, for example, should be avoided (see Section 20.5.2). It is absolutely essential, however, that all metallic components are securely earthed. If there is any doubt about earthing, the operation should not be permitted.

Operations in a sounding pipe are safe at any time in the presence of a wash water mist.

20.5.6 Inert Gas

Precautions are not normally required against static electricity in the presence of inert gas because the gas prevents the existence of a flammable gas mixture. However, as mentioned in Section 20.4.4, very high electrostatic potentials are possible due to particulates in suspension in inert gas. If it is believed that the tank is for any reason no longer in an inert condition dipping, ullaging and sampling operations should be restricted. Restrictions would thus be required in the event of a breakdown of the inert gas system:

● During discharge;

● Leading to the ingress of air;

● Re-inerting of a tank after such a breakdown;

● Initial inerting of a tank containing a flammable gas mixture.

Because of the very high potential that may be carried on inert gas particulates, it is not wise to assume that corona discharges from introduced conducting equipment will be non-incendive. Therefore no object should be introduced until the initially very high potential has had a chance to decay to a more tolerable level; a wait of 30 minutes after stopping the injection of inert gas is sufficient for this purpose. After 30 minutes, equipment may be introduced subject to the same precautions as for water mists caused by washing.

20.6 EARTHING, BONDING AND CATHODIC PROTECTION

20.6.1 Earthing and Bonding Practice

Earthing and bonding minimise the dangers arising from:

● Faults between electrically live conductors and non-current-carrying metal work.

● Atmospheric discharges (lightning).

● Accumulations of electrostatic charge.

Earthing is achieved by the establishment of an electrically continuous low resistance path between a conducting body and the general mass of the earth. Earthing may occur inherently through intimate contact with the ground or water, or it may be provided deliberately by means of an electrical connection between the body and the ground.

Bonding occurs where a suitable electrically continuous path is established between conducting bodies.

Bonding may be effected between two or more bodies without involving earthing, but more commonly earthing gives rise to bonding with the general mass of the earth acting as the electrical connection. Bonding may arise by construction through the bolting together of metallic bodies, thus affording electrical continuity, or may be effected by the provision of an additional bonding conductor between them.

Most earthing and bonding devices intended to protect against electrical faults or lightning are permanently installed parts of the equipment which they protect, and their characteristics must conform to the national standards in the country concerned or to classification societies' rules, where relevant. Earthing and bonding to guard against static electricity are often associated with movable equipment and must be established whenever the equipment is set up.

The acceptable resistance in the earthing system depends upon the type of hazard that it is required to guard against. To protect electrical systems and equipment the resistance value is chosen so as to ensure the correct operation of the protective device (e.g. cut-out or fuse) in the electrical circuit. For lightning protection the value depends on national regulations, and is typically in the range of 5-25 ohms. To avoid the accumulation of static electricity the earth resistance value need not be less than 1 megohm and in most cases may be considerably higher.

20.6.2   Ship to Shore Electric Currents

The subject of ship to shore currents is quite separate from static electricity.

Large currents can flow in electrically conducting pipework and flexible hose systems between the ship and shore. The sources of these currents are:

- Cathodic protection of the jetty or the hull of the ship provided by either a DC impressed current system or by sacrificial anodes.

- Stray currents arising from galvanic potential differences between ship and shore or leakage effects from electrical power sources.

An all-metal loading or discharge arm provides a very low resistance connection between ship and shore and there is a very real danger of an incendive arc when the ensuing large current is suddenly interrupted during the connecting or disconnecting of the arm at the tanker manifold. Similar arcs can occur with flexible hose strings containing metallic connections between the flanges of each length of hose. It is therefore recommended practice to insert an insulating flange within the length of the loading arms and at the connection of flexible hose strings to the shore pipeline system. An alternative solution with flexible hose strings is to include in each string one length only of hose without internal bonding. The insertion of such a resistance completely blocks the flow of current through the loading arm or the hose string. At the same time the whole system remains earthed either to the ship or to the shore.

In the past it was usual to connect the ship and shore systems by a bonding wire via a flame-proof switch before the cargo connection was made and to maintain this bonding wire in position until after the cargo connection was broken. The use of this bonding wire had no relevance to electrostatic charging. It was an attempt to short circuit the ship/shore electrolytic/cathodic protection systems and to reduce the ship/shore voltage to such an extent that currents in hoses or in metal arms would be negligible. However, because of the large current availability and the difficulty of achieving a sufficiently small electrical resistance in the ship/shore bonding wire, this method has been found to be quite ineffective for its intended purposes and, furthermore, a possible hazard to safety. The use of ship/shore bonding wires is therefore being abandoned in favour of the insulating flanges described above. While some national and local regulations still require mandatory connection of a bonding cable, it should be noted that the IMO 'Recommendations for the Safe Transport, Handling, and Storage of Dangerous Substances in Port Areas' urge port authorities to discourage the use of ship/shore bonding cables and to adopt the recommendation concerning the use of an insulating flange or a single length of non-conducting hose as described above.

Insulating flanges should be designed to avoid accidental short circuiting. A typical design of an insulating flange arrangement is shown in Appendix D. Points to be borne in mind when fitting an insulating flange are:

- When the ship to shore connection is wholly flexible, as with a hose, the insulating flange should be inserted at the jetty end where it is not likely to be disturbed.

- When the connection is partly flexible and partly metal arm the insulating flange should be connected to the metal arm.

- For all-metal arms, care should be taken to ensure that, wherever it is convenient to fit the flange, it is not short-circuited by guy wires.

Current flow can also occur through any other electrically conducting path between ship and shore, for example mooring wires or a metallic ladder or gangway. These connections may be insulated to avoid draining the dock cathodic protection system by the added load of the ship's hull. However, it is extremely unlikely that a flammable atmosphere would be present at these locations while contact is interrupted.

Switching off cathodic protection systems of the impressed current type either ashore or on the ship is not, in general, considered to be a feasible method of minimising ship/shore currents in the absence of an insulating flange or hose. A jetty which is handling a succession of ships would need to have this cathodic protection switched off almost continuously and would therefore lose its corrosion resistance. Further, if the jetty system remains switched on, it is probable that the difference of potential between ship and shore will be less if the ship also keeps its cathodic protection system energised. In any case, the polarisation in an impressed current system takes many hours to decay after the system has been switched off, so that the ship would have to be deprived of full protection not only while alongside but also for a period before arrival in port.

20.6.3 Ship to Ship Electric Currents

The principles for controlling arcing during ship to ship transfer operations are the same as in ship to shore operations.

In ships dedicated to ship to ship transfers, an insulating flange or a non-conducting length of hose should be used in the hose string. However, when transferring static accumulator oils it is essential that these measures are not taken by both ships, leaving an insulated conductor between them upon which an electrostatic charge could accumulate. For the same reason, when such a ship is involved in ship to shore cargo transfers care should be taken to ensure that there is no insulated conductor between ship and shore through, for example, the use of two insulating flanges on one line.

In the absence of insulation between the ships, the electrical potential between them should be reduced as much as possible. If both have properly functioning impressed current cathodic protection systems, this is probably best achieved by leaving them running. Likewise if one has an impressed system and the other a sacrificial system, the former should remain in operation. However, if either ship is without cathodic protection, or its impressed system has broken down, consideration should be given to switching off the impressed system, if any, on the other well before the two ships come together.

Chapter 21

Pressure Surge

This Chapter contains a brief explanation of the phenomenon of pressure surge in pipelines and discusses the ways in which it can be prevented.

21.1 INTRODUCTION

A pressure surge is generated in a pipeline system when there is an abrupt change in the rate of flow of liquid in the line. In tanker operations it is most likely to occur as a result of one of the following during loading:

- Closure of an automatic shut down valve.

- Slamming shut of a shore non-return valve.

- Slamming shut of a butterfly type valve.

- Rapid closure of a power operated valve.

If the pressure surge in the pipeline results in pressure stresses or displacement stresses in excess of the strength of the piping or its components, there may be a rupture leading to an extensive spill of oil.

21.2 GENERATION OF PRESSURE SURGE

When a pump is used to convey liquid from a feed tank down a pipeline and through a valve into a receiving tank, the pressure at any point in the system while the liquid is flowing has three components:

- Pressure on the surface of the liquid in the feed tank. In a tank with its ullage space communicating to atmosphere this pressure is that of the atmosphere.

- Hydrostatic pressure at the point in the system in question.

- Pressure generated by the pump. This is highest at the pump outlet, decreasing commensurately with friction along the line downstream of the pump and through the valve to the receiving tank.

Of these three components, the first two can be considered constant during pressure surge and need not be considered in the following description, although they are always present and have a contributory effect on the total pressure.

Rapid closure of the valve superimposes a transient pressure upon all three components, owing to the sudden conversion of the kinetic energy of the moving liquid into strain energy by compression of the fluid and expansion of the pipe wall. To illustrate the sequence of events the simplest hypothetical case will be considered, i.e. when the valve closure is instantaneous, there is no expansion of the pipe wall, and dissipation due to friction between the fluid and the pipe wall is ignored. This case gives rise to the highest pressures in the system.

When the valve closes, the liquid immediately upstream of the valve is brought to rest instantaneously.

This causes its pressure to rise by an amount P. In any consistent set of units:

$P = wav$

where: w is the mass density of the liquid.
a is the velocity of sound in the liquid.
v is the change in linear velocity of the liquid i.e. from its linear flow rate before closure.

The cessation of flow of liquid is propagated back up the pipeline at the speed of sound in the fluid, and as each part of the liquid comes to rest its pressure is increased by the amount P. Therefore a steep pressure front of height P travels up the pipeline at the speed of sound; this disturbance is known as a pressure surge.

Upstream of the surge, the liquid is still moving forward and still has the pressure distribution applied to it by the pump. Behind it the liquid is stationary and its pressure has been increased at all points by the constant amount P. There is still a pressure gradient downstream of the surge but a continuous series of pressure adjustments takes place in this part of the pipeline which ultimately result in a uniform pressure throughout the stationary liquid. These pressure adjustments also travel through the liquid at the speed of sound.

When the surge reaches the pump the pressure at the pump outlet (ignoring the atmospheric and hydrostatic components) becomes the sum of the surge pressure P and the output pressure of the pump at zero throughput (assuming no reversal of flow), since flow through the pump has ceased. The process of pressure equalization continues downstream of the pump. Again taking the hypothetical worst case, if the pressure is not relieved in any way, the final result is a pressure wave that oscillates throughout the length of the piping system. The maximum magnitude of the pressure wave is the sum of P and the pump outlet pressure at zero throughput. The final pressure adjustment to achieve this condition leaves the pump as soon as the original surge arrives at the pump and travels down to the valve at the speed of sound. One pressure wave cycle therefore takes a time $2L/a$ from the instant of valve closure, where L is the length of the line and a is the speed of sound in the liquid. This time interval is known as the pipeline period.

In this simplified description, therefore, the liquid at any point in the line experiences an abrupt increase in pressure by an amount P followed by a slower, but still rapid, further increase until the pressure reaches the sum of P and the pump outlet pressure at zero throughput.

In practical circumstances the valve closure is not instantaneous and there is thus some relief of the surge pressure through the valve while it is closing. The results are that the magnitude of the pressure surge is less than in the hypothetical case, and the pressure front is less steep.

At the upstream end of the line some pressure relief may occur through the pump and this would also serve to lessen the maximum pressure reached. If the effective closure time of the valve is several times greater than the pipeline period, pressure relief through the valve and the pump is extensive and a hazardous situation is unlikely to arise.

Downstream of the valve an analogous process is initiated when the valve closes, except that as the liquid is brought to rest there is a fall of pressure which travels downstream at the velocity of sound. However, the pressure drop is often relieved by gas evolution from the liquid so that serious results may not occur immediately, although the subsequent collapse of the gas bubbles may generate shock waves similar to those upstream of the valve.

21.3 ASSESSMENT OF PRESSURE SURGES

21.3.1 Effective Closure Time of the Valve

In order to determine whether a serious pressure surge is likely to occur in a pipeline system the first step is to compare the time taken by the valve to close with the pipeline period.

The effective closure time, i.e. the period during which the rate of flow is in fact decreasing rapidly, is usually significantly less than the total time of movement of the valve spindle. It depends upon the design of the valve, which determines the relationship between valve port area and spindle position. Substantial flow reduction is usually achieved only during the closure of the last quarter or less of the valve port area.

If the effective valve closure time is less than, or equal to, the pipeline period, the system is liable to serious pressure surges. Surges of reduced, but still significant, magnitude can be expected when the effective valve closure time is greater than the pipeline period, but they become negligible when the effective valve closure period is several times greater than the pipeline period.

21.3.2 Derivation of Total Pressure in the System

In the normal type of ship/shore system handling petroleum liquids, where the shore tank communicates to the atmosphere, the maximum pressure applied across the pipe wall at any point during a pressure surge is the sum of the hydrostatic pressure, the output pressure of the pump at zero throughput and the surge pressure. The first two of these pressures are usually known.

If the effective valve closure time is less than or equal to the pipeline period, the value of the surge pressure used in determining the total pressure during the surge should be P, derived as indicated in Section 21.2. If it is somewhat greater than the pipeline period, a smaller value can be used in place of P and, as already indicated, the surge pressure becomes negligible if the effective valve closure time is several times greater than the pipeline period.

21.3.3 Overall System Design

In this Chapter the simple case of a single pipeline has been considered. In practice the design of a more complex system may need to be taken into account. For example, the combined effects of valves in parallel or in series have to be examined. In some cases the surge effect may be increased; this can occur with two lines in parallel if closure of the valve in one line increases the flow in the other line before this line in its turn is shut down. On the other hand, correct operation of valves in series in a line can minimise surge pressure.

Transient pressures produce forces in the piping system which can result in large piping displacements, pipe rupture, support failure, and damage to machinery and other connected equipment. Therefore the structural response of the piping system to fluid induced loads resulting from fluid pressures and momenta must be considered in the design. In addition restraints are usually required to avoid damage ensuing from large movements of the piping itself. An important consideration in the selection of the restraints is the fact that the piping often consists of long runs of straight pipe which will expand considerably under thermal loads. The restraints must both allow this thermal expansion and absorb the surge forces without overstressing the pipe.

21.4 REDUCTION OF PRESSURE SURGE HAZARD

21.4.1 General Precautions

If as a result of the calculations summarised in Section 21.3 it is found that the potential total pressure exceeds or is close to the strength of any part of the pipeline system it is advisable to obtain expert advice.

Where manually operated valves are used, good operating procedures should avoid pressure surge problems. It is important that a valve at the end of a long pipeline should not be closed suddenly against the flow; all changes in valve settings should be made slowly.

Where motorised valves are installed, several steps can be taken to alleviate the problem:

- Reduce the linear flow rate, i.e. the rate of transfer of cargo, to a value which makes the likely surge pressure tolerable.

- Increase the effective valve closure time. In very general terms total closure times should be of the order of 30 seconds, and preferably more. Valve closure rates should be steady and reproducible, although this may be difficult to achieve if spring return valves or actuators are needed to ensure that valves fail safe to the closed position. A more uniform reduction of flow may be achieved by careful attention to valve port design, or by the use of a valve actuator which gives a very slow rate of closure over, say, the final 15% of the port closure.

- Use a pressure relief system, surge tanks or similar devices to absorb the effects of the surge sufficiently quickly.

21.4.2 Limitation of Flow Rate to Avoid the Risk of a Damaging Pressure Surge

In the operational context, pipeline length and, very often, valve closure times are fixed and the only practical precaution against the consequences of an inadvertent rapid closure, e.g. during topping off, is to limit the linear flow rate of the oil to a maximum value v_{max}. This flow rate is related to the maximum tolerable surge pressure P_{max}. by the equation:

$$P_{max} = wav_{max} \text{ (see Section 21.2)}$$

If the internal diameter of the pipeline is d, the corresponding maximum tolerable volumetric flow rate Q_{max}. is given by:

$$Q_{max} = \frac{\pi d^2}{4} v_{max}$$

$$= \frac{\pi}{4} \frac{1}{wa} d^2 P_{max}$$

With sufficient accuracy,

a, the velocity of sound in petroleum, is 1300 metres/second

w, the density of oils, is 850 kilograms/cubic metre so that, approximately,

$$Q_{max} = 7.1 \times 10^{-7} d^2 P_{max}$$

where Q_{max} is in cubic metres/second, d in metres and P_{max} in Newtons/square metre.

In two alternative sets of units:

$$Q_{max} = 0.025 d^2 P_{max}$$

where Q_{max} is in cubic metres/hour, d in metres and P_{max} in kilograms force/square metre;

or $Q_{max} = 0.16 d^2 P_{max}$

$$= \frac{d^2 P}{6} \text{ max approximately}$$

where Q_{max} is in cubic metres/hour, d in inches and P_{max} in kilograms force/square centimetre.

Chapter 22

Fire-Fighting – Theory and Equipment

This Chapter describes the types of fire that may be encountered, together with the means of extinguishing fires. Descriptions are given of fire-fighting equipment to be found on tankers and recommendations made for terminal fire-fighting equipment.

22.1 THEORY OF FIRE-FIGHTING

Fire requires a combination of fuel, oxygen and a source of ignition. Most combustible or flammable substances, some only when heated, give off gas which burns if ignited when mixed with an appropriate quantity of oxygen, as in air.

Fires can be controlled and extinguished by the removal of heat, fuel or air. The main aim when fighting fires must therefore be to reduce the temperature or to remove the fuel or to exclude the supply of air with the greatest possible speed.

22.2 TYPES OF FIRE

22.2.1 Combustible Material Fires

Examples of such fires are bedding, clothing, cleaning rags, wood, canvas, rope and paper fires.

Cooling by large quantities of water, or the use of extinguishing agents containing a large proportion of water, is of primary importance when fighting fires of such ordinary combustible material. Cooling the source and surrounding area should continue long enough to prevent any possibility of re-ignition.

22.2.2 Liquid Petroleum Fires

Foam is an efficient agent for extinguishing most liquid petroleum fires. It should be applied so as to flow evenly and progressively over the burning surface, avoiding undue agitation. This can best be achieved by directing the foam jet against any vertical surface adjacent to the fire, both in order to break the force of the jet and to build up an unbroken smothering blanket. If there is no vertical surface the jet should be advanced in oscillating sweeps with the wind, taking care to avoid plunging it into the liquid. Foam spray streams, while limited in range, are also effective.

Volatile oil fires of limited size can be extinguished by water fog or water spray. Dry chemical powder or vaporising halon liquids are also effective in dealing with such fires.

Non-volatile oil fires which have not been burning for too long can be extinguished by water fog or water spray if the whole of the burning surface is accessible. The surface of the liquid transfers its heat rapidly to the water droplets which present a very large cooling surface and the flame can be extinguished with advancing and oscillating sweeps of fog or spray across the whole width of the fire.

Any oil fire which has been burning for some time is more difficult to extinguish with water, since the oil will have been heated to a progressively greater depth and cannot readily be cooled to a point where it ceases to give off gas. Furthermore, the use of a water jet may spread the burning oil by splashing or overflow. Spreading can also occur through agitation of the oil caused by violent boiling of water. Water should only be applied to oil fires as a spray or fog, although jets of water can play a valuable role in cooling hot bulkheads and tank walls.

The best way of dealing with such fires in tanks is by means of a smothering agent, such as foam, carbon dioxide, or in some cases dry chemical, coupled if possible with sealing off the tank and cooling adjacent areas or spaces.

The risk of re-ignition of a liquid petroleum fire must be borne constantly in mind. Having extinguished such a fire, a watch should be maintained and fire-fighting equipment and personnel kept in a state of immediate readiness.

22.2.3   Liquefied Petroleum Gas Fires

Fires involving escaping liquefied petroleum gas should, where possible, be extinguished by stopping the gas flow. If the flow of gas cannot be stopped it may be safer to allow the fire to continue to burn, at the same time using water spray to cool and control the effect of radiant heat.

Extinguishing the flame may result in a wide spread of un-ignited gas and subsequent wider spread of flame if it is re-ignited.

In order to reach and close the valve controlling the flow of gas, it may be necessary to extinguish flames from small leaks in its vicinity. In this case dry powder extinguishers should be used.

Water jets should never be used directly into a liquefied petroleum gas fire. Foam will not extinguish such fires.

22.2.4   Electrical Equipment Fires

These may be caused by short circuit, overheating or the spreading of a fire from elsewhere. The immediate action should be to de-energize the equipment, and a non-conductive agent, such as carbon dioxide, halon or dry chemical, should then be used to extinguish the fire.

22.3   EXTINGUISHING AGENTS – COOLING

22.3.1   Water

Water is the most common cooling agent. This is largely because water possesses very good heat absorbing qualities and is available in ample quantities at terminals and on ships.

A water jet, although excellent for fighting fires involving combustible materials, should not be used on burning oil, or on burning cooking oil or fat in galleys, because of the danger of spreading the fire.

Water spray and water fog may be used effectively against oil fires and for making a screen between the fire-fighter and the fire.

Owing to the danger of electrical shock, water should not be directed towards any electrical equipment.

A wetting agent may be added to water when it is to be used on tightly packed combustible materials. This has the effect of lowering its surface tension and thus increasing its effective penetration.

22.3.2 Foam

Foam has a limited heat absorbing effect and should not normally be used for cooling.

22.4 EXTINGUISHING AGENTS – SMOTHERING

22.4.1 Foam

Foam is an aggregation of small bubbles, of lower specific gravity than oil or water, which flows across the surface of a burning liquid and forms a coherent smothering blanket. It will also reduce the surface temperature of the liquid by the absorption of some heat.

There are a number of different types of foam concentrates available. These include standard protein foam, fluoro-protein foams and synthetic concentrates. The synthetics are divided into aqueous film forming foam (AFFF) and hydrocarbon surfactant type foam concentrates. Normally the protein, fluoro-protein and AFFF concentrates are used at 3% to 6% by volume concentration in water. Hydrocarbon surfactant concentrates are available for use at 1% to 6% by volume concentration.

High expansion foam has an expansion ratio from about 150:1 to 1500:1. It is made from hydrocarbon surfactant concentrates and is used to extinguish a fire in an enclosed space by filling the compartment rapidly with foam, thus preventing the movement of free air. The foam generator, which may be fixed or mobile, sprays the foam solution on to a fine mesh net through which air is driven by a fan. High expansion foam is unsuitable for use in outside locations as it cannot readily be directed on to a hot fire and is quickly dispersed in light winds.

Medium expansion foam has an expansion ratio from about 15:1 up to 150:1. It is made from the same concentrates as high expansion foam, but its aeration does not require a fan. Portable applicators can be used to deliver considerable quantities of foam on to spill fires, but their throw is limited and the foam is liable to be dispersed in moderate winds.

Low expansion foam has an expansion ratio from about 3:1 up to about 15:1. It is made from protein based or synthetic concentrates and can be applied to spill or tank fires from fixed monitors or portable applicators. Good throw is possible and the foam is resistant to wind.

Foam applicators should be directed away from liquid petroleum fires until any water in the system has been flushed clear.

Foam should not come into contact with any electrical equipment.

The various foam concentrates are basically incompatible with each other and should not be mixed in storage. However, some foams separately generated with these concentrates are compatible when applied to a fire in sequence or simultaneously. The majority of foam concentrates can be used in conventional foam making devices suitable for producing protein foams. The systems should be thoroughly flushed out and cleaned before changing agents, as the synthetic concentrates may dislodge sediment and block the proportioning equipment.

Some of the foams produced from the various concentrates are compatible with dry chemical powder and are suitable for combined use. The degree of compatibility between the various foams and between the foams and dry chemical agents varies and should be established by suitable tests.

The compatibility of foam compounds is a factor to be borne in mind when considering joint operations with other services.

Foam concentrates may deteriorate with time depending on the storage conditions. Storage at high temperatures and in contact with air will cause sludge and sediment to form. This may affect the extinguishing ability of the expanded foam. Samples of the foam concentrate should therefore be returned periodically to the manufacturer for testing and evaluation.

22.4.2 Carbon Dioxide

Carbon dioxide is an excellent smothering agent for extinguishing fires, when used in conditions where it will not be widely diffused. Carbon dioxide is therefore effective in enclosed areas such as machinery spaces, pumprooms and electrical switch rooms where it can penetrate into places that cannot be reached by other means. On an open deck or jetty area, carbon dioxide is comparatively ineffective.

Carbon dioxide does not damage delicate machinery or instruments and, being a non-conductor, can be used safely on or around electrical equipment.

Due to the possibility of static electricity generation, carbon dioxide should not be injected into any space containing a flammable atmosphere which is not on fire.

Carbon dioxide is asphyxiating and cannot be detected by sight or smell. No one should enter confined or partially confined spaces when carbon dioxide extinguishers have been used unless supervised and protected by suitable breathing apparatus and lifeline. Canister type respirators should not be used. Any compartment which has been flooded with carbon dioxide must be fully ventilated before entry without breathing apparatus.

22.4.3 Steam

Steam is inefficient as a smothering agent because of the substantial delay that may occur before sufficient air is displaced to render the atmosphere incapable of supporting combustion. Steam should not be injected into any space containing an unignited flammable atmosphere due to the possibility of static electricity generation.

22.4.4 Sand

Sand is relatively ineffective as an extinguishing agent and is only useful on small fires on hard surfaces. Its basic use is to dry up small spills.

22.5   FLAME INHIBITORS

22.5.1 General

Flame inhibitors are materials which interfere chemically with the combustion process, and thereby extinguish the flames. However cooling or removal of fuel is necessary if re-ignition is to be prevented.

22.5.2 Dry Chemical Powder

Dry chemical powder is discharged from an extinguisher as a free flowing cloud. It is most effective in dealing initially with a fire resulting from an oil spill on a jetty or on the deck of a tanker but can also be used in confined spaces. It is especially useful on burning liquids escaping from leaking pipelines and joints. It is a non-conductor and therefore suitable for dealing with electrical fires. It must be directed into the flames.

Dry chemical powder has a negligible cooling effect and affords no protection against re-ignition, arising, for example, from the presence of hot metal surfaces.

Certain types of dry chemical powder can cause a breakdown of a foam blanket and only those labelled 'foam compatible' should be used in conjunction with foam.

Dry chemical powder clogs and becomes useless if it is allowed to become damp when stored or when extinguishers are being filled.

22.5.3 Vaporising Liquids (Halons)

Vaporising liquids, in the same way as dry chemical powder, have a flame inhibiting effect and also have a slight smothering effect. There are a number of different liquids available, all halogenated hydrocarbons, often identified by a system of halon numbers.

The halons are most effective in enclosed spaces such as computer centres, storage rooms, tanker engine or pump rooms, generator enclosures and similar locations.

All halons are considered to be toxic to some degree because contact with hot surfaces and flames causes them to break down, yielding toxic substances. All personnel should therefore evacuate the area where halons are to be used, although it is possible to start the discharge of halons before the evacuation is complete as the normal concentrations encountered in extinguishing fires are acceptable for brief periods. After the fire has been extinguished the area should be thoroughly ventilated. If it is necessary to enter the area before ventilating, suitable breathing apparatus should be used.

Halon gases are known to have significant ozone depleting properties and, under the terms of the Montreal Protocol, production of Halon is to be phased out by the year 2000. New shipboard installations have been prohibited since July 1992.

Carbon tetrachloride should not be used as it is highly toxic.

22.6 TANKER FIRE-FIGHTING EQUIPMENT

The requirements for ships' fire-fighting equipment are laid down by the regulations of the particular country in which the tanker is registered. These regulations are generally based on the principles of the International Convention for the Safety of Life at Sea (SOLAS), 1974, as amended.

22.7 TANKER FIXED FIRE-FIGHTING INSTALLATIONS – COOLING

All tankers are provided with a water fire-fighting system consisting of pumps, a fire main with hydrant points, fire hoses complete with couplings, and jet nozzles or, preferably, jet/ spray nozzles. A sufficient number of hydrants are provided and located so as to ensure that two jets of water can reach any part of the ship. Certain bulkheads are sometimes fitted with permanent water spray lines.

An International Shore Fire Connection should be provided on tankers so that an external water supply can be coupled to any hydrant in the ship's fire main. These connections should be available for immediate use (see Appendix E).

22.8 TANKER FIXED FIRE-FIGHTING INSTALLATIONS – SMOTHERING

One or more, or a combination of, the different smothering systems listed below may be installed on board tankers.

22.8.1 Carbon Dioxide Flooding System

This system is designed to fight fires in the engine room, boiler room and pumproom. The system normally consists of a battery of large carbon dioxide cylinders. The carbon dioxide is piped from the cylinder manifold to suitable points having diffusing nozzles. An alarm should be activated in the compartment before the carbon dioxide is released to give personnel time to evacuate the compartment.

22.8.2 Foam Systems

These are used for fighting fire in the cargo spaces, on the cargo deck, in the pumproom or in the engine spaces. A foam system has storage tanks containing foam concentrate. Water from the fire pumps picks up the correct proportion of foam concentrate from the tank through a proportioner and the foam solution is then conveyed through permanent supply lines to offtake points.

22.8.3 Water Fog

Water fog is supplied through a system of high pressure water lines and fog nozzles. A ring of nozzles around the inside of the tank opening effectively blankets a cargo tank hatch fire. Some ships are also fitted with fixed pressurised water fog protection for boiler rooms, machinery spaces, and pumprooms.

22.8.4 Water Curtain

Some ships have a fixed system to give a protective water curtain between the cargo deck and the superstructure.

22.8.5 Inert Gas System

The purpose of an inert gas system is to prevent cargo tank fires or explosions. It is not a fixed fire-fighting installation, but in the event of a fire, the system may be of assistance in extinguishing it.

22.8.6 Steam Smothering System

> **Steam smothering systems may be fitted in older tankers. Their use should be discouraged because of their inefficiency and the risk of static electricity generation.**

22.9 TERMINAL FIRE-FIGHTING EQUIPMENT

The type and quantity of fire-fighting equipment should be related to the size, location and frequency of use of the terminal; other relevant factors are the layout of, and the petroleum products handled by, the terminal.

In ports with many terminals or in congested industrial locations the local authority or port authority may provide the main fire-fighting capability. Arrangements may exist between oil terminals or with other industries in the same area for assistance in the event of a fire.

Because of these many variables it is impractical here to make comprehensive recommendations on terminal fire-fighting equipment. Each terminal should be studied individually when deciding upon the type, location and use of such equipment.

The OCIMF publication "Guide on Marine Terminal Fire Protection and Emergency Evacuation" should be referred to for further guidance.

22.10 TERMINAL PORTABLE FIRE-FIGHTING EQUIPMENT

22.10.1 General

Portable fire extinguishers should be made available at each berth to allow terminal personnel to attack an outbreak of fire immediately in order to limit the area of fire, to extinguish the fire and thereafter to prevent re-ignition.

22.10.2 Foam Extinguishers

Small foam extinguishers with capacities of about 10 litres are too limited to be effective in most cases in the event of a fire at a terminal.

Pre-mix foam appliances in the order of 100 litres capacity are most effective for use at berths. These produce 1000 litres of foam and it is desirable to have a jet length of about 12 metres.

22.10.3 Dry Chemical Extinguishers

Dry chemical (foam compatible) extinguishers are available in a range of capacities. The length of the application hose may have to be limited, in accordance with the manufacturer's recommendation, to maintain nozzle velocity throughout total discharge.

22.10.4 Carbon Dioxide Extinguishers

Carbon dioxide extinguishers have little value at berths or on jetties except at points where minor electrical fires could occur.

Electrical sub-stations located on jetties should be provided with an adequate number of carbon dioxide extinguishers or may have a fixed carbon dioxide system installed.

22.11 TERMINAL FIXED FIRE-FIGHTING EQUIPMENT

22.11.1 Fire Water Mains and Pumps

Fire water pipelines, either sea or fresh water, should extend as near to the heads of jetties as possible with a number of accessible water take off (hydrant) points which should be spaced not more than two or three standard hose lengths apart. The take off (hydrant) points generally consist of headers with individually valved outlets fitted with a fire hose connection suitable for the particular type of fire hose coupling in use locally. Isolating valves should be fitted so as to maintain the efficiency of the system in the event of a fracture.

The hydraulics of fire water or foam pipeline systems dictate the characteristics of the fixed pumping capacities required. It may be desirable to consider whether such fixed pumping units should have two independent sources of power or whether mobile pumps should be available for use in the event of a breakdown of the fixed pumping unit; these may also be used for boosting fire water main pressure.

Terminals should have a suitable connection or adaptor fitted with an International Shore Fire Connection through which water could be supplied to a tanker's fire main if required (see Appendix E).

The minimum capacities and pressures for fire water mains are dependent upon whether the system is to be used for cooling or for the production of foam, and upon the length of jet required.

At some locations, precautions against the freezing of fire water mains may be necessary.

22.11.2 Foam Mains

Where pipelines for foam solution or concentrate are provided the lines should have a number of accessible take off (hydrant) points which should be spaced not more than two or three standard hose lengths apart. The take off (hydrant) points generally consist of a header fitted with two outlets individually valved and fitted with a fire hose connection suitable for the particular type of fire hose coupling in use locally. Isolating valves should be fitted so as to maintain the integrity of the line in the event of fracture. Suitable pipeline drain valves and wash out facilities should be provided. A foam solution pipeline of this type should cater for a design minimum of 115 cubic metres/hour of solution.

Foam concentrate can be distributed through a smaller bore pipe system to the tanks supplying the inductors of fixed or mobile foam making appliances.

Fixed pipelines for generated (aerated) foam are of limited value owing to pressure losses in the system and lack of projection.

22.11.3 Monitors and Cannons

The terms 'monitor' and 'cannon' may be used interchangeably; in this guide the term monitor is used to mean both.

In general monitors may be used for foam or water, although specific types may be designed solely for foam. Large capacity monitors would normally be on a fixed mounting or on a mobile unit.

The effective height of the liquid stream required from a monitor is dictated by the particular use envisaged. If the monitor is required to assist in the event of a tanker fire, an important consideration is the height of freeboard which, for large tankers, can be in excess of 20 metres. Minimum requirements for monitor operations are a jet length of 30 metres and a jet height of 15 metres in still air.

Monitors may be mounted on fixed towers, remotely controlled either from the tower base or at a distance. Tower base controls may need special protection. Fixed tower installations may have the drawback that smoke may obscure vision and sighting when the wind direction is unfavourable.

Foam and water monitors can also be installed on articulated or telescopic booms and be remotely operated. This provides additional flexibility over fixed monitors; for example, if the tanker is loaded the boom can be lowered and extended over the tanker to apply the foam gently with a minimum of disturbance.

Two basic types of boom are available. One has only a monitor at its top while the other has a monitor and a platform or basket to carry personnel. There are advantages for the latter unit in that it can be used to place fire-fighters on or take them off the vessel if the gangway is unusable owing to the fire. In addition, personnel can be elevated to observe the fire and direct the fire-fighting.

Ideally, booms or towers should be installed on tugs. Booms have advantages over stationary elevated towers on tugs for both fire-fighting and tug operations. With the boom lowered, the tug can manoeuvre under hawsers or other obstructions and then elevate the boom to the desired position. Fixed monitors on towers or on the deck of a tug do not have this flexibility.

22.11.4 Fixed Water Spray or Drencher System

A fixed water spray or drencher system installed for fire protection should incorporate drencher heads having 12 millimetres minimum orifice openings, rather than small holes drilled in a pipe header which can become clogged due to corrosion or by painting over the holes.

The design of a fire water system should ensure that drencher systems or similar fixed cooling arrangements do not materially reduce the volume of water available for fire-fighting.

22.12 WATER-BORNE FIRE-FIGHTING EQUIPMENT

Water borne equipment is highly effective in fire-fighting at a terminal. Such a capability is normally best provided by working tugs fitted with fire-fighting equipment, including foam facilities, which should be capable of tackling a deck fire on the largest tanker likely to use the port. In very special circumstances consideration may be given to the provision of a specifically equipped fire-fighting tender.

Fire-fighting craft, especially those at terminals with buoy mooring berths, should have a connection for an International Shore Fire Connection (see Appendix E) for use in boosting pressure in, or supplies to, a tanker's fire water mains, or a suitable adaptor for this purpose. The craft should also have a connection to enable them to supply water to, or boost pressure in, a terminal fire main.

22.13 PROTECTIVE CLOTHING

The most effective fire protective clothing presently available is made of light weight fire resistant fabric incorporating an aluminium covering, and is sometimes referred to as a fire proximity suit. This type of suit is not suitable for direct entry into fire areas. Heavier weight suits, termed fire suits, permit personnel actually to enter the fire area wearing breathing apparatus.

Although early suits were made of asbestos, this type is not now recommended. Asbestos absorbs and transmits heat much more quickly than newer types of material, and clothing made of asbestos provides protection only for a short period. Asbestos must be kept dry, otherwise there is a danger that the wearer will be scalded when exposed to fire. Personnel wearing gloves should be standing by ready to remove asbestos clothing that has become very hot.

All protective clothing should be kept serviceable and dry, and should be properly fastened while being worn.

On tankers, protective clothing should be stowed near lockers that contain breathing apparatus.

Chapter 23

Pyrophoric Iron Sulphide

This Chapter deals with the formation of pyrophoric iron sulphides in cargo tanks and the dangers to safe tanker operation from pyrophoric oxidation.

23.1 PYROPHORIC OXIDATION

In an oxygen-free atmosphere where hydrogen sulphide gas is present (or specifically where the concentration of hydrogen sulphide exceeds that of the oxygen), iron oxide is converted to iron sulphide. When the iron sulphide is subsequently exposed to air, it is oxidised back to iron oxide and either free sulphur or sulphur dioxide gas is formed. This oxidation can be accompanied by the generation of considerable heat so that individual particles may become incandescent. Rapid exothermic oxidation with incandescence is termed pyrophoric oxidation. Pyrophoric iron sulphide i.e. iron sulphide capable of pyrophoric oxidation in air, can ignite flammable hydrocarbon gas/air mixtures.

23.2 FORMATION OF PYROPHORS

23.2.1 General

It can be seen from the above that the formation of pyrophors is therefore dependent on three factors:

- Presence of iron oxide (rust).

- Presence of hydrogen sulphide gas.

- Lack of oxygen.

However, it also depends on the comparative influence of these factors. The presence of oxygen will inhibit the conversion of iron oxide to iron sulphide. Also, while the concentration of hydrogen sulphide gas has a direct influence on the formation of pyrophors, the degree of porosity of the iron oxide and the rate of flow of the gas over its surface will influence the rate of sulphidation. Experiments have supported the view that there is no safe level of hydrogen sulphide below which a pyrophor cannot be generated.

23.2.2 In Terminal Operations

In terminal operations, pyrophoric iron sulphide is well recognised as a potential source of ignition. Pyrophoric deposits are apt to accumulate in storage tanks in sour crude service and in process equipment handling sour streams. When such tanks or equipment are taken out of service, it is normal practice to keep all internal surfaces thoroughly wet during ventilation so that there can be no pyrophoric reaction before the equipment is made hydrocarbon gas free. Deposits and sludge must be kept wet until removed to a safe area where subsequent ignition will cause no damage. Numerous fires have occurred when deposits have dried out prematurely.

23.2.3   In Marine Operations

While pyrophoric iron sulphide is a widely recognised ignition source in shore-based operations, it has rarely been cited as the cause of a marine ignition and in those few cases the hydrogen sulphide levels were very high. Presumably marine operations have been free of this hazard because the cargo tanks of non-inerted ships normally contain some oxygen in the vapour space as a result of tank breathing.

23.2.4   In Inerted Cargo Tanks

The use of inert gas on crude carriers may, by decreasing the initial oxygen level as well as that of subsequent replenishments, increase the possibility of forming pyrophoric deposits. Although tanker flue gas normally contains from one to five percent oxygen, this level can be further reduced by absorption into the crude cargo. Furthermore, as the cargo tanks are kept pressurised with inert gas with a low oxygen content no air will enter the ullage space. If the pressure needs to be increased it will again be done with inert gas having a low oxygen content.

23.3   PREVENTION OF PYROPHORIC IGNITION IN CARGO TANKS

The industry-wide conversion to the use of inert gas systems on crude carriers has probably increased the possibility of forming pyrophoric deposits, but as long as the cargo tanks remain inerted there is no danger of ignition from a pyrophoric exothermic reaction. However, it is imperative that the atmosphere in the tank is not allowed to become flammable. Flammable atmospheres would inevitably arise if the tanks are discharged while the inert gas plant is inoperable.

This does not mean that the probability of ignition is high if discharge without atmospheric control takes place. Various factors may inhibit pyrophor formation or a pyrophoric reaction. These factors include:

- Lack of sufficiently thick deposits of iron oxide.

- Inclusion of elemental sulphur and crude oil in tank deposits.

- Introduction of oxygen by re-pressurising.

These inhibiting factors are not, however, predictable nor can one be confident that they will always be effective. Hence the degree of risk is judged to be high enough to require that atmosphere control is always maintained during and after discharge. To ensure that atmosphere control can be maintained, the following practices should be observed:

- Diligent maintenance of inert gas plants.

- Spares should be kept on hand for critical parts which cannot be obtained quickly or which can fail abruptly (e.g. the fans).

- In the event of an inert gas plant failure prior to or during cargo or ballast discharge, discharge should not commence or continue until the inert gas plant operation is restored, or an alternative source of inert gas is provided.

There is evidence that any pyrophoric deposit formed during the loaded passage will not necessarily be de-activated during the subsequent ballast passage. Therefore the atmosphere in the tanks should be maintained in an inert or non-flammable condition both throughout the voyage and during the discharge of ballast. The correct use of inert gas and gas-freeing procedures given in Chapters 9 and 10 should ensure that a flammable atmosphere is avoided.

Chapter 24

The Flammability Hazards Associated with the Handling, Storage and Carriage of Residual Fuel Oils

This Chapter deals with the flammability hazards associated with residual fuel oils and provides information on flashpoint and vapour composition measurement together with recommended precautionary procedures to be adopted when handling, storing or carrying residual fuel oils.

*It should be noted that this Chapter refers **only** to residual fuel oils and **not** distillate fuels.*

24.1 NATURE OF HAZARD

Residual fuel oils are capable of producing light hydrocarbons in the tank headspace such that the vapour composition may be near to or within the flammable range. This can occur even when the storage temperature is well below the measured flashpoint. This is not normally a function of the origin or manufacturing process of the fuel, although fuels containing cracked residues may show a greater tendency to generate light hydrocarbons.

Although light hydrocarbons may be present in the headspaces of residual fuel oil tanks, the risk associated with them is small unless the atmosphere is within the flammable range and an ignition source is present. In such a case an incident could result. It is therefore recommended that residual fuel oil headspaces are regarded as being potentially flammable.

24.2 FLASHPOINT AND HEADSPACE FLAMMABILITY MEASUREMENT

24.2.1 Flashpoint

Fuel oils are classified for their safety in storage, handling and transportation by reference to their closed cup flashpoint. However, information on the relationship between the calculated flammability of a headspace atmosphere and the measured flashpoint of the residual fuel oil has shown that there is no fixed correlation. A flammable atmosphere can therefore be produced in a tank headspace even when a residual fuel oil is stored at a temperature below its flashpoint.

24.2.2 Headspace Flammability

Traditionally, gas detectors such as explosimeters have been used to check that enclosed spaces are gas free and they are entirely suited to this purpose. They have also been used to measure the "flammability" of headspaces in terms of percentage of the lower flammability limit (LFL).

Such detectors rely on a calibration carried out normally on a single hydrocarbon, such as methane, which may have LFL characteristics that are far removed from the hydrocarbons actually present in the headspace. When using an explosimeter to assess the degree of hazard in non-inerted residual fuel oil tank headspaces, it is recommended that the instrument is calibrated with a pentane/air or hexane/air mixture. This will result in a more conservative estimate of the flammability but the readings should still not be regarded as providing a precise measurement of the vapour space condition.

When taking measurements, the manufacturer's operating instructions for the instrument should be closely followed and the instrument's calibration should be frequently checked as oxidation catalyst detectors (pellisters) are likely to be susceptible to poisoning when exposed to residual fuel oil vapours.

In view of the problems associated with obtaining accurate measurements of the flammability of residual fuel tank headspaces using readily available portable equipment, the measured % LFL only broadly ranks fuels in terms of relative hazard. Care should therefore be exercised in interpretation of the figures obtained by such gas detectors.

24.3 PRECAUTIONARY MEASURES

24.3.1 Storage and Handling Temperatures

When carried as fuel, temperatures of the residual fuel oil in the fuel system should conform to relevant codes of practice at all times and excessive local heating should be avoided.

24.3.2 Filling and Venting

When tanks are being filled, tank headspace gas will be displaced through vent pipes. Particular care should be taken to ensure that flame screens/traps are in good condition and that there are no ignition sources in the area immediately surrounding the venting system.

When filling empty or near empty tanks, the heating coils should be shut down and cool. Fuel oil contacting hot, exposed heating coils could possibly lead to a flammable atmosphere being rapidly generated.

24.3.3 Headspace Classification

All residual fuel oil tank headspaces should be classified as "hazardous" and suitable precautions taken. Electrical equipment within the space must meet the appropriate safety standards.

24.3.4 Hazard Reduction

The flammability of the headspace of residual fuel oil tanks should be monitored regularly. Should a measured value in excess of recommended levels be detected (IMO Resolution A.565(14) refers to a level in excess of 50% LFL), action should be taken to reduce the vapour concentration by purging the headspace with low pressure air. Gases should be vented to a safe area with no ignition sources in the vicinity of the outlet. On completion of venting, gas concentrations within the tank should continue to be monitored and further venting undertaken if necessary.

When residual fuel oil is carried as cargo on board tankers fitted with inert gas, it is recommended that the inert gas is utilised and that the headspace is maintained in an inert condition.

24.3.5 Ullaging and Sampling

All operations should be conducted such as to take due care to avoid the hazards associated with static electrical charges (see Section 7.2).

Appendix A

This Appendix comprises the Ship/Shore Safety Check List, Guidelines relating to the Check List and a specimen letter for issue by the terminal representative to masters of tankers at terminals.

SHIP/SHORE SAFETY CHECK LIST

Ship's Name:_____

Berth: _____   Port:_____

Date of Arrival:_____   Time of Arrival_____

INSTRUCTIONS FOR COMPLETION:

The safety of operations requires that all questions should be answered affirmatively by clearly ticking (✓) the appropriate box. If an affirmative answer is not possible, the reason should be given and agreement reached upon appropriate precautions to be taken between the ship and the terminal. Where any question is considered to be not applicable, then a note to that effect should be inserted in the remarks column.

A box in the columns 'ship' and 'terminal' indicates that checks should be carried out by the party concerned.

The presence of the letters **A**, **P** or **R** in the column 'Code' indicates the following:

A – any procedures and agreements should be in writing in the remarks column of this Check List or other mutually acceptable form. In either case, the signature of both parties should be required.

P – in the case of a negative answer, the operation should not be carried out without the permission of the Port Authority.

R – indicates items to be re-checked at intervals not exceeding that agreed in the declaration.

PART 'A' - BULK LIQUID GENERAL

General	Ship	Terminal	Code	Remarks
1. Is the ship securely moored?	☐	☐	R	Stop cargo at: ___ kts wind vel. Disconnect at: ___ kts wind vel. Unberth at: ___ kts wind vel.
2. Are emergency towing wires correctly positioned?	☐	☐	R	
3. Is there safe access between ship and shore?	☐	☐	R	
4. Is the ship ready to move under its own power?	☐	☐	PR	
5. Is there an effective deck watch in attendance on board and adequate supervision on the terminal and on the ship?	☐	☐	R	
6. Is the agreed ship/shore communication system operative?	☐	☐	AR	
7. Has the emergency signal to be used by the ship and shore been explained and understood?	☐	☐	A	
8. Have the procedures for cargo, bunker and ballast handling been agreed?	☐	☐	AR	
9. Have the hazards associated with toxic substances in the cargo being handled been identified and understood?	☐	☐		
10. Has the emergency shutdown procedure been agreed?	☐	☐	A	
11. Are fire hoses and fire-fighting equipment on board and ashore positioned and ready for immediate use?	☐	☐	R	
12. Are cargo and bunker hoses/arms in good condition, properly rigged and appropriate for the service intended?	☐	☐		
13. Are scuppers effectively plugged and drip trays in position, both on board and ashore?	☐	☐	R	
14. Are unused cargo and bunker connections properly secured with blank flanges fully bolted?	☐	☐		
15. Are sea and overboard discharge valves, when not in use, closed and visibly secured?	☐	☐		
16. Are all cargo and bunker tank lids closed?	☐	☐		
17. Is the agreed tank venting system being used?	☐	☐	AR	
18. Has the operation of the P/V valves and/or high velocity vents been verified using the checklift facility, where fitted?	☐	☐		
19. Are hand torches of an approved type?	☐	☐		

General	Ship	Terminal	Code	Remarks
20. Are portable VHF/UHF transceivers of an approved type?	☐	☐		
21. Are the ship's main radio transmitter aerials earthed and radars switched off?	☐	☐		
22. Are electric cables to portable electrical equipment disconnected from power?	☐	☐		
23. Are all external doors and ports in the accommodation closed?	☐	☐	R	
24. Are window-type air conditioning units disconnected?	☐	☐		
25. Are air conditioning intakes which may permit the entry of cargo vapours closed?	☐	☐		
26. Are the requirements for use of galley equipment and other cooking appliances being observed?	☐	☐	R	
27. Are smoking regulations being observed?	☐	☐	R	
28. Are naked light regulations being observed?	☐	☐	R	
29. Is there provision for an emergency escape?	☐	☐		
30. Are sufficient personnel on board and ashore to deal with an emergency?	☐	☐	R	
31. Are adequate insulating means in place in the ship/shore connection?	☐	☐		
32. Have measures been taken to ensure sufficient pumproom ventilation?	☐	☐	R	
33. If the ship is capable of closed loading, have the requirements for closed operations been agreed?	☐	☐	R	
34. Has a vapour return line been connected?	☐	☐		
35. If a vapour return line is connected, have operating parameters been agreed?	☐	☐		
36. Are ship emergency fire control plans located externally?	☐	☐		

If the ship is fitted, or required to be fitted, with an Inert Gas System the following questions should be answered.

Inert Gas System	Ship	Terminal	Code	Remarks
37. Is the Inert Gas System fully operational and in good working order?	☐	☐	P	
38. Are deck seals in good working order?	☐	☐	R	
39. Are liquid levels in P/V breakers correct?	☐	☐	R	
40. Have the fixed and portable oxygen analysers been calibrated and are they working properly?	☐	☐	R	
41. Are fixed IG pressure and oxygen content recorders working?	☐	☐	R	
42. Are all cargo tank atmospheres at positive pressure with an oxygen content of 8% or less by volume?	☐	☐	PR	
43. Are all the individual tank IG valves (if fitted) correctly set and locked?	☐	☐	R	
44. Are all the persons in charge of cargo operations aware that in the case of failure of the Inert Gas Plant, discharge operations should cease and the terminal be advised?	☐			

If the ship is fitted with a crude oil washing (COW) system, and intends to crude oil wash, the following questions should be answered.

Crude Oil Washing	Ship	Terminal	Code	Remarks
45. Is the Pre-Arrival Crude Oil Washing Check List, as contained in the approved Crude Oil Washing Manual, satisfactorily completed?	☐	☐		
46. Is the Crude Oil Washing Check List for use before, during and after Crude Oil Washing, as contained in the approved Crude Oil Washing Manual, available and being used?	☐	☐	R	

If the ship is planning to tank clean alongside, the following questions should be answered.

Tank Cleaning	Ship	Shore	Remarks
Are tank cleaning operations planned during the ship's stay alongside the shore installation?	Yes/No*		
If so, have the Port Authority and terminal authority been informed?	Yes/No*	Yes/No*	

* Delete Yes or No as appropriate

PART 'B' - BULK LIQUID CHEMICALS

Bulk Liquid Chemicals	Ship	Terminal	Code	Remarks
1. Is information available giving the necessary data for the safe handling of the cargo, and where applicable a manufacturer's inhibition certificate?	☐	☐		
2. Is sufficient and suitable protective equipment (including self-contained breathing apparatus) and protective clothing ready for immediate use?	☐	☐		
3. Have counter measures against accidental personal contact with the cargo been agreed?	☐	☐		
4. Is the cargo handling rate compatible with the automatic shutdown system, if in use?	☐	☐	A	
5. Are cargo system gauges and alarms correctly set and in good order?	☐	☐		
6. Are portable vapour detection instruments readily available for the products to be handled?	☐	☐		
7. Has information on fire-fighting media and procedures been exchanged?	☐	☐		
8. Are transfer hoses of suitable material, resistant to the chemical action of the cargoes?	☐	☐		
9. Is cargo handling being performed with portable pipelines?	☐	☐	P	

PART 'C' - BULK LIQUEFIED GASES

Bulk Liquefied Gases	Ship	Terminal	Code	Remarks
1. Is information available giving the necessary data for the safe handling of the cargo including, as applicable, a manufacturer's inhibition certificate?	☐	☐		
2. Is the water spray system ready for use?	☐	☐		
3. Is sufficient suitable protective equipment (including self-contained breathing apparatus) and protective clothing ready for immediate use?	☐	☐		
4. Are hold and inter-barrier spaces properly inerted or filled with dry air as required?	☐			
5. Are all remote control valves in working order?	☐	☐		
6. Are the required cargo pumps and compressors in good order, and have maximum working pressures been agreed between ship and shore?	☐	☐	A	
7. Is reliquefaction or boil off control equipment in good order?	☐			
8. Is the gas detection equipment properly set for the cargo, calibrated and in good order?	☐	☐		
9. Are cargo system gauges and alarms correctly set and in good order?	☐	☐		
10. Are emergency shutdown systems working properly?	☐	☐		
11. Does the shore know the closing rate of ship's automatic valves; does the ship have similar details of shore system?	☐	☐	A	Ship: .... Shore: ....

Bulk Liquefied Gases	Ship	Terminal	Code	Remarks
12. Has information been exchanged between ship and shore on the maximum/minimum temperatures/ pressures of the cargo to be handled?	☐	☐	A	
13. Are cargo tanks protected against inadvertent overfilling at all times while any cargo operations are in progress?	☐	☐		
14. Is the compressor room properly ventilated, the electrical motor room properly pressurised and the alarm system working?	☐	☐		
15. Are cargo tank relief valves set correctly and actual relief valve settings clearly and visibly displayed? Tank No. 1 .... Tank No. 2 .... Tank No. 3 .... Tank No. 4 .... Tank No. 5 .... Tank No. 6 .... Tank No. 7 .... Tank No. 8 .... Tank No. 9 .... Tank No. 10	☐			

Declaration

We the undersigned have checked, where appropriate jointly, the items on this check list and have satisfied ourselves that the entries we have made are correct to the best of our knowledge.

We have also made arrangements to carry out repetitive checks as necessary and agreed that those items with the letter '**R**' in the column '**Code**' should be re-checked at intervals not exceeding _____ hours.

For Ship	For Shore
Name:	Name:
Rank:	Position:
Signature:	Signature:
Date: Time:	

SHIP/SHORE SAFETY CHECK LIST GUIDELINES

Introduction

Before liquid bulk dangerous substances are pumped into or out of any ship, or into a shore installation, the master of the ship and the berth operator should:

- Agree in writing on the handling procedures including the maximum loading or unloading rates;

- Complete and sign, as appropriate, the Ship/Shore Safety Check List, showing the main safety precautions to be taken before and during such handling operations; and

- Agree in writing on the action to be taken in the event of an emergency during handling operations.

The following guidelines have been produced to assist berth operators and ship masters in their joint use of the Ship/Shore Safety Check List.

The Mutual Safety Examination

A tanker presenting itself to a loading or discharging terminal needs to check its own preparations and its fitness for the safety of the intended cargo operation. Additionally, the master of a ship has a responsibility to assure himself that the terminal operator has likewise made proper preparations for the safe operation of his terminal.

Equally the terminal needs to check its own preparations and to be assured that the tanker has carried out its checks and has made appropriate arrangements.

The Ship/Shore Safety Check List, by its questions and requirements for exchange of written agreements for certain procedures, should be considered a minimum basis for the essential considerations which should be included in such a mutual examination.

Some of the Check List questions are directed to considerations for which the ship has prime responsibility, others apply to both ship and terminal.

All items lying within the responsibility of the tanker should be personally checked by the tanker's representative and similarly all items which are the terminal's responsibility should be personally checked by the terminal representative. In carrying out their full responsibilities however, both representatives, by questioning the other, by sighting of records and, where felt appropriate, by joint visual inspection should assure themselves that the standards of safety on both sides of the operation are fully acceptable.

The joint declaration should not be signed until such mutual assurance is achieved.

Thus all applicable questions should result in an affirmative mark in the boxes provided. If a difference of opinion arises on the adequacy of any arrangements made or conditions found, the operation should not be started until measures taken are jointly accepted.

A negative answer to the questions coded "**P**" does not necessarily mean that the intended operation cannot be carried out. In such cases, however, permission to proceed should be obtained from the Port Authority.

Items coded "**R**" should be re-checked at intervals not exceeding that agreed in the declaration.

Where an item is agreed to be not applicable to the ship, to the terminal or to the operation envisaged, a note to that effect should be entered in the "Remarks" column.

Whilst the Ship/Shore Safety Check List is based upon cargo handling operations, it is recommended that the same mutual examination, using the Check List as appropriate, be carried out when a tanker presents itself at a berth for tank cleaning after carriage of liquid bulk dangerous substances.

Deviations

The conditions under which the operation takes place may change during the process. The changes may be such that safety can no longer be regarded as guaranteed. The party noticing or causing the unsafe condition is under an obligation to take all necessary actions, which may include stopping the operation, to re-establish safe conditions. The presence of the unsafe condition should be reported to the other party and where necessary, co-operation with the other party should be sought.

Tank Cleaning Activities

The questions on tank cleaning are provided in the list in order to inform the terminal and the port authorities of the ship's intentions regarding these activities.

GUIDELINES FOR COMPLETING THE SHIP/SHORE SAFETY CHECK LIST

PART 'A' - BULK LIQUID GENERAL

1.   Is the ship securely moored?

In answering this question, due regard should be given to the need for adequate fendering arrangements.

Ships should remain adequately secured in their moorings. Alongside piers or quays, ranging of the ship should be prevented by keeping all mooring lines taut; attention should be given to the movement of the ship caused by wind, currents, tides or passing ships and the operation in progress.

The wind velocity at which loading arms should be disconnected, cargo operations stopped or the vessel unberthed, should be stated.

Wire ropes and fibre ropes should not be used together in the same direction (i.e. breasts, springs, head or stern) because of the difference in their elastic properties.

Once moored, ships fitted with automatic tension winches should not use such winches in the automatic mode.

Means should be provided to enable quick and safe release of the ship in case of an emergency. In ports where anchors are required to be used, special consideration should be given to this matter.

Irrespective of the mooring method used, the emergency release operation should be agreed, taking into account the possible risks involved.

Anchors not in use should be properly secured.

2.   Are emergency towing wires correctly positioned?

Emergency towing wires (fire wires) should be positioned both on the off-shore bow and quarter of the ship. At a buoy mooring, emergency towing wires should be positioned on the side opposite to the hose string.

There are various methods for rigging emergency towing wires currently in use. Some terminals may require a particular method to be used and the ship should be advised accordingly.

3.   Is there safe access between ship and shore?

The access should be positioned as far away from the manifolds as practicable.

The means of access to the ship should be safe and may consist of an appropriate gangway or accommodation ladder with a properly secured safety net fitted to it.

Particular attention to safe access should be given where the difference in level between the point of access on the vessel and the jetty or quay is large or likely to become large.

When terminal access facilities are not available and a ship's gangway is used, there should be an adequate landing area on the berth so as to provide the gangway with a sufficient clear run of space and so maintain safe and convenient access to the ship at all states of tide and changes in the ship's freeboard.

Near the access ashore, appropriate life-saving equipment should be provided by the terminal. A lifebuoy should be available on board the ship near the gangway or accommodation ladder.

The access should be safely and properly illuminated during darkness.

Persons who have no legitimate business on board, or who do not have the master's permission, should be refused access to the ship.

The terminal should control access to the jetty or berth in agreement with the ship.

4.   Is the ship ready to move under its own power?

The ship should be able to move under its own power at short notice, unless permission to immobilise the ship has been granted by the Port Authority and the terminal manager.

Certain conditions may have to be met for permission to be granted.

5.   Is there an effective deck watch in attendance on board and adequate supervision on the terminal and on the ship?

The operation should be under constant control both on ship and shore.

Supervision should be aimed at preventing the development of hazardous situations; if however such a situation arises, the controlling personnel should have adequate means available to take corrective action.

The controlling personnel on ship and shore should maintain an effective communication with their respective supervisors.

All personnel connected with the operations should be familiar with the dangers of the substances handled.

6.   Is the agreed ship/shore communication system operative?

Communication should be maintained in the most efficient way between the responsible officer on duty on the ship and the responsible person ashore.

When telephones are used, the telephone both on board and ashore should be continuously manned by a person who can immediately contact his respective supervisor. Additionally, the supervisor should have a facility to override all calls. When RT/VHF systems are used the units should preferably be portable and carried by the supervisor or a person who can get in touch with his respective supervisor immediately. Where fixed systems are used the guidelines for telephones should apply.

The selected system of communication, together with the necessary information on telephone numbers and/or channels to be used, should be recorded on the appropriate form. This form should be signed by both ship and shore representatives.

The telephone and portable RT/VHF systems should comply with the appropriate safety requirements.

7. Has the emergency signal to be used by the ship and shore been explained and understood?

The agreed signal to be used in the event of an emergency arising ashore or on board should be clearly understood by shore and ship personnel.

8. Have the procedures for cargo, bunker and ballast handling been agreed?

The procedures for the intended operation should be pre-planned. They should be discussed and agreed upon by the ship and shore representatives prior to the start of the operations. Agreed arrangements should be formally recorded and signed by both ship and terminal representatives. Any change in the agreed procedure that could affect the operation should be discussed by both parties and agreed upon. After agreement has been reached by both parties, substantial changes should be laid down in writing as soon as possible and in sufficient time before the change in procedure takes place. In any case, the change should be laid down in writing within the working period of those supervisors on board and ashore in whose working period agreement on the change was reached.

The operations should be suspended and all deck and vent openings closed on the approach of an electrical storm.

The properties of the substances handled, the equipment of ship and shore installation, the ability of the ship's crew and shore personnel to execute the necessary operations and to sufficiently control the operations are factors which should be taken into account when ascertaining the possibility of handling a number of substances concurrently.

The manifold areas both on board and ashore should be safely and properly illuminated during darkness.

The initial and maximum loading rates, topping off rates and normal stopping times should be agreed, having regard to:

- The nature of the cargo to be handled.

- The arrangement and capacity of the ship's cargo lines and gas venting systems.

- The maximum allowable pressure and flow rate in the ship/shore hoses and loading arms.

- Precautions to avoid accumulation of static electricity.

- Any other flow control limitations.

A record to this effect should be formally made as above.

9. Have the hazards associated with toxic substances in the cargo being handled been identified and understood?

Many tanker cargoes contain components which are known to be hazardous to human health. In order to minimise the impact on personnel, information on cargo constituents should be available during the cargo transfer to enable the adoption of proper precautions. In addition, some port states require such information to be readily available during cargo transfer and in the event of an accidental spill.

The information provided should identify the constituents by chemical name, name in common usage, UN number and the maximum concentration expressed as a percentage by volume.

10. Has the emergency shutdown procedure been agreed?

An emergency shutdown procedure should be agreed between ship and shore, formally recorded and signed by both the ship and terminal representative.

The agreement should state the circumstances in which operations have to be stopped immediately .

Due regard should be given to the possible introduction of dangers associated with the emergency shutdown procedure.

11. **Are fire hoses and fire-fighting equipment on board and ashore positioned and ready for immediate use?**

Fire-fighting equipment both on board and ashore should be correctly positioned and ready for immediate use.

Adequate units of fixed or portable equipment should be stationed to cover the ship's cargo deck and on the jetty. The ship and shore fire main systems should be pressurised, or be capable of being pressurised at short notice.

Both ship and shore should ensure that their fire main systems can be inter-connected in a quick and easy way utilising, if necessary, the international shore fire connection.

12. **Are cargo and bunker hoses/arms in good condition, properly rigged and appropriate for the service intended?**

Hoses should be in a good condition and properly fitted and rigged so as to prevent strain and stress beyond design limitations.

All flange connections should be fully bolted and any other types of connections should be properly secured.

It should be ensured that the hoses/arms are constructed of a material suitable for the substance to be handled taking into account its temperature and the maximum operating pressure.

Cargo hoses should be properly marked and identifiable with regard to their suitability for the intended operation.

13. **Are scuppers effectively plugged and drip trays in position, both on board and ashore?**

Where applicable all scuppers on board and drain holes ashore should be properly plugged during the operations. Accumulation of water should be drained off periodically.

Both ship and jetty manifolds should ideally be provided with fixed drip trays; in their absence portable drip trays should be used.

All drip trays should be emptied in an appropriate manner whenever necessary but always after completion of the specific operation.

When only corrosive liquids or refrigerated gases are being handled, the scuppers may be kept open, provided that an ample supply of water is available at all times in the vicinity of the manifolds.

14. **Are unused cargo and bunker connections properly secured with blank flanges fully bolted?**

Unused cargo and bunker line connections should be closed and blanked. Blank flanges should be fully bolted and other types of fittings, if used, properly secured.

15. **Are sea and overboard discharge valves, when not in use, closed and visibly secured?**

Experience shows the importance of this item in pollution avoidance on ships where cargo lines and ballast systems are interconnected. Remote operating controls for such valves should be identified in order to avoid inadvertent opening.

If appropriate, the security of the valves in question should be checked visually.

16. Are all cargo and bunker tank lids closed?

Apart from the openings in use for tank venting (refer to question 17) all openings to cargo tanks should be closed and gastight.

Except on gas tankers, ullaging and sampling points may be opened for the short periods necessary for ullaging and sampling.

Closed ullaging and sampling systems should he used where required by international, national or local regulations and agreements.

17. Is the agreed tank venting system being used?

Agreement should be reached, and recorded, as to the venting system for the operation, taking into account the nature of the cargo and international, national or local regulations and agreements.

There are three basic systems for venting tanks:

1. Open to atmosphere via open ullage ports, protected by suitable flame screens.

2. Fixed venting systems which includes inert gas systems.

3. To shore through other vapour collection systems.

18. Has the operation of the P/V valves and/or high velocity vents been verified using the checklift facility, where fitted?

The operation of the P/V valves and/or high velocity vents should be checked using the testing facility provided by the manufacturer. Furthermore, it is imperative that an adequate check is made, visually or otherwise at this time to ensure that the checklift is actually operating the valve. On occasion a seized or stiff vent has caused the checklift drive pin to shear and the ship's personnel to assume, with disastrous consequences, that the vent was operational.

19. Are hand torches of an approved type? and,

20. Are portable VHF/UHF transceivers of an approved type?

Battery operated hand torches and VHF radio-telephone sets should be of a safe type which is approved by a competent authority. Ship/shore telephones should comply with the requirements for explosion-proof construction except when placed in a safe space in the accommodation.

VHF radio-telephone sets may operate in the internationally agreed wave bands only.

The above mentioned equipment should be well maintained. Damaged units, even though they may be capable of operation, should not be used.

21. Are the ship's main radio transmitter aerials earthed and radars switched off?

The ship's main radio station should not be used during the ship's stay in port, except for receiving purposes. The main transmitting aerials should be disconnected and earthed.

Satellite communications equipment may be used normally unless advised otherwise.

The ship's radar installation should not be used unless the master, in consultation with the terminal manager, has established the conditions under which the installation may be used safely.

22. Are electric cables to portable electrical equipment disconnected from power?

The use of portable electrical equipment on wandering leads should be prohibited in hazardous zones during cargo operations and the equipment preferably removed from the hazardous zone.

Telephone cables in use in the ship/shore communication system should preferably be routed outside the hazardous zone. Wherever this is not feasible, the cable should be so positioned and protected that no danger arises from its use.

23. Are all external doors and ports in the accommodation closed?

External doors, windows and portholes in the accommodation should be closed during cargo operations. These doors should be clearly marked as being required to be closed during such operations, but at no time should they be locked.

24. Are window type air conditioning units disconnected? and,

25. Are air conditioning intakes which may permit the entry of cargo vapours closed?

Window type air conditioning units should be disconnected from their power supply.

Air conditioning and ventilator intakes which are likely to draw in air from the cargo area should be closed.

Air conditioning units which are located wholly within the accommodation and which do not draw in air from the outside may remain in operation.

26. Are the requirements for the use of galley equipment and other cooking appliances being observed?

Open fire systems may be used in galleys whose construction, location and ventilation system provides protection against entry of flammable gases.

In cases where the galley does not comply with the above, open fire systems may be used provided the master, in consultation and agreement with the terminal representative, has ensured that precautions have been taken against the entry and accumulation of flammable gases.

On ships with stern discharge lines which are in use, open fire systems in galley equipment should not be allowed unless the ship is constructed to permit their use in such circumstances.

27. Are smoking regulations being observed?

Smoking on board the ship may only take place in places specified by the master in consultation with the terminal manager or his representative.

No smoking is allowed on the jetty and the adjacent area except in buildings and places specified by the terminal manager in consultation with the master.

Places which are directly accessible from the outside should not be designated as places where smoking is permitted. Buildings, places and rooms designated as areas where smoking is permitted should be clearly marked as such.

28. Are naked light regulations being observed?

A naked light or open fire comprises the following: flame, spark formation, naked electric light or any surface with a temperature that is equal to or higher than the minimum ignition temperature of the products handled in the operation.

The use of open fire on board the ship, and within a distance of 25 metres of the ship, should be prohibited, unless all applicable regulations have been met and agreement reached by the port authority, terminal manager and the master. This distance may have to be extended for ships of a specialised nature such as gas tankers.

29. **Is there provision for an emergency escape?**

In addition to the means of access referred to in question 3, a safe and quick emergency escape route should be available both on board and ashore. On board the ship it may consist of a lifeboat ready for immediate use, preferably at the after end of the ship.

30. **Are sufficient personnel on board and ashore to deal with an emergency?**

At all times during the ship's stay at a terminal, a sufficient number of personnel should be present on board the ship and in the shore installation to deal with an emergency.

31. **Are adequate insulating means in place in the ship/shore connection?**

Unless measures are taken to break the continuous electrical path between ship and shore pipework provided by the ship/shore hoses or metallic arms, stray electric currents, mainly from corrosion prevention systems, can cause electric sparks at the flange faces when hoses are being connected and disconnected.

The passage of these currents is usually prevented by an insulating flange inserted at each jetty manifold outlet or incorporated in the construction of metallic arms. Alternatively, the electrical discontinuity may be provided by the inclusion of one length of electrically discontinuous hose in each hose string.

It should be ascertained that the means of electrical discontinuity is in place, is in good condition and that it is not being by-passed by contact with an electrically conductive material.

32. **Have measures been taken to ensure sufficient pumproom ventilation?**

Pumprooms should be mechanically ventilated and the ventilation system, which should maintain a safe atmosphere throughout the pumproom, should be kept running throughout the operation.

33. **If the ship is capable of closed loading, have the requirements for closed operations been agreed?**

It is a requirement of many terminals that when the ship is ballasting, loading and discharging, it operates without recourse to opening ullage and sighting ports. Such ships will require the means to enable closed monitoring of tank contents, either by a fixed gauging system or by using portable equipment passed through a vapour lock, and preferably backed up by an independent overfill alarm system.

34. **Has a vapour return line been connected?**

If required, a vapour return line may have to be used to return flammable vapours from the cargo tanks to shore.

35. **If a vapour return line is connected, have operating parameters been agreed?**

The maximum and minimum operating pressures and any other constraints associated with the operation of the vapour return system should be discussed and agreed by ship and shore personnel.

36. **Are ship emergency fire control plans located externally?**

A set of fire control plans should be permanently stored in a prominently marked weathertight enclosure outside the deckhouse for the assistance of shoreside fire-fighting personnel. A crew list should also be included in this enclosure.

If the ship is fitted, or required to be fitted, with an Inert Gas System the following questions should be answered.

37. **Is the Inert Gas System fully operational and in good working order?**

The inert gas system should be in safe working condition with particular reference to all interlocking trips and associated alarms, deck seal, non-return valve, pressure regulating control system, main deck IG line pressure indicator, individual tank IG valves (when fitted) and deck P/V breaker.

Individual tank IG valves (if fitted) should have easily identified and fully functioning open/close position indicators.

38. **Are deck seals in good working order?**

It is essential that the deck seal arrangements are in a safe condition. In particular, the water supply arrangements to the seal and the proper functioning of associated alarms should be checked.

39. **Are liquid levels in P/V breakers correct?**

Checks should be made to ensure the liquid level in the P/V breaker complies with manufacturer's recommendations

40. **Have the fixed and portable oxygen analysers been calibrated and are they working properly?**

All fixed and portable oxygen analysers should be calibrated and checked as required by the company and/or manufacturer's instructions. The in-line oxygen analyser/recorder and sufficient portable oxygen analysers should be working properly.

41. **Are fixed IG pressure and oxygen content recorders working?**

All recording equipment should be switched on and operating correctly.

42. **Are all cargo tank atmospheres at positive pressure with an oxygen content of 8% or less by volume?**

Prior to commencement of cargo operations, each cargo tank atmosphere should be checked to verify an oxygen content of 8% or less by volume. Inerted cargo tanks should at all times be kept at a positive pressure.

43. **Are all the individual tank IG valves (if fitted) correctly set and locked?**

For both loading and discharge operations it is normal and safe to keep all individual tank IG supply valves (if fitted) open in order to prevent inadvertent under or over pressurisation. In this mode of operation each tank pressure will be the same as the deck main IG pressure and thus the P/V breaker will act as a safety valve in case of excessive over or under pressure. If individual tank IG supply valves are closed for reasons of potential vapour contamination or de-pressurisation for gauging, etc., then the status of the valve should be clearly indicated to all those involved in cargo operations. Each individual tank IG valve should be fitted with a locking device under the control of a responsible officer.

44. **Are all the persons in charge of cargo operations aware that in the case of failure of the Inert Gas Plant, discharge operations should cease, and the terminal be advised?**

In the case of failure of the IG plant, the cargo discharge, de-ballasting and tank cleaning should cease and the terminal to be advised.

Under no circumstances should the ship's officers allow the atmosphere in any tank to fall below atmospheric pressure.

Section 10 of the IMO publication entitled "Crude Oil Washing Systems" contains operational check lists for the use of the crew at each discharge in accordance with Regulation 13B of Annex I to MARPOL 73/78. If the ship is fitted with a crude oil washing (COW) system, and intends to crude oil wash, the following questions should be answered.

45. **Is the Pre-Arrival Crude Oil Washing Check List, as contained in the approved Crude Oil Washing Manual, satisfactorily completed?**

    The approved Crude Oil Washing Manual contains a Pre-Arrival Crude Oil Washing Check List, specific to each ship, which should be completed by a responsible ship's officer prior to arrival at every discharge port where crude oil washing is intended.

46. **Is the Crude Oil Washing Check List for use before, during and after Crude Oil Washing, as contained in the approved Crude Oil Washing Manual, available and being used?**

    The approved Crude Oil Washing Manual contains a Crude Oil Washing Check List, specific to each ship, for use before, during and after crude oil washing operations. This Check List should be completed at the appropriate times and the terminal representative should be invited to participate.

PART 'B' - BULK LIQUID CHEMICALS

1. **Is information available giving the necessary data for the safe handling of the cargo, and where applicable, a manufacturer's inhibition certificate?**

    Information on the product to be handled should be available on board the ship and ashore before and during the operation.

    This information should include:

    - A cargo stowage plan.

    - A full description of the physical and chemical properties, including reactivity, necessary for the safe containment of the cargo.

    - Action to be taken in the event of spills or leaks.

    - Counter measures against accidental personal contact.

    - Fire-fighting procedures and fire-fighting media.

    - Procedures for cargo transfer.

    When cargoes required to be stabilised or inhibited are to be handled, information should be exchanged thereon.

2. **Is sufficient and suitable protective equipment (including self-contained breathing apparatus) and protective clothing ready for immediate use?**

    Suitable protective equipment (including self-contained breathing apparatus and protective clothing), appropriate to the specific dangers of the product handled, should be readily available in sufficient numbers for operational personnel both on board and ashore.

3. **Have counter measures against accidental personal contact with the cargo been agreed?**

    Sufficient and suitable means should be available to neutralise the effects and remove small quantities of spilled products. However, it is possible that unforeseen personal contact may occur.

    To limit the consequences, sufficient and suitable counter measures should be taken.

    Information on how to handle such contact having regard to the special properties of the products, should be studied and available for immediate use.

    A suitable safety shower and eye rinsing equipment should be fitted and ready for instant use in the immediate vicinity of places on board and ashore where operations regularly take place. Measures should be taken to maintain the water at a safe temperature.

4. **Is the cargo handling rate compatible with the automatic shutdown system, if in use?**

    Automatic shutdown valves may be fitted on the ship and shore. The action of these is automatically initiated by a certain level being reached in the tank being loaded either on board or ashore. In cases where such systems are used, the cargo handling rate should be so adjusted that a pressure surge evolving from the automatic closure of any such valve does not exceed the safe working pressure of either the ship or shore pipeline system.

    Alternative means, such as a recirculation system and buffer tanks, may be fitted to relieve the pressure surge created.

    A written agreement should be made between the ship and shore supervisors indicating whether the cargo handling rate will be adjusted or alternative systems will be used.

The safe handling rate should be noted in this agreement and also in the formally recorded agreement for cargo, bunker and ballast handling which has been agreed and signed by both ship and terminal representatives. (Refer to Part 'A' - Bulk Liquid General, Question 8)

5.   **Are cargo system gauges and alarms correctly set and in good order?**

Ship and shore cargo system gauges and alarms should be regularly checked to ensure they are in good working order.

In cases where it is possible to set alarms to different levels, the alarm should be set to the required level.

6.   **Are portable vapour detection instruments readily available for the products to be handled?**

The equipment provided should be capable of measuring, where appropriate, flammable and/or toxic levels.

Suitable equipment should be available to calibrate those instruments capable of measuring flammability. Calibration should be carried out before the operation commences.

7.   **Has information on fire-fighting media and procedures been exchanged?**

Information should be exchanged on the availability of fire-fighting equipment and the procedures to be followed in the event of a fire on board or ashore.

Special attention should be given to any products which are being handled which may be water reactive or require specialised fire-fighting procedures.

8.   **Are transfer hoses of suitable material, resistant to the chemical action of the cargoes?**

Each transfer hose should be indelibly marked so as to allow the identification of the products for which it is suitable, its specified maximum working pressure, the test pressure and last date of testing at this pressure, and, if used at temperature other than ambient, its maximum and minimum service temperatures.

9.   **Is cargo handling being performed with portable pipelines?**

During cargo operations where the use of portable cargo lines on board or ashore is unavoidable, care should be taken to ensure that these lines are correctly positioned and assembled so that no additional danger exists from their use. Where necessary, the electrical continuity of these lines should be checked.

The use of non-permanent equipment inside tanks is not generally permitted unless the approval of the Port Authority has been obtained.

Non-permanent cargo lines should be kept as short as possible.

Whenever cargo hoses are used to make connections within the ship or shore permanent pipeline system, these connections should be secured and kept as short as possible and be electrically continuous to the ship or shore pipeline respectively.

PART 'C' - BULK LIQUEFIED GASES

1.   Is information available giving the necessary data for the safe handling of the cargo including where applicable, a manufacturer's inhibition certificate?

Information on each product to be handled should be available on board the ship and ashore before and during the operation.

Cargo information, in a written format, should include:

- A cargo stowage plan.

- A full description of the physical and chemical properties necessary for the safe containment of the cargo.

- Action to be taken in the event of spills or leaks.

- Counter-measures against accidental personal contact.

- Fire-fighting procedures and fire fighting media.

- Procedures for cargo transfer, gas freeing, ballasting, tank cleaning and changing cargoes.

- Special equipment needed for the safe handling of the particular cargo(es).

- Minimum allowable inner hull steel temperatures; and

- Emergency procedures.

When cargoes required to be stabilised or inhibited are to be handled, ships should be provided with a certificate from the manufacture stating:

- Name and amount of inhibitor added.

- Date inhibitor was added and the normally expected duration of its effectiveness.

- Any temperature limitations affecting the inhibitor; and

- The action to be taken should the length of the voyage exceed the effective lifetime of the inhibitor.

2.   Is the water spray system ready for use?

In cases where flammable and/or toxic products are handled, water spray systems should be regularly tested. Details of the last tests should be exchanged.

During operations the systems should be kept ready for immediate use.

3.   Is sufficient suitable protective equipment (including self-contained breathing apparatus) and protective clothing ready for immediate use?

Suitable protective equipment, including self-contained breathing apparatus, eye protection and protective clothing appropriate to the specific dangers of the product handled, should be available in sufficient quantity for operations personnel both on board and ashore.

Storage places for this equipment should be protected from the weather and be clearly marked.

All personnel directly involved in the operation should utilise this equipment and clothing whenever the situation requires.

Personnel required to use breathing apparatus during operations should be trained in its safe use. Untrained personnel and personnel with facial hair should not be selected for operations involving the use of breathing apparatus.

4.   **Are hold and inter-barrier spaces properly inerted or filled with dry air as required?**

The spaces that are required to be inerted by the IMO Gas Carrier Codes should be checked by ship's personnel prior to arrival.

5.   **Are all remote control valves in working order?**

All ship and shore cargo system remote control valves and their position indicating systems should be regularly tested. Details of the last tests should be exchanged.

6.   **Are the required cargo pumps and compressors in good order, and have maximum working pressures been agreed between ship and shore?**

Agreement in writing should be reached on the maximum allowable working pressure in the cargo line system during operations.

7.   **Is reliquefaction or boil off control equipment in good order?**

It should be verified that reliquefaction and boil off control systems, if required, are functioning correctly prior to commencement of operations.

8.   **Is the gas detection equipment properly set for the cargo, calibrated and in good order?**

Span gas should be available to enable calibration of gas detection equipment. Fixed gas detection equipment should be calibrated for the product to be handled prior to commencement of operations. The alarm function should have been tested and the details of the last test should be exchanged.

Portable gas detection instruments, suitable for the products handled, capable of measuring flammable, and/or toxic levels, should be available.

Portable instruments capable of measuring in the flammable range should be calibrated for the product to be handled before operations commence.

9.   **Are cargo system gauges and alarms correctly set and in good order?**

Ship and shore cargo system gauges should be regularly checked to ensure that they are in good working order.

In cases where it is possible to set alarms to different levels, the alarm should be set to the required level.

10.   **Are emergency shutdown systems working properly?**

Where possible, ship and shore emergency shutdown systems should be tested before cargo transfers.

11.   **Does the shore know the closing rate of ship's automatic valves; does the ship have similar details of shore system?**

Automatic shutdown valves may be fitted in the ship and the shore systems. Among other parameters, the action of these valves can be automatically initiated by a certain level being reached in the tank being loaded either on board or ashore.

Where valves are fitted and used, the cargo handling rate should be so adjusted that a pressure surge evolving from the automatic closure of any such valve does not exceed the safe working pressure of either the ship or shore pipeline system.

Alternatively, means may be fitted to relieve the pressure surge created, such as recirculation systems and buffer tanks.

A written agreement should be made between the ship and shore supervisor indicating whether the cargo handling rate will be adjusted or alternative systems will be used; the safe cargo handling rate should be noted in this agreement.

12. Has information been exchanged between ship and shore on the maximum/minimum temperatures/pressures of the cargo to be handled?

Before operations commence, information should be exchanged between ship and shore representatives on cargo temperature/pressure requirements.

This information should be agreed in writing.

13. Are cargo tanks protected against inadvertent overfilling at all times while any cargo operations are in progress?

Automatic shutdown systems are normally designed to shut the liquid valves, and if discharging, to trip the cargo pumps, should the liquid level in any tank rise above the maximum permitted level. This level must be accurately set and the operation of the device tested at regular intervals.

If ship and shore shutdown systems are to be inter-connected then their operation must be checked before cargo transfer begins.

14. Is the compressor room properly ventilated, the electrical motor room properly pressurised and the alarm system working?

Fans should be run for at least 10 minutes before cargo operations commence and then continuously during cargo operations.

Audible and visual alarms, provided at airlocks associated with compressor/motor rooms, should be regularly tested.

15. Are cargo tank relief valves set correctly and actual relief valve settings clearly and visibly displayed?

In cases where cargo tanks are permitted to have more than one relief valve setting, it should be verified that the relief valve is set as required by the cargo to be handled and that the actual setting of the relief valve is clearly and visibly displayed on board the ship. Relief valve settings should be recorded on the check list.

Specimen Letter for Issue to Masters of Tankers at Terminals

Company ....

Terminal ....

Date ....

The Master
SS/MV..

Port: ....

Dear Sir,

Responsibility for the safe conduct of operations whilst your ship is at this terminal rests jointly with you, as master of the ship, and with the responsible terminal representative. We wish, therefore, before operations start, to seek your full co-operation and understanding on the safety requirements set out in the Ship/Shore Safety Check List which are based on safe practices widely accepted by the oil and the tanker industries.

We expect you, and all under your command, to adhere strictly to these requirements throughout your stay alongside this terminal and we, for our part, will ensure that our personnel do likewise, and co-operate fully with you in the mutual interest of safe and efficient operations.

Before the start of operations, and from time to time thereafter, for our mutual safety, a member of the terminal staff, where appropriate together with a responsible officer, will make a routine inspection of your ship to ensure that the questions on the Ship/Shore Safety Check List can be answered in the affirmative. Where corrective action is needed we will not agree to operations commencing or, should they have been started, we will require them to be stopped.

Similarly, if you consider safety is endangered by any action on the part of our staff or by any equipment under our control you should demand immediate cessation of operations.

THERE CAN BE NO COMPROMISE WITH SAFETY.

Please acknowledge receipt of this letter by countersigning and returning the attached copy.

Signed: ....
Terminal Representative

Terminal Representative on Duty is: ....

Position or Title: ....

Telephone No.: ....

UHF/VHF Channel: ....

Signed: ....
Master

SS/MV ....

Date: ....Time...................................

Appendix B

Fire Instructions

IN CASE OF FIRE DO NOT HESITATE TO RAISE THE ALARM

TERMINAL FIRE ALARM:

At this terminal the fire alarm signal is:

....

....

IN CASE OF FIRE:

1. Sound one or more blasts of the ship's whistle, each blast of not less than ten seconds duration supplemented by a continuous sounding of the general alarm system.

2. Contact the terminal.

   Telephone number.......................................

   UHF/VHF communication channel...................................

ACTION – SHIP

- **Fire on your ship**

  - Raise alarm

  - Fight fire and prevent fire spreading

  - Inform terminal

  - Cease all cargo/ballast operations and close all valves

  - Stand by to disconnect hoses or arms

  - Bring engines to standby

- **Fire on another ship or ashore**

  Stand by, and when instructed:

  - Cease all cargo/ballast operations and close all valves

  - Disconnect hoses or arms

  - Bring engines and crew to standby, ready to unberth

ACTION – TERMINAL

- **Fire on a Ship**

  - Raise alarm

  - Contact ship

  - Cease all cargo/ballast operations and close all valves

  - Stand by to disconnect hoses or arms

  - Stand by to assist fire fighting

  - Inform all ships

  - Implement terminal emergency plan

- **Fire Ashore**

  - Raise alarm

  - Cease all cargo/ballast operations and close all valves

  - Fight fire and prevent fire spreading

  - If required stand by to disconnect hoses or arms

  - Inform all ships

  - Implement terminal emergency plan

IN THE CASE OF FIRE THE TERMINAL PERSONNEL WILL DIRECT THE MOVEMENT OF VEHICULAR TRAFFIC ASHORE

Appendix C

Oil Cargo Hose

1 GENERAL

Oil cargo hose should conform to recognised standard specifications as laid down by a National Authority such as the British Standards Institution (BS1435) or as recommended by the Oil Companies International Marine Forum (OCIMF) and confirmed by established hose manufacturers. Hose should be of a grade and type suitable for the service and operating conditions in which it is to be used.

Special hose is required for use with high temperature cargoes such as hot asphalt. Special hose is also required for use with low temperature cargoes.

As a general indication of hose which may be supplied for normal cargo handling duty, the information given in Sections 2 to 6 of this Appendix is condensed from the British Standard BS1435. Reference may also be made to the OCIMF publication "Guide to Purchasing, Manufacturing and Testing of Loading and Discharge Hoses for Offshore Moorings".

2 TYPES AND APPLICATIONS

For normal duty there are three basic types of hose:

- **Rough bore (R):**

  This type of hose is heavy and robust with an internal lining supported by a steel wire helix. It is used for cargo handling at terminal jetties. A similar hose is made for submarine and floating use (type R x M).

- **Smooth bore (S):**

  Smooth bore hose is also used for cargo handling at terminal jetties but is of lighter construction than the rough bore type and the lining is not supported by a wire helix. A similar hose is made for submarine and floating use (type S x M).

- **Lightweight (L):**

  Lightweight hose is for discharge duty or bunkering only, where flexibility and light weight are important considerations.

All of these types of hose may be supplied in electrically continuous or electrically discontinuous construction.

There are also a number of special hose types having the same basic construction, but modified for particular purposes such as for submarine pipelines and floating hose strings. These can be made for sinking or floating and can have individual floats or integral flotation.

3 PERFORMANCE

Hose is classified according to its rated pressure and that stipulated by the manufacturer should not be exceeded. The manufacturer applies a vacuum test to hoses used for suction and discharge service.

Hose of normal standards is usually manufactured for products having a minimum temperature of -20°C to a maximum of 82°C and an aromatic hydrocarbon content not greater than 25%. Hose is normally suitable for sunlight and ambient temperatures ranging from -29°C to 52°C.

4 MARKING

Each length of hose manufactured to the British Standard or the OCIMF Guidelines should be marked by the manufacturers with:

- The manufacturer's name or trademark.

- Identification with the standard specification for manufacture.

- Factory test pressure.

- Month and year of manufacture.

- Manufacturer's serial number.

- Indication that the hose is electrically continuous or electrically discontinuous.

5 FLOW VELOCITIES

The maximum permissible flow velocity through a hose is limited by the construction of the hose. The hose manufacturer's recommendations and certification should give details. Operators should however, take other factors into account when deciding flow velocities. These should include, but not be limited to, the following:

- The factor of safety being applied.

- Any limitations imposed by flow velocities in the ships fixed piping system.

- Weather conditions causing movement of the hose.

- Age and condition of the hose.

- Amount of use and method of storing the hose.

- Other local considerations.

For conventional buoy and SPM facilities, the relevant OCIMF Guidelines should be applied; for dock facilities, the BS1435 standards are applicable.

The following tables are indicative of flow rates for hose supplied under the British Standard or the OCIMF Guidelines.

Velocity 12 metres/second			
Nominal Inside Diameter of Hose		Throughput	
Inches	Millimetres	Cubic Metres Per Hour	Barrels Per Hour
6	152	788	4,950
8	203	1,400	8,810
10	254	2,180	13,700
12	305	3,150	19,800
16	406	5,600	35,200
20	508	8,750	55,000
24	610	12,600	79,300
30	762	19,700	123,000

Table 1: *Throughput v. Inside Diameter at Velocity of 12m/s*

Velocity 15 metres/second			
Nominal Inside Diameter of Hose		Throughput	
Inches	Millimetres	Cubic Metres Per Hour	Barrels Per Hour
6	152	985	6,190
8	203	1,750	11,000
10	254	2,730	17,200
12	305	3,940	24,700
16	406	7,000	44,000
20	508	10,900	68,000
24	610	15,700	99,100
30	762	24,600	154,000

Table 2: *Throughput v. Inside Diameter at velocity of 15m/s*

6   TESTING OF HOSES

Periodic testing of hoses should be in accordance with the requirements of the specification to which the hose was manufacurered and/or as detailed in the OCIMF publication "Guide for the Handling, Storage, Inspection and Testing of Hoses in the Field".

7   HOSE FLANGE STANDARDS

Flange dimensions and drilling should conform to the common standard of ANSI B16.5, BS1560 Series 150, or equivalent as recommended for flanges on shore pipeline and ship manifold connections.

8   OPERATING CONDITIONS

For oil cargo hose to be used in normal duties:

- Oil temperatures in excess of those stipulated by the manufacturer, generally 82°C, should be avoided.

- The maximum permissible working pressure stipulated by the manufacturer should be adhered to and surge pressures should be avoided.

- The hose life will be shorter in white oil service than with black oils.

- The life of a hose can be extended by transferring it from white oil to black oil duties during its service, but any hose so transferred should be clearly and permanently marked.

9   EXTENDED STORAGE

New hoses in storage before use, or hoses removed from service for a period of two months or more, should, as far as practicable, be kept in a cool, dark, dry store in which air can circulate freely. They should be drained and washed out with fresh water and laid out horizontally on solid supports spaced to keep the hose straight. No oil should be allowed to come into contact with the outside of the hose.

If the hose is stored outside it should be well protected from the sun.

Recommendations for hose storage are given in the OCIMF publication "Guide for the Handling, Storage, Inspection and Testing of Hoses in the Field".

10   HOSE WEIGHTS

Weights of Hose Strings for Conventional Buoy Moorings

The following tables give the approximate weights of hose strings in tonnes (including fittings, floats and pick-up buoy) with all hoses full of crude oil S.G. 0·850. The assumed total lift is 7·5 metres above deck level, with the tanker on light draught.

Size of Tanker	Water Depth in Berth										
	Feet Metres	180 54	150 46	120 37	100 30	90 27	80 24	70 21	60 18	50 15	40 12	30 9
20 inches I.D. Hoses												
500,000 DWT		19.5	18.7	18.0	17.5	17.3						
330,000　,,		16.9	16.2	15.4	14.9	14.7	14.5					
270,000　,,		16.4	15.7	14.9	14.4	14.2	13.9	13.7				
200,000　,,		15.9	15.1	14.4	13.9	13.7	13.4	13.2	12.9			
100,000　,,		14.3	13.6	12.9	12.4	12.1	11.9	11.6	11.4	11.2		
70,000　,,		13.8	13.1	12.4	11.9	11.6	11.4	11.1	10.9	10.6	10.4	
50,000　,,		13.4	12.7	12.0	11.5	11.2	11.0	10.7	10.5	10.3	10.0	9.8
35,000　,,		13.1	12.3	11.6	11.1	10.8	10.6	10.4	10.1	9.9	9.6	9.4
18,000　,,		12.4	11.7	11.0	10.5	10.2	10.0	9.7	9.5	9.2	9.0	8.7
16 inches I.D. Hoses												
500,000 DWT		13.5	13.0	12.4	12.0	11.8						
330,000　,,		11.8	11.2	10.7	10.3	10.1	9.9					
270,000　,,		11.4	10.9	10.3	10.0	9.8	9.6	9.4				
200,000　,,		11.1	10.5	10.0	9.6	9.4	9.2	9.1	8.9			
100,000　,,		10.1	9.5	8.9	8.6	8.4	8.2	8.0	7.8	7.7		
70,000　,,		9.7	9.2	8.6	8.2	8.1	7.9	7.7	7.5	7.3	7.1	
50,000　,,		9.4	8.9	8.3	8.0	7.8	7.6	7.4	7.2	7.1	6.9	6.7
35,000　,,		9.2	8.6	8.1	7.7	7.5	7.3	7.2	7.0	6.7	6.6	6.4
18,000　,,		8.7	8.2	7.6	7.3	7.1	6.9	6.7	6.5	6.4	6.2	6.0
12 inches I.D. Hoses												
500,000 DWT		8.9	8.6	8.2	8.0	7.8						
330,000　,,		7.8	7.4	7.0	6.8	6.7	6.6					
270,000　,,		7.6	7.2	6.8	6.6	6.5	6.4	6.2				
200,000　,,		7.3	7.0	6.6	6.4	6.2	6.1	6.0	5.9			
100,000　,,		6.6	6.3	5.9	5.7	5.6	5.4	5.3	5.2	5.1		
70,000　,,		6.4	6.1	5.7	5.5	5.3	5.2	5.1	5.0	4.9	4.7	
50,000　,,		6.3	5.9	5.5	5.3	5.2	5.1	4.9	4.8	4.7	4.6	4.4
35,000　,,		6.1	5.7	5.4	5.1	5.0	4.9	4.8	4.6	4.5	4.4	4.3
18,000　,,		5.8	5.4	5.1	4.8	4.7	4.6	4.5	4.4	4.2	4.1	4.0
10 inches I.D. Hoses												
500,000 DWT		6.2	5.9	5.7	5.5	5.4						
330,000　,,		5.4	5.1	4.9	4.7	4.6	4.5					
270,000　,,		5.2	5.0	4.7	4.6	4.5	4.4	4.3				
200,000　,,		5.1	4.8	4.6	4.4	4.3	4.2	4.1	4.0			
100,000　,,		4.6	4.3	4.1	3.9	3.8	3.7	3.6	3.5	3.4		
70,000　,,		4.4	4.2	3.9	3.8	3.7	3.6	3.5	3.4	3.3	3.2	
50,000　,,		4.3	4.1	3.8	3.7	3.6	3.5	3.4	3.3	3.2	3.1	3.0
35,000　,,		4.2	3.9	3.7	3.5	3.4	3.3	3.2	3.1	3.0	2.9	2.8
18,000　,,		4.0	3.7	3.5	3.3	3.2	3.1	3.0	2.9	2.8	2.7	2.6
8 inches I.D. Hoses												
500,000 DWT		4.4	4.2	4.1	4.0	3.9						
330,000　,,		3.9	3.7	3.5	3.4	3.3	3.2					
270,000　,,		3.7	3.6	3.4	3.3	3.2	3.1	3.0				
200,000　,,		3.6	3.5	3.3	3.2	3.1	3.0	2.9	2.8			
100,000　,,		3.3	3.1	2.9	2.8	2.7	2.6	2.5	2.4	2.3		
70,000　,,		3.2	3.0	2.8	2.7	2.6	2.5	2.4	2.3	2.2	2.1	
50,000　,,		3.1	2.9	2.8	2.6	2.5	2.4	2.3	2.2	2.1	2.0	1.9
35,000　,,		3.0	2.9	2.7	2.5	2.4	2.3	2.2	2.1	2.0	1.9	1.8
18,000　,,		2.9	2.7	2.5	2.4	2.3	2.2	2.1	2.0	1.9	1.8	1.7

Weight of Hose Strings for Single Buoy Moorings

The following table gives the approximate weights of hose strings in tonnes (including fittings, floats and pick-up buoy) with all hoses full of crude oil of S.G.0.850. The assumed lift is 7·5 metres above deck level, with the tanker on light draught.

Size of Tanker	Inside Diameter of Hose in Inches				
	20	16	12	10	8
500,000 DWT	16.4	11.4	8.2	6.6	4.7
330,000 ,,	13.6	9.4	6.8	5.4	3.9
270,000 ,,	13.0	9.1	6.5	5.2	3.7
200,000 ,,	12.5	8.7	6.2	5.0	3.6
100,000 ,,	10.8	7.5	5.4	4.3	3.1
70,000 ,,	10.0	7.1	5.1	4.1	2.9
50,000 ,,	9.8	6.8	4.9	3.9	2.8
35,000 ,,	9.4	6.5	4.7	3.7	2.7
18,000 ,,	8.7	6.0	4.3	3.5	2.5

Appendix D

Typical Insulating Flange Joint

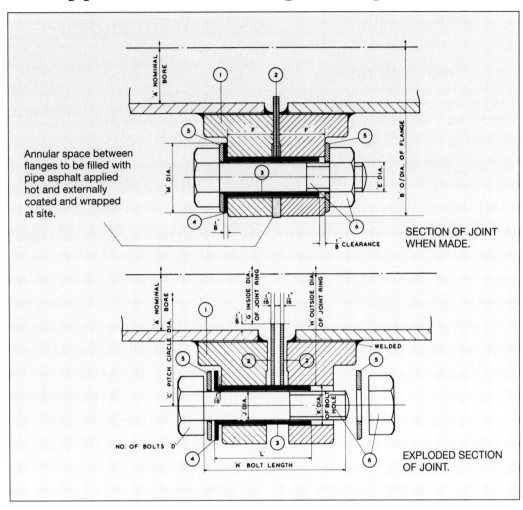

Annular space between flanges to be filled with pipe asphalt applied hot and externally coated and wrapped at site.

SECTION OF JOINT WHEN MADE.

EXPLODED SECTION OF JOINT.

SCHEDULE OF DIMENSIONS IN INCHES

A	1	1½	2	2½	3	4	6	8	10	12	13¼	15¼
B	4¼	5	6	7	7½	9	11	13½	16	19	21	23½
C	3⅛	3⅞	4¾	5½	6	7½	9½	11¾	14¼	17	18¾	21¼
D	4	4	4	4	4	8	8	8	12	12	12	16
E	½	½	⅝	⅝	⅝	⅝	¾	¾	⅞	⅞	1	1
F	9/16	11/16	¾	⅞	15/16	15/16	1	1⅛	1 3/16	1¼	1⅜	1 7/16
G	¾	1¼	1¾	2¼	2¾	3¾	5¾	7¾	9¾	11¾	13	15
H	2⅜	3⅛	3⅞	4⅝	5⅛	6⅝	8½	10¾	13⅛	15⅞	17½	20
J	9/16	9/16	11/16	11/16	11/16	11/16	13/16	13/16	15/16	15/16	1 1/16	1 1/16
K	¾	¾	⅞	⅞	⅞	⅞	1	1	1⅛	1⅛	1¼	1¼
L	1¼	1½	1⅝	1⅞	2	2	2⅛	2⅜	2½	2⅝	2⅞	3
M	1 5/16	1 5/16	1½	1½	1½	1½	1¾	1¾	1 15/16	1 15/16	2⅛	2⅛
N	2¼	2½	2¾	3	3¼	3¼	3½	3¾	4	4	4½	4½

SCHEDULE OF MATERIALS

ITEM	MATERIAL	DESCRIPTION
1	Steel	Flange to ANSI B 16.5 – Bolt holes drilled to suit dimensions scheduled opposite. Can be screw-on, slip on, or weld neck
2	Klingerite	Joint rings 1/16" thick. See note
3	Tufnol	Bolt insulating sleeves – Crow Grade
4	Tufnol	Bolt washer ⅛" thick – Crow Grade
5	Steel	Plain round washer B.S.
6	Steel	B.S.W. Bright bolts and nuts

Appendix E

International Shore Fire Connection

The purpose of the International Shore Fire Connection is to connect the fire water supply from shore to the ship fire main or to interconnect the fire mains of two ships. The shore fire connection provides a standardised joint between two systems where each might otherwise have couplings or connections that do not match.

All ships, jetties and apparatus likely to require an emergency source of fire water or to provide it should have at least one shore fire connection.

The flange on the connection should have the dimensions shown on the relevant drawing overleaf. It should have a flat face on one side and on the other should be a coupling that will fit the hydrant or hose on the ship or shore as appropriate.

The connection should be kept readily available together with a gasket of any material suitable for $1.0N/mm^2$ services, and with four 16mm bolts, 50mm in length, and eight washers.

Fire hose having a shore fire connection on the end is led to its counterpart and the flange joints are bolted together. If the shore fire connection is permanently fixed to a hydrant or pipe then a portable connection for use on a hose must be available in case the opposite fire main has only a fixed connection.

If fixed on a vessel, the connection should be accessible from either side of the vessel and should be plainly marked. The shore fire connection should be ready for use when a ship is in port.

INTERNATIONAL SHORE FIRE CONNECTION

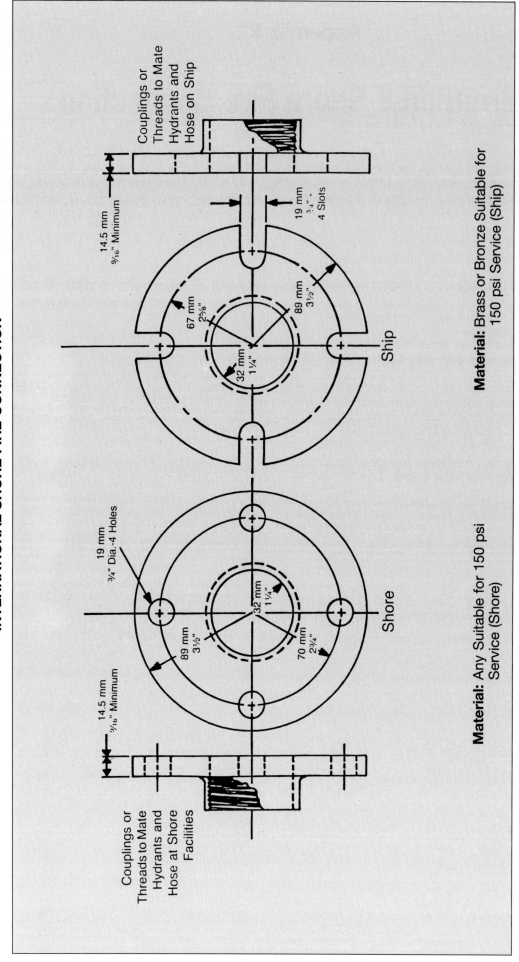

Couplings or Threads to Mate Hydrants and Hose on Ship

14.5 mm 9/16" Minimum

19 mm 3/4" - 4 Slots

67 mm 2⅝"

89 mm 3½"

32 mm 1¼"

Ship

Couplings or Threads to Mate Hydrants and Hose at Shore Facilities

14.5 mm 9/16" Minimum

19 mm 3/4" Dia.-4 Holes

89 mm 3½"

32 mm 1¼"

70 mm 2¾"

Shore

Material: Brass or Bronze Suitable for 150 psi Service (Ship)

Material: Any Suitable for 150 psi Service (Shore)

For Both —

> **Flange Surface:** Flate Face
> **Gasket Material:** Any Suitable for 150 psi Service
> **Bolts:** Four (⅝ inch) Diameter, 50mm (2 inches) long
> Threaded to within 25mm (1 inch) of the bolt head
> **Nuts:** Four, to Fit Bolts
> **Washers:** Four, to Fit Bolts

Appendix F

Hot Work Permit

This permit to work relates to any work involving temperature conditions which are likely to be of sufficient intensity to cause ignition of combustible gases, vapour or liquids in or adjacent to the area involved. Before completing this form, refer to the accompanying guidance notes, and to Section 2.8.

- **GENERAL**

    This permit is valid from...hrs   Date ....

    to...............................hrs   Date...

    Location of hot work..

    ....

    Has an enclosed space entry permit been issued?   Yes / No

    Reason if 'No': ....

    Description of hot work ....

    ....

    Personnel carrying out hot work ....

    Person responsible for hot work ....

    Person responsible for safety ....

- **SECTION 1**

    1.1 Has the hot work area been checked with a combustible gas indicator for hydrocarbon vapours?   Yes / No

    Time ....

    1.2 Has the surrounding area been made safe?   Yes / No

    Time ....

- **SECTION 2**

2.1 Has the hot work area been checked with a combustible gas indicator for hydrocarbon vapours?   Yes / No

2.2 Has the equipment or pipeline been gas freed?   Yes / No

2.3 Has the equipment or pipeline been blanked?   Yes / No

2.4 Is the equipment or pipeline free of liquid?   Yes / No

2.5 Is the equipment isolated electrically?   Yes / No

2.6 Is the surrounding area safe?   Yes / No

2.7 Is additional fire protection available?   Yes / No

2.8 Special conditions/precautions ....

....

In the circumstances noted it is considered safe to proceed with this hot work.

Signed .... Master

.... Person in charge of hot work team

- **SECTION 3**

The work has been completed and all persons under my supervision, materials and equipment have been withdrawn.

Authorised officer in charge .... Time .... Date.......................

   First copy for display at work area
   Second copy for ship or terminal records.

GUIDANCE NOTES FOR HOT WORK PERMIT

- **GENERAL**

(a) Starting/finishing time must not exceed the Authorised Signatories'/Responsible Officer's working hours.

(b) Specific location of hot work to be given.

(c) Description of hot work to include type of equipment to be used.

- **SECTION 1:**

Applies to all hazardous work not involving naked flame or continuous spark production, and would include use of electrical equipment, use of air driven rotary equipment, sand or grit blasting, hammering and mechanical chipping and movement of equipment or materials over or near to machinery that is operating.

- **SECTION 2:**

Applies to all hot work involving high temperatures, open flame, electric arc or continuous source of sparks etc. This type of work includes but is not limited to welding, burning and grinding.

> **TESTS FOR COMBUSTIBLE GAS SHOULD BE CARRIED OUT IMMEDIATELY BEFORE COMMENCEMENT OF HOT WORK AND AT FREQUENT INTERVALS AS LONG AS THE WORK IS IN PROGRESS.**

Appendix G

Cold Work Permit

This permit relates to any work in a hazardous or dangerous area which will not involve generation of temperature conditions likely to be of sufficient intensity to cause ignition of combustible gases, vapours or liquids in or adjacent to the area involved.

- **GENERAL**

  This permit is valid from..hrs   Date ....

  to..hrs   Date...

  Location of cold work ....

  ....

  Has enclosed space entry permit been issued?   Yes / No

  Description of cold work ....

  ....

  Personnel carrying out cold work ....

  ....

  Responsible person in attendance ....

- **SECTION 1**

  Preparation and checks to be carried out by Officer in Charge of cold work to be performed.

  1.1   The equipment/pipeline has been prepared as follows:

  Vented to atmosphere: Yes / No   Drained: Yes / No

  Washed: Yes / No   Purged: Yes / No

  Other: ....

  1.2   The equipment/pipeline has been isolated as follows:

  Lines Blanked: Yes / No   Lines Disconnected: Yes/No

  Valves Closed: Yes / No   Other: ....

  1.3   Is equipment free from:

  Oil: Yes / No   Gas: Yes / No H_2S: Yes / No   Steam: Yes / No

  Pressure: Yes / No

  1.4   Is surrounding area free from hazards?   Yes / No

  1.5   If work is to be performed on electrical equipment has that equipment been isolated?

  Yes / No

- **SECTION 2**

    Information and instructions to person carrying out cold work:

    2.1 The following personal protection must be worn ....

    ....

    2.2 Equipment/pipeline contained following material in service ....

    ....

    2.3 Equipment expected to contain the following hazardous material when opened ....

    ....

    2.4 Special conditions/precautions ....

    ....

    In the circumstances noted it is considered safe to proceed with this cold work.

    Signed .... Master/Responsible Officer

    .... Person carrying out work task
    or in charge of cold work team

- **SECTION 3**

    The cold work has been completed and all persons under my supervision, materials and equipment have been withdrawn.

    Authorised person in charge .... Time .... Date ....

    First copy for display at work area
    Second copy for ship or terminal records.

GUIDANCE NOTES FOR COLD WORK PERMIT

(a) Starting/finishing time must not exceed the Authorised Signatories'/Responsible Officer's working hours.

(b) Specific location of cold work to be given.

(c) Description of work to include type of equipment to be used.

(d) This permit should be used for but not be limited to the following cold work:

      1. Blanking/de-blanking.

      2. Disconnecting and connecting pipework.

      3. Removing and fitting of valves, blanks, spades or blinds.

      4. Work on pumps etc.

      5. Clean up (oil spills).

Appendix H

Electrical Isolation Certificate (EIC)

No. ....

DRIVE No. AND/OR EQUIPMENT DESCRIPTION

WORK TO BE DONE

WORK TO BE DONE BY

ON WORK PERMIT No. ....

METHOD OF ISOLATION

AUTHORISED BY

TIME   DATE

SUPPLY ISOLATED BY

EIC RECEIVED BY

WORK COMPLETED BY

WORK CLEARED BY

SUPPLY RECONNECTION
AUTHORISED BY

SUPPLY RECONNECTED BY

THE PERSON ENGAGED ON THE ABOVE WORK MUST HOLD THIS CERTIFICATE UNTIL THE JOB IS COMPLETED WHEN HE WILL SIGN IT, HAVE IT CLEARED BY HIS IMMEDIATE SUPERVISOR AND RETURN IT TO THE ISSUING AUTHORITY.

Appendix I

Enclosed Space Entry Permit

This permit relates to entry into any enclosed space as described in Chapter 11.

- **General**

  Location/Name of Enclosed Space...

  Reason for Entry...

  This permit is valid   from .... hrs   Date ....   *(See Note 1)*

                         to .... hrs   Date ....

- **Section 1 – Pre-Entry Preparations**
  (To be checked by the master or responsible officer)

  ☐ Has the space been segregated by blanking off or
     isolating all connecting pipelines?   ....

  ☐ Have valves on all pipelines serving the space been
     secured to prevent their accidental opening?   ....

  ☐ Has the space been cleaned?   ....

  ☐ Has the space been thoroughly ventilated?   ....

  ☐ Pre-entry atmosphere tests: *(See Note 2)*

       Readings   Oxygen.................. % vol (21%)
                     Hydrocarbon .... % LFL (Less than 1%)
                     Toxic Gases............ ppm (specify gas & PEL)   *(See Note 3)*

  ☐ Have arrangements been made for frequent atmosphere
     checks to be made while the space is occupied and after
     work breaks?   ....

  ☐ Have arrangements been made for the space to be
     continuously ventilated throughout the period of
     occupation and during work breaks?   ....

  ☐ Is adequate illumination provided?   ....

  ☐ Is rescue and resuscitation equipment available for
     immediate use by the entrance to the space?   ....

  ☐ Has a responsible person been designated to stand by
     the entrance to the space?   ....

☐ Has the Officer of the Watch (bridge, engine room, cargo control room) been advised of the planned entry? ....

☐ Has a system of communication between the person at the entrance and those entering the space been agreed and tested? ....

☐ Are emergency and evacuation procedures established and understood? ....

☐ Is there a system for recording who is in the space? ....

☐ Is all equipment used of an approved type? ....

- **Section 2 – Pre-Entry Checks**
  (To be checked by the the person authorised as leader of the team entering the space)

☐ Section 1 of this permit has been completed fully. ....

☐ I am aware that the space must be vacated immediately in the event of ventilation failure or if atmosphere tests change from agreed safe criteria. ....

☐ I have agreed the communication procedures. ....

☐ I have agreed upon a reporting interval of .... minutes. ....

☐ Emergency and evacuation procedures have been agreed and are understood. ....

To be signed by:

Master or responsible officer .... Date.................. Time.......................

Authorised team leader .... Date.................. Time.......................

Responsible person supervising entry .... Date.................. Time.......................

THIS PERMIT IS RENDERED INVALID SHOULD VENTILATION OF THE SPACE STOP OR IF ANY OF THE CONDITIONS NOTED IN THE CHECK LIST CHANGE

Notes:

1.   The Entry Permit should contain a clear indication as to its maximum period of validity which, in any event, should not exceed a normal working day.

2.   In order to obtain a representative cross-section of the compartment's atmosphere, samples should be taken from several depths and through as many openings as possible. Ventilation should be stopped for about 10 minutes before the pre-entry atmosphere tests are taken (see Section 11.3.1).

3.   Tests for specific toxic contaminants, such as benzene and hydrogen sulphide, should be undertaken depending on the nature of the previous contents of the space.

Index

Ballast spaces
monitoring of 7.8

Ballast tanks
over pressurisation 7.14.1, 7.14.2, 7.14.3
under pressurisation 7.14.4, 7.14.5

Barges
- *see* Boats alongside

Battery equipment
portable 2.4.4

Bearings
cargo pump, inspection of 2.17.8, 6.3.2

Benzene
and other aromatic hydrocarbons 16.4
cargo information 5.1.1, 5.2.2
in enclosed spaces 9.3.4, 10.6.11, 11.2, 11.3.3
toxicity 11.2.3, 16.4.1, 16.4.2

Berthing
exchange of information 3.1
general precautions at berths *Chapter 4*
preparation for arrival 3.2

Berths
access to 4.12.8
mooring at 3.2.2, 3.2.3, 3.5
- *see also* Adjacent berths; Jetty

Bilges
cleanliness of 2.14.4, 2.17.2

Bitumen carrier
hot cargo 7.6.14

Boats alongside
barges 13.2.10
during an emergency 14.4
during cargo operations 9.1.2
- *see also* Tugs

Boiler tubes
soot blowing 2.14.2

Bonding
- *definitions*
ship/shore 6.10
static electricity *Chapter 20*
tank cleaning hoses 9.2.6

Booms
earthing 2.7
fire-fighting equipment mounted on 22.11.3

Breathing apparatus
air line 11.5.3
cartridge/canister face masks 11.5.4, 22.4.2
hose mask (fresh air) 11.5.5
maintenance 11.5.6
pumproom escape 2.17.8
readiness for use 11.4.2, *Appendix A*
self contained 11.5.2, 14.2.13
stowage 11.5.7
training 11.5.8

Bunkers
checking of headspace for flammability 2.1
hazards associated with *Chapter 24*
information exchange 5.1.1, 5.2.1
safety 2.14.6
- *see also* Residual fuel

Buoy moorings
berthing information 3.2.2
hoses for 6.6.4, *Appendix C*
precautions at 4.1.3
types of 3.6

Buoyancy
security of 3.3.1

Butane
addition to crude oil 17.6.1
flammable limits of *Table* 15-1, *Table* 15-2

Butterfly valves
- *see* Valves

Cables
ship/shore bonding 6.10.2, 20.6.2
- *see also* Wandering leads

Cannons
- *see* Monitors

Cans
petroleum in 13.2

Carbon dioxide
fire-fighting 22.2.4, 22.10.4
flooding 22.8.1
properties of 22.4.2
static hazard 12.10, 20.4.5

Carbon monoxide
hazards of 16.7.5

Carbon tetrachloride
toxicity 22.5.3
- *see also* Vaporising liquids

Cargo

alarms, testing of   6.4
changeover, combination carriers   12.14
deck   13.2.9
distribution   3.1.2, 5.3, 5.5
handling   *Chapter 6, Chapter 7, Appendix A*
information   3.1.2, 5.1, 5.2, *Appendix A*
jettison   14.7
leakage in double hull spaces   8.5
nets   13.2.3
packaged   *Chapter 13*
pipeline draining   2.17.7
tank lids   6.2.1, *Appendix A*
toxicity   1.4, 7.2.4
- *see also* Discharging; Loading; Hoses;
   Manifolds; Measuring and Sampling;
   Metal cargo arms; Pipelines; Pumps;
   Tank; Valves

Cargo arms
- *see* Hoses; Metal cargo arms; Pipelines

Cathodic protection
- *definitions*
anodes   2.11
hull/jetty   3.1.3, 6.10, *Chapter 20*
in cargo tanks   2.11

Check lists
combination carriers   12.14
ship/shore safety   4.1.4, 5.7, 7.6.10,
   Appendix A

Chemical indicator tubes
toxic gases, measurement of   18.6

Cigarette lighters
precautions for use   2.2.2

Cleaning liquids
precautions for use   2.14.3
tank cleaning additives   9.5

Climatic conditions
cold weather precautions   2.15, 4.4.1
electrical storms   6.8.3, 20.6.1
lightning   6.8.3
still air/wind   6.8.2, 7.6.13, 17.4.2, 17.5

Clingage
- *definitions*

Closed discharging
operations   7.9.3

Closed loading
cargoes containing H_2S 16.5
operations   7.6.3
very high vapour pressure cargoes   7.6.13

Clothing
electrostatic hazard   2.6
- *see also* Protective clothing; Synthetic
   clothing

Cold weather
precautions   2.15, 4.4.1
- *see also* Climatic conditions

Cold work
- *definitions*
electrical repairs   19.4.2
permit   4.1.4, 4.12, 11.6.6, *Appendix G*
safety tests for   11.3.2, *Appendix G*

Combination carrier
- *definitions, Chapter 12*
ballast spaces   10.11.4, 12.11, 20.4.2
cargo changeover   10.11.7, 12.14
discharge plan   7.9.1, 12.4.2
hatch covers   10.11.3, 12.7
inert gas system   10.11, 12.12
loading plan   7.6.1, 12.4.2
Oil/Bulk/Ore (OBO)   12.2.1
Oil/Ore (O/O)   12.2.2
openings in cargo tanks   12.8
pressure/vacuum breakers   10.8.1
slack holds   10.11.2, 12.4
slops   10.11.6, 12.10
sloshing   10.11.2, 12.4.1, 12.4.3
stability   7.6.1, 7.9.1, 12.4.2
tank washing   12.9, *Chapter 9*
typical section (OBO)   *Figure 12-1*
typical section (O/O)   *Figure 12-2*
venting of holds   12.6
void spaces   10.11.4, 12.3

Combustible (flammable)
- *definitions*

Combustible gas indicator (explosimeters)
- *definitions*
area testing   2.9.1, 9.1.6, 10.6.11, 11.3.2,
   24.2.2
benzene, unsuitability for   11.3.3, 16.4
catalytic filament type   18.1, 18.2
dilution tubes   18.2.3
non-catalytic heated filament type   18.1,
   18.3, 18.10
oxygen, unsuitability for   18.2.1

Combustion equipment
maintenance   2.14.1

Command centre
- *see* Emergency

Communications
buoy mooring   3.6, 4.1.3
cargo and ballast handling   4.1.3, 4.3, 4.5,
   5.1, 5.6, 7.1.3, 7.6.5, 7.12.4

Flexible cables
- *see* Wandering leads

Flue gas
carbon monoxide   16.7.5
inert gas quality   10.3
sulphur dioxide   16.7.4

Foam (froth)
- *definitions*
concentrate *definitions*,   22.4.1
cooling   22.3.2
extinguishers   22.10.2
fire-fighting, theory and equipment
    Chapter 22
fixed installation   22.8.2, 22.11.2
mains   22.11.2
monitors (cannons)   22.11.3
petroleum fires, use on   22.2.2
solution *definitions*,   22.4.1, 22.11.2

Fog
- *see* Water

Footwear
static charge   20.4.6

Free fall
- *definitions*
failure of IG system   7.10
precautions   9.2.7, 12.10, 20.4.1

Free surface effect
combination carriers   7.6.1, 7.9.1, 12.4.2
double hull tankers   8.1

Freezing
deck water seals   2.15
fire hydrants   4.4.1
fire main   2.15, 4.4.1
metal arms, cargo   6.7.5
steam winches/windlasses   2.15

Froth
- *see* Foam

Funnel
fire/sparks   2.14.1

Galleys
equipment, safe operation of   2.3, 4.1.4, 4.9,
    Appendix A
steam cookers/boilers   4.9.2
stoves   4.9.1, *Appendix A*

Gangways
access   4.6.1, 4.6.2, 4.6.3
aluminium   2.10
operating envelope restrictions   7.5.4

Gas
cylinders   13.2.3, 13.3
density   1.3, 15.3, 17.1, 17.2.1
detection   1.4, 2.8, 2.17.8, 9.3.2, 11.3.1,
    11.6.7, 12.13, 14.2.2, *Figure 17-1*
dispersion   17.3, 17.4
emission, from ballasted cargo tanks   9.4.8
evolution   17.1, 17.2, 17.2.1, 17.6.1
flammability   1.1, 10.1, 15.2.4, 15.2.6
flue   10.3, 16.7.2, 16.7.4, 16.7.5, 23.2.4
free *definitions*,   7.6.15, *Chapter 9*, 10.6.10,
    17.2.5, 17.4, 17.5
free certificate *definitions*,   12.9, 19.4.3, 4.12.5
freeing   8.7, *Chapter 9*, 10.3, 17.2.5, 17.5
indicators, catalytic filament   18.1, 18.2,
    18.10, *Figure 18-1*
indicators, non-catalytic heated filament
    18.1, 18.3, 18.10
indicators   9.1.6, *Chapter 18*
inert - *see* Inert gas
liquefied, packaged   13.3
masks, canister   11.5.2, 11.5.4, 22.4.2
masks, hose type   11.5.5
measurement (toxic)   7.2.3, 18.6
measuring equipment   9.1.6, *Chapter 18*
meter, refractive index   18.1, 18.4
sampling, filters   18.10
sampling, lines   9.1.6, 10.6.7, 18.9
sampling, procedures   7.2, 10.6.7, 11.3.1,
    18.9.2
tests, for entry   2.8, 9.1.6, 9.2.11, 9.3.4,
    10.6.11, 11.3, *Chapter 18*
tests, for tank washing   9.2.3, 9.2.5, 9.2.9
venting   7.6.3, 9.3.2, 12.6, *Chapter 17*

Gauging
closed   7.2.5, 7.7.5
- *see also* Measuring and sampling

General cargo
berth, tanker operations at   6.11.3
ships, at adjacent berth   6.11.2

Glands
inspection of   6.3.2

Grounding
- *see* Earthing

Halon
- *definitions*
use of   22.2.4
vaporising liquids   22.5.3

Harbour authorities
in an emergency   14.2.10, 14.2.15

Ice formation
   on ballast vents   7.14.4
   in fire hydrants   4.4.1
   on metal arms   6.7.5
   - see also Climatic conditions; Freezing

IGS
   - see Inert gas system

IMDG (International Maritime Dangerous Goods) Code
   packaged cargo   13.1

Incendive spark
   anodes   2.11
   gas indicators   18.2.4
   portable tank washing machines   9.2.6
   use of tools   2.9.2, 2.10

Induced charge
   electrostatic   12.10, Chapter 20

Inert condition
   - definitions
   dipping/ullaging/sampling in   5.4, 7.2.3, 20.5.6
   fixed inert gas systems   Chapter 10
   for crude oil washing   9.4.4, 10.6.8
   for handling static accumulator oils   7.4.3
   for tank washing   9.4, 9.5
   inspection of tanks in   5.4, 10.6.11, 10.7.2, 11.2.2

Inert gas
   - definitions
   assistance in fire-fighting   22.8.5
   ballast passage   10.6.6
   cold weather precautions   2.15
   combination carriers   12.12, Appendix A
   composition Table 16-3
   condensate water   10.7.4
   crude oil carriers   10.12.2
   distribution system definitions
   effect on flammability   15.2.3, Figure 15-1
   electrostatic charge, precautions   20.4.4, 20.5.6
   emergency supply   10.9
   failure of   7.10, 10.6.5, 10.6.7, 23.3
   health hazard   10.7.1
   hose clearing   7.11.3
   leakage   10.6.4, 10.6.11, 10.11.3, 10.11.4
   maintenance of supply   10.6.5
   plant definitions
   pressurising   7.6.2, 10.6, 10.8
   procedures   7.6.2, 7.9.2, 7.10, 9.1.6, 10.6
   product carriers   7.10, 10.6.5, 10.10, 10.12.3
   purging   Chapter 10, 15.2.3, 17.2.4
   quality   10.3
   repairs to system   10.13
   requirements for   3.1.4

Inert gas (contd.)
   residual fuel oil tanks   24.3.4
   scrubbers   10.7.4, 10.13, 11.1
   sources of   10.2
   system (IGS) definitions,   Chapter 10
   topping up   10.6.6, 12.7.1
   toxic components   7.2.3, 10.6.11, 10.7.1, 16.7
   water seal   10.5, 10.13

Inerted tanks
   crude carriers   23.2.4
   entry into   5.4, 10.6.11, 10.7.3
   formation of pyrophors in   23.2.4
   inspection of   5.4, 10.6.11, 10.7.2, 11.2.2

Inerting
   - definitions
   double hull spaces   8.5, 8.6
   tanks   10.4, 10.5, 10.6.1

Inflatable work boats
   for tank repairs   11.6.8

Information
   exchange of   3.1, 3.2.1, 3.2.2, 3.2.3, 4.1.4, 5.1, 5.2, 5.3, 5.5, 5.6

Inspection plates
   precautions   6.3.2

Insulating flange
   - definitions
   ship/shore   6.10.1, 20.6.2, 20.6.3, Appendix A, Appendix D

Insulation
   electrical, testing of   2.4.1, 19.3.3

Interface detector
   - definitions
   precautions for use   9.2.4

International shore fire connection
   use of   4.4.1, 22.7, 22.11.1, 22.12, Appendix A
   description of   Appendix E

Intoxicated
   persons   4.6.5

Intrinsically safe
   - definitions
   equipment, use of   2.4.2, 4.11

Iron sulphide, pyrophoric
   - see Pyrophoric iron sulphide

Jettison of cargo
precautions before   14.7

Jetty
access   4.12.8
fendering capacity   3.4
moorings at   3.2.2, 3.5
traffic movement and control   4.12.8, 14.2.8

Lamps
air driven   2.4.3, 11.6.4, 13.2.5
portable   2.4, 4.10.2, 11.6.4

Language difficulties
avoiding   4.5

Lead (Pb)
in cargo   5.1.1, 5.2
tetraethyl/tetramethyl   13.4, 16.6

Leaded gasoline
tank entry   9.2.10

Leakage
inert gas   10.6.4, 10.6.11, 10.11.3, 10.11.4
oil   2.13, 3.1.3, 6.9, 8.2, 8.5, 9.4.5, 11.2.1, 12.11

Level alarms
testing   6.4

LFL
- *see* Lower flammable limit

Lifebuoys
gangway safety   4.6.1

Lifelines
gangway safety   4.6.1, 22.4.2
use in a rescue   11.7, 22.4.2

Lighters
cigarette   2.2.2

Lightning
earthing and bonding   20.6.1
electrical storms   6.8.3

Lights
during darkness   4.6.3, 6.5.4, 13.2.3
explosion proof   2.17.5
naked *definitions,*   2.2, 4.7.1, 4.7.2, 6.11.4, *Appendix A*

Liquefied gases
packaged   13.3

Liquefied petroleum gas (LPG)
fires involving 22.2.3

Loading
cargo   7.6
cargo containing H$_2$S   16.5
cessation of, by terminal   7.6.10, *Appendix A*
checks following   7.6.12
closed   7.6.3
commencement of   7.6.4, 7.6.5, 7.6.6, 7.6.7
communication system   5.1.1, 7.6.5, 7.6.7
double hull tankers   8.1
from the top   7.6.15
heated products   7.6.14
high vapour pressure cargoes   7.6.13, 17.6
inspection of cargo tanks before   5.4
overall *definitions,*   7.6.15, 20.4.1
packaged petroleum   13.2
plans   5.3
rates   5.1, 5.2, 7.4.3, 7.6.9, 7.6.13, 7.6.14, 20.3.1, *Appendix A, Appendix C*
readiness   7.1.2
static accumulator oils   7.4.3, 20.3.1
topping off   7.6.11

Lower flammable limit
- *definitions*
and toxicity   1.4
crude oil vapours   10.1
effect of inert gas   15.2.3
gas free tanks   9.3.2, 9.3.3, 9.3.4, 17.2.2, 24.2.2
general   1.1, 10.1, 15.2.2
measuring   9.1.6
tank cleaning   9.5
too lean atmosphere   9.2.1, 9.2.3

Magnesium
anodes   2.11

Manifolds
ship/shore cargo connection   6.5
forces on   6.6.2, 6.7.2, 6.7.3
stern loading   7.6.6
shore   3.1.4, 3.2.2, 6.5, *Appendix A*
tanker   3.1.3, 3.2.2, 6.5, 6.6.2, 6.6.3, 6.6.4, 6.7.1, 6.7.2, 6.7.3, 6.7.6, 6.7.7, 7.6.6, *Appendix A*
vapour return   7.7.2, *Figure 7-2*

Manning requirements
in an emergency   4.1.2

Matches
use of   2.2.2

Measuring and sampling
cargo and ballast handling   7.2
cargoes containing toxic substances   7.2.4
double hull spaces   8.2

Measuring and sampling (contd.)
precautions during   7.4.3, *Table 7-1, Figure 7-1*
- *see also* Sampling; Ullage

Medical facilities
communication with, in an emergency
14.2.14

Mercaptans
information on   5.1.1, 5.2.2

Metal cargo arms
clearing   7.11
damage to due to pressure surge   7.3
emergency release of   6.5.5
forces on   3.5.2, *Appendix A*
ice formation on   6.7.5
mechanical couplers   6.7.6
operating envelope   6.7.1, 7.5.4
parking lock   6.7.4, 6.7.5
precautions whilst connected   6.7.8
risk of arcing   20.6.2
wind forces on   6.7.2, 6.7.7

Monitors (cannons)
fire-fighting readiness   4.4.1
foam   22.4.1
general   22.11.3

Moorings
arrangements   3.1.3, 3.1.4, 3.2, 3.5, 3.6,
4.2, 4.3, 7.6.7
buoy   3.2.2, 3.6, 4.1.3, 4.3, 7.6.6
communications   3.2.2, 3.6.2, 3.6.3
emergency release of   3.7.1
equipment   3.2.3, 3.5
lines   3.5.3
management of   4.2
plan   3.2.2, 3.5
safety of personnel   3.5.1
security of   3.5.2
self stowing winches   3.5.5
shore   3.1.4, 3.5.6, 4.2, 5.6, 6.2
shore   3.5.6, 3.6.2
tending   4.2, 6.7.8, 7.6.7
tension winches   3.5.4
towing off wires   3.7.2, *Appendix A*
tugs, requirement for   3.1.3, 4.2
winch brake design capacity *definitions,*   3.5.5
winch design heaving capacity *definitions*
- *see also* Conventional buoy moorings;
Single point moorings

Naked lights
- *see* Lights, naked

Navigation
- *see* Purpose and Scope

Nitrogen oxides
electrolytic sensors   18.8.2
in inert gas   16.7.1

Non-catalytic heated filament gas indicator
filters   18.10
operation of   18.3

Non-conductors
static   20.1.4

Non-gas free compartments
entry into   *Chapter 11*

Non-inerted tanks
electrostatic hazards *Table 7-1,*   7.4.3
measuring and sampling   7.2.2

Non-return valves
- *see* Valves

Non-static accumulator oils
flammable atmosphere above   20.5.4

Non-volatile petroleum
- *definitions*
and hydrocarbon vapours   11.2.1
classification   1.2, 15.2.6
loading overall   7.6.15
reporting   5.1.1

Notices
crude oil washing lines   9.4.10
entry to enclosed spaces   11.4.1
fire instructions   *Appendix B*
naked lights   2.2.4, 4.7.1, 4.7.2, 4.8.2
on tanker   4.7.1
on terminal   4.7.2
pumproom entry   2.17.4
smoking   2.2.4, 4.7.1, 4.7.2, 4.8.2
tank entry   11.4.1

Oil spillage and leakage
accidental   6.9
auto ignition   2.13
general   2.14.4
into double hull spaces   8.2

Oil/Bulk/Ore (OBO) carrier
- *see* Combination carrier

Oil/Ore (O/O) carrier
- *see* Combination carrier

Opening up equipment
in enclosed spaces   11.6.2
inert gas plant   10.13

Residual fuel oil
bunker safety   2.14.6
flammability hazards   *Chapter 24*
- *see also* Bunkers

Respiratory
protective equipment   11.5
- *see also* Breathing apparatus; Bunkers

Responsible officer/person
- *definitions*
checks by   2.8.7, 5.2.1, 11.4.1, 11.6.9

Resuscitator
- *definitions*
general   11.8
readiness of   11.4.2, 11.7

Ropes
mooring   3.5.3
synthetic fibre   7.2.2, 9.2.4, 20.1.2, 20.5.2
wire   3.5.3

Rotating shafts
inspection of glands/bearings   6.3.2

RVP
- *see* Reid vapour pressure

Safety net
for gangway   4.6.1

Sampling
double hull spaces   8.2
filters in lines   18.10
gas measuring equipment   9.1.6, 18.9
inert gas failure   7.10
lines, tank atmosphere   9.1.6
manual, gas inhalation   7.2.1
procedures   18.9.2
residual fuel oils   24.3.5
static accumulator oils   *Table 7-1,*
   Table 7-2, 7.4, 10.6.7, 20.5
tanks   7.2.1, 7.2.2
toxic cargoes   7.2.4, *Chapter 16*
vapour recovery   7.7.5
- *see also* Measuring and sampling; Ullage

Satellite communications
and ignition hazard   2.7, 4.11.4

Scale
and gas release   11.2.1
and hot work   2.8.4, 9.2.11, 11.6.5
in enclosed spaces   11.6.1
removal   11.6.5

Screen
door   6.1.2
- *see also* Flame screen

Scupper
plugs   6.9.3, *Appendix A*

Sea islands
offshore facilities   6.10.3

Sea valves
- *see* Valves

Security
notices   4.7.1, 4.7.2
of buoyancy   3.3.1
unauthorised persons   4.6.4

Sediment
- *see* Scale

Segregated ballast
contaminated   8.9
retention   7.5.4
tank lids   6.2.5

Self stowing mooring winches
- *definitions*
general   3.5.5

Ship/barge transfer
precautions   7.12.2, 20.6.3

Ship/ship transfer
precautions   7.12.1, 7.12.3, 7.12.4, 20.6.3

Ship/shore safety checklist
purpose   5.7
use of *Appendix A*

Shipyard safety
- *see* Purpose and Scope

Shore fire services
communication with   14.2.3, 14.5.2
practice with tanker personnel   14.3.7

Shore moorings
- *see* Moorings

Short term exposure limit
- *see* Permissible exposure limit

Sighting and ullaging ports
use of   6.2.2, 7.2.3

Signals
emergency *Appendix A*
ship/shore   5.6

Single point moorings
berthing information   3.2.2

Single point moorings (contd.)
    loading at   7.6.5, 7.6.7
    mooring at   3.6.3, 4.3
    precautions at   4.1.3

Slops
    combination carriers   10.11.6, 12.9, 12.10
    free fall of   9.2.7
    loading overall   7.6.15
    on board   3.1.3, 3.1.4, 5.2.1, 5.2.2

Sloshing
    slack tanks   12.4.3

Sludge
    - *see* Scale

Slugs
    of water   20.4.2

Smoking
    alongside   4.1.4, 4.6.5, 4.7, 4.8.1, 6.11.5, 13.2.3, *Appendix A*
    at sea   2.2.1
    designated areas   4.8.2
    notices   2.2.4, 4.7, 4.8

Smothering systems
    extinguishing agents   22.4
    packaged cargo   13.2.6

SOLAS
    - *definitions*

Sounding
    during washing   9.2.3, 9.2.4, 20.5.5
    pipes   7.4.3, *Figure 7-1,* 20.5.3, 20.5.5
    ports   6.2.2, 7.6.3

Sour crude oil
    - *definitions*
    precautions when handling   16.5
    reporting   5.1, 5.2

Spillage of oil
    in engine room   2.14.4
    in pumproom   2.17, 6.9.2

Spontaneous combustion
    - *definitions*
    prevention of   2.12, 13.2.3

Spools
    ballast/cargo connection   8.9

Spray
    arrestors, pumproom   2.17.8
    water   7.13.3, 9.2.8, 13.2.7, 22.1.4, 22.2.2, 22.3.1

Stability
    combination carriers   7.6.1, 7.9.1, 12.4.2
    double hull tankers   8.1

Static accumulator oils
    - *definitions, Chapter 20*
    dipping/ullaging/sampling   *Table 7-1, Table 7-2,* 7.2.2, 7.4.2, 7.4.3, 20.5.3
    discharge of cargo   7.4.4, 7.4.5
    loading   *Table 7-1,* 7.4.3, 20.3.1, 20.5.3

Static electricity
    - *definitions, Chapter 20*
    charge accumulation   7.2.2, 7.4, 8.6, 9.2.8, 20.1.3, 20.3, 24.3.5
    charge relaxation   20.1.3, 20.3.1
    charge separation   20.1.2
    clothing   2.6, 20.4.6
    conductors   7.4.2, 20.1
    dipping/ullaging/sampling   *Table 7-1, Table 7-2,* 7.2.2, 7.4, 9.2.4, 20.5
    discharges   7.7.8, 20.1.4
    free fall   9.2.7, 12.10, 20.4.1
    general precautions   7.2.2, 20.2
    induction   *Chapter 20*
    inert gas   8.6, 10.6.1, 10.6.7, 20.4.4, 20.5.6
    intermediate conductors   20.1.4
    non-conductors   20.1.4
    non-inerted tanks   *Table 7-1*
    principles   20.1
    static accumulator oils   7.4, 20.3
    steam   9.2.4, 9.2.9, 20.1.2, 20.4.3
    synthetic materials   20.4.7
    tank washing   9.2.4, 9.2.8, *Chapter 20*
    water mist   7.13.3, 9.4.6, 20.4.2, 20.4.3

Static non- accumulator oils
    - *definitions*
    dipping/ullaging/sampling   *Table 7-1,* 7.4.2

Stays
    earthing   2.7

Steam
    electrostatic hazard   9.2.4, 9.2.9, 20.1.2, 20.4.3
    fire-fighting   22.4.3, 22.8.6
    smothering system   22.8.6
    tank washing   9.2.3, 9.2.4, 9.2.9, 9.5

Steam winches
    cold weather precautions   2.15

STEL
    - *see* Short term exposure limit

Stern discharge/loading
    area classification   4.10.1
    fire-fighting equipment   4.4.1

TLV
- *see* Threshold limit value

TML
- *see* Tetramethyl lead

Too lean
atmosphere   9.2.1, 9.2.3
- *see also* Atmosphere

Tools
hand   2.9.2, 4.12.17, 11.6.3
non-sparking   2.9.2
power   2.9.1, 4.12.7, 11.6.3, *Appendix F*
use in enclosed space   11.6.3
use of   2.9
- *see also* Work permit

Topping off
- *definitions*
tanks on board   7.6.11

Topping up
- *definitions*
inert gas, combination carrier   12.7.1
inert gas, double hull space   8.6
inert gas, maintaining pressure   10.5

Torch
- *see* Flashlight

Towers
fire-fighting   22.11.3

Towing off wires
making fast   3.7.2
use of   *Appendix A*

Toxic
- *definitions*
gases   5.2.2, 9.1.6, 10.6.11, 11.2, 11.4,
    Chapter 16, 18.6, Appendix A
- *see also* Benzene; Hydrogen sulphide;
    Toxicity

Toxicity
aromatics   16.4
benzene   9.3.4, 11.2, 15.4.2, 16.4.2
carbon monoxide   16.7.1, 16.7.5
halon   22.5.3
hydrocarbon gas   1.4, 16.3
hydrogen sulphide   1.4, 9.3.4, 11.2.3, 16.5
leaded gasoline   9.2.10, 16.6
liquid petroleum   16.2
nitrogen oxides   16.7.3
petroleum   *Chapter 16*
petroleum gases   1.4, 9.3.4, 16.3
sulphur dioxide   16.7.4

Transfers
ship/barge   7.12.2, 20.6.3
ship/ship   7.12.1, 7.12.3, 7.12.4, 20.6.3

Transmitter
radio   2.4.4, 2.7, 4.5, 4.11.2

Trimming
ventilators   6.1.3

Trips
cargo pump   2.17.8, 6.4

True vapour pressure (TVP)
- *definitions*
and volatility   1.1, 15.1.1
depth of gas layer   *Figure 17-6*
discharging   5.2.2
information exchange   5.2.2
loading   5.1.1, 5.2.1, 7.6.13, 17.2.1, 17.6.1,
    Figure 17-6

Tugs
alongside   3.3.2, 6.11.4
in emergency   14.2.3, 14.2.4, 14.2.12
fire-fighting   14.2.12, 22.11.3, 22.12
requirements   3.1

TVP
- *see* True vapour pressure

TWA
- *see* Time weighted average

UFL
- *see* Upper flammable limit

UHF/VHF
transceivers   2.4.4, 2.7, 4.5, 4.11.2, 14.2.4,
    Appendix A

Ullage
- *definitions*
equipment   20.5.2
inerted   5.4, 7.2.3, 7.10, 10.6.5, 10.6.7,
    20.5.6
manual, inhalation of gas   7.2.1, 10.7.2
ports   6.2.2, 7.2, 7.6.3
residual fuel oil   24.3.5
static accumulator oils   *Figure 7-1, Table 7-1,*
    20.5.3
static electricity hazards   20.5
synthetic fibre ropes   *Table 7-1,* 9.2.4, 20.5.2
- *see also* Measuring; Sampling

Unauthorised access
to ship or terminal   4.6.4, 4.7.1, 4.12.8
to dangerous area   7.6.6, 7.9.8

Wandering leads (contd.)
    mechanical damage   2.4.1
    proper use of   2.4.2, *Appendix A*
    use in a hazardous area   4.10.2,

Washing machines
    crude oil   2.11, 9.4, 10.6.8
    electrostatic hazards   9.2.3, 9.2.4, 20.2, 20.3, 20.4
    fixed   2.11, 9.4.3, 10.6.8
    portable   8.8, 9.2.3, 9.2.4, 9.2.6, 20.2

Water
    dips, in cargo tanks   5.2.2
    fire-fighting   22.7
    fog *definitions,*   22.2.2, 22.3.1, 22.8.3
    jet   22.2.2, 22.2.3, 22.3.1
    mist   7.13.3, 9.4.6, 20.4.2, 20.5.5
    seals, cold weather precautions   2.15
    slug   20.4.2
    spray *definitions,*   7.13.3, 9.2.8, 13.2.7, 22.2.2, 22.3.1, 22.11.4
    wall (curtain)   22.8.4

Weights of hoses
    - *see* Hoses, weights

Welding
    hot work   2.8

Winches
    brake holding capacity   3.5.5
    self stowing   3.5.5
    steam, cold weather precautions   2.15
    tension   3.5.4
    - *see also* Moorings

Wind
    conditions   3.5, 3.5.3, 4.2, 6.8.2, 7.6.13, 17.4.2, 17.5
    - *see also* Climatic conditions

Windlasses
    cold weather precautions   2.15

Work boats
    inflatable   11.6.8

Work permit
    - *definitions*
    in enclosed spaces   11.6.1
    samples of   *Appendix F, Appendix G*
    cold   4.1.4, 4.12.1, 11.6.6, *Appendix G*
    conditions   4.11.2, 4.12.1, 4.12.2, *Appendix F, Appendix G*
    gangs (contractors)   11.6.9
    hot   *Figure 2-1,* 2.8.1, 4.1.4, 4.12.1, 4.12.2, 4.12.4, 4.12.5, 11.6.7, 19.4.3, *Appendix F*
    on a tanker   4.12.4
    on a berth   4.12.3, 19.4.3
    tools   2.9, 4.12.7

Zinc
    anodes   2.11

Zone, hazardous
    - *see* Hazardous zone